THE
MEETING
OF
SCIENCE
AND
SPIRIT

AN OMEGA BOOK

This New Age series of Paragon House is dedicated to classic and contemporary works about higher human development and the nature of ultimate reality. *Omega Books* encompasses the fields of mysticism and spirituality, psychic research and paranormal phenomena, the evolution of consciousness, and the human potential for self-directed growth in body, mind, and spirit.

Ask your bookseller for these other Omega Books:

MYSTICS, MAGICIANS, AND MEDICINE PEOPLE:
Tales of a Wanderer by Doug Boyd

SWAMI
  by Doug Boyd

SYNCHRONICITY: Science, Myth, and the Trickster
  by Allan Combs and Mark Holland

KUNDALINI, EVOLUTION AND ENLIGHTENMENT
  edited by John White

General Editor: John White

THE
MEETING
OF
SCIENCE
AND
SPIRIT

Guidelines for
a New Age

JOHN WHITE

P A R A G O N H O U S E / New York

First edition 1990
Published in the United States by
Paragon House
90 Fifth Avenue
New York, NY 10011

Manufactured in the United States of America

Library of Congress Cataloging-in-Publication Data

White, John Warren, 1939-
    The meeting of science and spirit : guidelines for a new age /
John White. — 1st ed.
        p.   cm. — (Omega books)
    ISBN 1-55778-302-0
    1. New Age movement.   2. Religion and science—
1946-   3. Spiritual life.
I. Title.   II. Series.
BP605.N48W55   1990
299'.93—dc20   89-70910
                                                                  CIP

10   9   8   7   6   5   4   3   2   1

This book is printed on acid-free paper.

Dedicated to friends,
past and present,
along the way to a New Age

Contents

I

Science—The Ascent of Humanity

II

Spirit—The Descent of the Divine

Invocation

O God, I surrender myself unto Thee.

Open my eyes that I may see
    the miracle and beauty of Thy creation.

Open my ears that I may hear
    Thy wisdom guiding me toward the light.

Open my mouth that I may speak truth
    to everyone in all situations.

Open my mind that I may understand
    that everything is from Thee for my perfection.

Open my arms that I may help
    all whom I meet with selfless service.

Open my heart that I may love
    all whom I encounter, compassionately and unconditionally.

Open my total being
    that I may experience Thy peace and wisdom
    and show others their at-one-ment with Thee.

Foreword: From God to Humanity

I t is said in metaphysics that the human being is the center of the universe. This is not meant egocentrically or astrophysically but rather that each of us is a point of confluence for higher and lower worlds, the visible and the invisible, the mundane and the sublime. Through a mysterious process the universe infolds upon itself to produce the human species that, although finite, is aware of infinity . . . is imperfect but aspires to perfection. The macrocosm produces the microcosm; as above, so below.

Each of us is thus a meeting point of the mental and material, consciousness and cosmos, inner and outer space. Every plane of reality, every level of being is contained within us. At the same time, paradoxically, we are contained within them. That is a profound topic to contemplate.

And contemplation reveals a holy purpose to that infolding, that involutionary descent which eventually leads through many twists and turns back to our act of contemplation. Humanity is involved in a mighty evolutionary drama of awakening to God, to the Creator, to the Great Mystery. A two-way process is at work/play behind that self-discovery in which the lower world reaches upward while the higher world reaches downward to encourage the lower to keep reaching.

On one hand, we recognize something beyond ourselves, something mysterious which is attractive, which gestures to us, calls us to attain deeper understanding, a greater scope of action, the possibility of becoming more than we are. Gropingly, painfully, we seek it, striving soulfully, ascending to ever-deeper awareness and ever-wider dominion. In its most technical aspect, that striving is called science.

On the other hand, that mysterious something reaches to us from what has traditionally been perceived as "on high." It descends in its majesty and power to beckon us toward it by revealing itself in ever-greater degree through visions, dreams, imagination, and inspired moments of discovery and creativity. Its traditional name is Spirit.

That involuntary evolutionary process is the mystery at the heart of creation. I became aware of the mystery at an early age and was impelled to try to solve it. Through various circumstances and life situations I gathered data, acquired knowledge, and sought wisdom. I was also impelled to communicate about it, to share the data, knowledge, and wisdom. I therefore undertook a career as a teacher and writer.

This book is a record of some of my explorations. These essays were produced over the last ten years or so but, upon reflection recently, it became apparent that they had an organic relationship and could be arranged to let the deep structure behind them become visible. The title describes that deep structure: the two-way process by which Spirit manifests a universe in search of Spirit. The subtitle describes the book's function: to assist Spirit in the feedback process by which humanity assumes its divine birthright.

The Meeting of Science and Spirit is about the human being as human becoming. We are Spirit materialized, engaged in spiritualizing matter. Like the Prodigal Son, we have journeyed to a far country and now long to go home because in the depths of our being we have never forgotten who we are and where we come from. We are striving to actualize that which is potential in us, that which is "home": godhood. We are awakening to ourselves in the paradoxical situation of seeming separate from our source and seeking to return to it, but discovering that Spirit has been our ever-present condition throughout the long journey from darkness to light, from ignorance to comprehension, from bondage to freedom, from fragmentation to wholeness. Thus, self-realization is God-realization.

That is what I write about here as I examine various aspects of the human scene, especially the much-discussed New Age movement and related topics. The selections move from the physical (neuroscience) to the spiritual (salvation for humanity), but all are concerned with clarifying what is true or false about the topics under examination and showing, first, what is detrimental or dangerous about them to the noetic process of self-transcendence and, second, what is useful about them for our enlightenment. They are intended to illumine an amorphous subject—the New Age movement—by placing New Age topics in a larger context and showing their ultimate significance.

Put another way, my central concern is human liberation through God-realization. I have sometimes taken the voice of objective journalist; at other times I've spoken subjectively as teacher, critic, and friend. Throughout I have tried to relate the data of science to the concerns of spirituality in the interest of enriching both. And because these pieces were composed separately for different audiences, there is some overlapping of ideas and phrasing. Since reality is seamless, one may come at a topic from different directions but should expect some restatement of data and key ideas as the various approaches converge, especially as certain expressions prove effective for conveying information. I have eliminated redundancy as best I could without doing damage to the text. What remains, I feel, simply gives it greater coherence and solidity. I trust that revisiting certain statements in new contexts will enlarge their significance for readers.

Portions of this book originally appeared in *Body, Mind & Spirit, Common Boundary, Holistic Living, Human Behavior, The Idea Exchange, Journal of Near-Death Studies, Man-Environment Systems, New Frontiers, New Realities, Science of Mind, UFO Venture Inward, Wildfire,* and *Yoga Journal.* "Enlightenment and the Spiritual Journey" and "The Judeo-Christian Tradition and the New Age" are expanded from essays in *What Is Enlightenment?* and appear with the kind permission of the publisher, Jeremy P. Tarcher.

The Meeting of Science and Spirit is intended to help the process of expanding and refining human consciousness by showing that science and spirit are complementary. The scientific and religio-spiritual establishments have been in conflict for centuries, albeit with notable and welcome exceptions such as Goethe, R. M. Bucke, Rudolf Steiner, and Pierre Teilhard de Chardin. In this century the rift began to close in an accelerated fashion as science was forced by the logic and data of its own methodology to acknowledge that matter was dematerializing into the void from which creation arises. Spiritually oriented people and organizations were likewise forced to acknowledge the validity of "godless" science which could peer inside the atom, listen to the galaxies, eradicate disease, illuminate the night, transport people through the skies and even land them on the moon.

May that healing of the division continue and quicken. Human survival depends on it. Materialism alone, no matter how technologically spectacular, will not save the world. Nor will a world-denying spirituality. Both matter and spirit are part of God, because God is the One-in-all. When the human species is conscious of matter and spirit as differing aspects of the Whole, of Ultimate Reality, rather than seeing them as opposites and rather than seeing one or the other as illusion or delusion, we will have arrived at the point in our celestial voyage which truly deserves to be called a New Age.

Introduction: What Is the New Age?

Civilization is rapidly approaching a critical juncture, a great divide in history. Many voices tell us that a major period or cycle is ending and another is beginning. Astrologers say Planet Earth is on the cusp between two ages; various metaphysicians and psychics point to the year 2000 as the turning point. Quite apart from the occult/esoteric field, others tell us that our world is at a watershed. Some environmentalists point to roughly the same period (within, say, a decade or generation of this century's end) as the time human influences on the global ecosystem will culminate in a dire manner unless checked. And in the political realm, forecasts also show the population reaching criticality in many parts of the world, placing unsupportable burdens on delivery systems for food, housing, transportation, medical care, and so forth. Although the arms race between superpowers seems to be abating, until all nuclear, biological, and chemical weapons stockpiles are dismantled, the threat of a military armageddon remains.

Will humanity survive these looming disasters? What is to come *can* be a better world if we don't destroy ourselves before then. Insofar as the problems facing us are of our own making, they originate in the human mind and can be solved there, but a problem cannot be solved at the level which generated it. The solution to our global crisis is not simply more of what caused it: ignorant exploitation of nonrenewable resources and undeveloped peoples, callous pursuit of political power and wealth, thoughtless application of technology and disposal of waste, rampant consumerism, greed—the entire spectrum of selfish desires and stupid actions arising from the egocentricity of Man. If all that is to be alleviated and eliminated, mere science and technology are not the answer. Something more, something from a higher level of awareness is needed, something beyond ego and its mindset. Lower mind is the problem; higher mind is the answer: a fundamental change of consciousness in the human race.

xvii

I contend that a change of consciousness is precisely what is happening now. Around the globe there are strong signs of an awakening to higher consciousness. Some call it the coming of the Age of Aquarius. Others speak of the consciousness revolution, the human potential movement, the Aquarian Conspiracy. Still others refer to it as the New Age.

Something unprecedented is happening in the world, something transformative. The human *condition* is changing, thanks to the human *potential*—our potential for self-transcendence and growth to enlightenment. In its grandest dimension, I see emerging a higher form of humanity which I have named *Homo noeticus*. That evolutionary advance is occurring right now, in accelerated fashion, all over the planet. Various lines of activity are converging (albeit in an uncoordinated fashion and at varying rates) to produce a "new breed." The burgeoning interest in psychic and mystical phenomena, in psychotechnologies, spiritual traditions, and sacred lifeways especially indicate a deepening and expansion of awareness going on around the globe: a Great Awakening to Ultimate Reality. That change of consciousness defines *Homo noeticus* and the New Age.

In its best aspect, then, the New Age movement is conscious evolution—a healthy response to promptings from the cosmos which would have us move toward the light and grow to a higher state of being. It is trite but true to say that man's extremity is God's opportunity. Thus, in response to global emergency, there is global emergence. That evolutionary advance could ultimately create a new and unified world culture based on life-affirming values, unconditional love, and the perennial wisdom demonstrated humanistically by Jesus of Nazareth. After all, the term *New Age* is conceptually derived from the Bible: "And I saw a new heaven and a new earth" (Revelation 21:1). However, the concept of a radically new social order is found in many traditions (both sacred and secular) which envision a change in human life, a change which resolves societal disharmonies and allows people to fulfill their deepest longings for peace, truth, self-expression, and freedom from the age-old problem of man's inhumanity to man and nature's privations. The most familiar is called the American dream, a profoundly spiritual vision expressed in words on the Great Seal of the United States, beneath the all-seeing eye of wisdom: *Novus ordo seclorum,* "the new order of the ages."

Publisher Jeremy Tarcher, writing about "New Age as Perennial Philosophy" in the *Los Angeles Times Book Review* (February 7, 1988) advises us not to think of the New Age as a specific period of time: "Rather, it is a metaphor for a process of striving for personal growth through which millions of people are trying to become more fully awake to their inherent capacities. . . . Like every other movement, whether religious, political, economic or philosophical, the New Age is ultimately based upon a group of assumptions about the place of humanity in the cosmos. At the heart of New Age thought is the idea that humans have many levels of consciousness and that, with the exception of a limited number of spiritual geniuses throughout history, we essentially live in a walking sleep that keeps us from a balanced, harmonious and direct relationship with God (however you understand that concept), nature, each other and ourselves." Tarcher notes that this idea is ancient, and in that sense the New Age is not new at all.

In a more psychological vein, graduate student of biology Ted Schultz writes about "A Personal Odyssey through the New Age" in the critical work edited by Robert Basil, *Not Necessarily the New Age:* "I think the New Age focus on higher principles—morality, meaning, development of creativity and intuition—provides a healthy and necessary balance in a society that emphasizes and rewards greed, materialism, and callousness toward one's fellow humans. Science can tell us whether a proposition about the natural world is or is not true; it cannot supply the morality or vision required to use this knowledge. . . . New Age teachings validate the realm of inner, subjective experience, thus satisfying a vital human need that is largely unfilled in modern, twentieth-century culture."[1]

Another voice of the movement, Florence Graves, editor and associate publisher of *New Age* magazine, states in the *New Age Journal's 1988 Guide to New Age Living* that the heart of New Age thinking is "a belief that we all have the power to effect deep changes—not only in our personal lives but also in the world. . . . There's a lot of confusion now surrounding *new age,* a term that has been used in the mass media to characterize everything from 'healing' crystals to progressive business consultants. . . . While new age thinking has both political and spiritual dimensions, it is neither a political party nor a religion. In fact, this amorphous cultural transition in the making has no creed, no dogma, no leaders. . . . We believe the best new age thinking reflects the age-old yet eminently relevant belief that the health of the individual and that of society are fundamentally interrelated. This holistic world view is in alignment with such down-to-earth subjects as environmentalism, holistic health, women's rights, social responsibility, and personal spirituality."

Likewise, David Spangler, an early proponent of New Age philosophy noted for his role at a spiritual community at Findhorn, Scotland, told *Science of Mind* magazine (January 1989): "I try to define the New Age in its highest sense, away from mere phenomena such as crystals and prophecies. . . . The New Age should represent that which helps us meet the challenges and opportunities of our time with imagination and hope, effectiveness and enthusiasm, wisdom and compassion. Anything else is not really New Age and may actually be a harmless diversion that dissipates our efforts and scatters the energies we need to face the personal and planetary tasks confronting us."

Unfortunately, however, there *is* an "anything else" in the New Age movement. All is not sweetness and light. Many who wear the label or speak the language are not truly in tune with its aim and spirit. Some are well-meaning but naïve, unaware of its larger dimensions. (*Body, Mind & Spirit* magazine, publisher of *The New Age Catalogue,* noted in its June 1989 issue that *Time* magazine's image of the quintessential New Age is a cultural dropout sitting under an aluminum pyramid in the Rockies, clutching an array of crystals while waiting for the UFOs to land. This image, I'm sorry to say, accurately portrays many New Agers.) Others are drawn by glitter, greed, and escapism. In its worst aspect, the movement is a grab bag of superficial, trivial, irrational, and even menacing ideas, attitudes, beliefs, products, and services, all of which amount to a sad caricature and prostitution of the real thing.

There is a dark side to the New Age movement. The worst of the Old Age permeates the thinking and behavior, the attitudes and values of some who profess to be spiritual and for a new society. What is the worst? It's called self-ignorance and delusion. It's called untested vision. It's called spiritual pride. It's called ego.

So beware of what has been called NABS (standing for New Age you-know-what). NABS takes many forms: crystal healing, aura cleansing, the Bermuda Triangle, gods from outer space, the hollow Earth theory, chakra balancing, the Harmonic Convergence, financial "abundance" games and pyramid prophecies. The lack of scientific support for many claims made in the name of the New Age is just plain ludicrous; the lack of logic and the acceptance of spurious information for many New Age beliefs is just plain pathetic. Whether it's holistic health, metaphysics, or spirituality, misrepresentation, pseudoscientific data, flawed logic, wishful thinking, and sheer delusion abound in the New Age movement. I comment on that sort of irrational nonsense throughout this book as a corrective to widespread confusion about the topics.

The dark side is not simply a matter of many New Agers being naïve or ineffectual dreamers who sprinkle fairy dust over everything. That's bad, but to be expected from the inexperienced. They have much to learn from the best of the Old Age in terms of being productive, analytic, efficient, dependable, and accountable in business and other endeavors. (I'd hate to list all the enterprises which have gone down the tubes because a bunch of starry-eyed people couldn't do things on time, distribute their products properly, or be counted on to perform the most rudimentary services—and consequently pay the bills.)

Another aspect is just as bad: exploitation and ripoff in the name of higher consciousness. I'm talking here about the spiritual materialists—

the crass hustlers who slickly package activities, goods, and services, labeling them "New Age." They tout them as the ultimate experience in the spiritual supermarket and then sell them at inflated prices. And the bogus psychotechnologies they devise are endless: meditation hats, enlightenment meters, cosmic stress-alert monitors, golden brainfood pills, superionized vitamin XYZ, holistic haircuts, transpersonal teabags, biosolaralphafeedback jewelry: You name it and someone will sell you a dozen, wholesale. The baser aspects of the New Age movement require what I call a "spiritual crap detector" so you can tell the spurious from the true, the leading edge from the lunatic fringe, an open mind from a hole in the head. (For more on spiritual crap detectors, see Appendix 5.)

So a new age doesn't automatically mean a good age. At present, the New Age movement is somewhere between the dark and the light. While it is a beautiful source of hope for a better world, it is also effervescing with empty-headed faddishness, gross commercialism, media hype, nonsense and quackery, antiscientific irrationalism, fraud, and even outright danger. Without self-examination and self-policing, it will run into public rejection and indifference. Its wares will be seen as foolish, its mindset as regressive, its activities as a waste of time. And, if that should happen, it will be thoroughly deserved.

In other words, criticism is badly needed because the movement which aims at purifying human awareness and human society is itself unaware and impure in many ways. Some criticism has indeed been made by fundamentalist Christians, who view the New Age movement as counterfeiting and subverting God's plan for humanity. For example, Constance Cumbey's *The Hidden Dangers of the Rainbow* and Dave Hunt's *Peace, Prosperity and the Coming Holocaust* maintain that people and groups in the New Age movement are at least deluded by Satan, if not demonically possessed or consciously dedicated to the Antichrist. Cumbey, Hunt, and other Christian critics claim to have "exposed" the New Age as spreading nazism and communism under the banner of higher consciousness. I am included in their condemnation for proposing *Homo noeticus* and for advocating meditation and other spiritual disciplines.

Such criticism plays fast and loose with the facts, is based on simplistic understanding, and is further distorted by paranoid fantasies. But there are also more thoughtful critics. I recommend *Not Necessarily the New Age,* which is primarily a debunking book. On a more lofty plane, cultural historian William Irwin Thompson describes his response to the New Age movement in his 1989 book *Imaginary Landscape: Making Worlds of Myth and Science:* "So as the New Age began to define the new as paleolithic shamanism, neolithic feminism, pharaonic architecture, and medieval Islamic geometry, I moved away."[2]

Transpersonal psychologist Ken Wilber is harsher. He told *Yoga Journal* (July/August 1988): "I don't know a single good theorist who would refer to him/herself as 'new age' in any sense. In fact, as far as I'm aware, most good theorists—philosophers, psychologists, and so on—hate being called 'new age' or being in any way associated with so-called new age trends, because of the flakiness of so many things called new age. . . . And when you subtract them from the scene, all you're left with are the flaky, unauthentic, narcissistic aspects" (p. 48).

Yes, there is narcissism, there is irrationality, there is depersonalization rather than transpersonalization; there is ripoff and even, in some areas, sinister machinations in the New Age movement. But something else is going on, in my judgment something sacred. Don't define the New Age by the worst, but by the best. By their fruits ye shall know them, not by their nuts and flakes.

Despite a significant dose of superficiality, gimmicks, and re-gressiveness, there is a genuine and infinitely valuable core truth to the New Age movement, so I'm not making a wholesale condemnation of any organization, philosophy, or practice. I speak as someone deeply involved in the New Age movement who recognizes that the essence of higher consciousness is never casting anyone out of your heart. There is goodness to be found everywhere in the movement because it is sustained by sincere, well-meaning, committed people who don't underestimate the dimensions of the task before them, who are aware of the limitations both of themselves and of their path to enlightenment, and who serve others selflessly to help manifest a new mode of being: a radically changed world inhabited by a new humanity. Consider, for example, some of the very positive developments and trends of the last few decades. They are largely independent of each other. They are proceeding at varying rates. They have their own factionalism and divisiveness. Some might even disown any New Age label. Nevertheless, in their totality they are manifestations of a common urge to transcend human limitations and to change society at its innermost level:

• The elevation of spirituality over religiosity in context of tolerance for, and exploration of, spiritual traditions and sacred lifeways. Burgeoning interest in, and acceptance of, innate psychic abilities and the reality of paranormal phenomena.
• Holistic health philosophy and practices which recognize alternatives to the "drug and slug" pills-and-surgery method and seek to combine them in ways appropriate for treating the whole person rather than merely the illness, while emphasizing the individual's responsibility for creating health.
• The self-reliance and local-sufficiency movement chronicled by

Mother Earth News, sections of *The Whole Earth Catalog,* and kindred publications.

• Natural foods and the associated emphasis on a healthy lifestyle, which includes good nutrition and proper diet as aids to personal growth.

• The push for energy conservation, renewable energy technology, and "small is beautiful"/appropriate technology.

• Environmentalism—meaning everything from saving whales and snails to "get those chemicals out of our water and soil and that pollution out of our sky," along with reforestation of denuded areas in Third World countries.

• The "new communities" movement, which has given rise to experiments in political authority and decision-making, cottage industries, alternate education, and global networking.

• The women's movement, which seeks a simple but fundamental goal essential to human happiness: equality of status and opportunity for the genders.

• The movement for civil rights, which seeks equality of opportunity and protection under the law for citizens regardless of race, creed, color, national or ethnic origin, marital status, affectional orientation, age, or disability. (Diversity must be respected and allowed full expression within legal bounds set up in recognition that violence, deceit, exploitation, and coercion are wrong and morally indefensible. Thus, ideally speaking, sexual freedom will lead to the elimination of pornography, prostitution, rape, child molestation, incest, and other heinous, abusive forms of sexual behavior.) Also, recognition of a person's autonomy will lead to the elimination of laws which regard women and children as chattel or possessions to be sold or bargained away in marriage.

• Respect for native peoples—their history, traditions, and contemporary plight.

• Ethical investing as a means of social reform.

• Emphasis on ethics in commerce, politics, and medicine to the point that those institutions are beginning to formulate explicit statements about their ethical principles and having professional ethicists to guide them.

• The hospice movement, thanatology, and death education, as well as reform of funeral industry practices.

• Socially conscious journalism and alternate news publications which cover events and issues generally ignored by mainstream publications or are treated superficially (as in *Time* magazine's 1987 cover story on the New Age).

• The blossoming of sports and recreation into a host of brand-new pastimes such as hang gliding, windsurfing, and triathalon and a veritable explosion of interest in older pursuits ranging from body building and mountain climbing to the martial arts, along with a parallel spillover of sports medicine and physical fitness into the public's awareness.

• The comprehensive critique of the scientific establishment's philosophical base of physicalism, objectivism, and reductionism.

• The grass-roots humanitarian efforts to feed the hungry (in Ethiopia; various food kitchens for street people), clothe the naked (The Farm gathering blankets for Guatemalan earthquake victims), treat the sick (the Seva Foundation's work to eliminate a form of eye disease in the Third World), shelter the homeless (Habitat for Humanity; varicus efforts on behalf of street people), aid prisoners (Amnesty International), and comfort the afflicted (Mother Teresa's centers).

• The efflorescence of the arts—everything from graphics and the plastic arts through music and dance to film and drama.

• The emergence of self-help groups and peer support groups dealing with a wide range of problems and painful situations from substance abuse and other addictions to Parents Without Partners, Widows and Widowers, and even Parents of Murdered Children.

• The coalition of antimilitaristic forces calling for the elimination of nuclear arms, the entire weapons industry, and the military-political-industrial power elite which supports it while urging governments to begin working for a world beyond war.

These are aspects of an emerging global culture which seek to found itself in love and wisdom, honesty and equality, peace and freedom. That emergence, that profoundly spiritual process, is self-transcendence and the experience of enlightenment. Behind that, less far along the path, are larger numbers of people who are entering the transpersonal realm to one degree or another. That, as I see it, has never before happened to the extent and degree it is happening now. Behind that group are still larger numbers of people who are entering the domain of self-actualization and development of a fully functional ego. And, although development of individualized self-sense or sense of self-autonomy is far, far away from final self-transcendence, even that is part of the spiritual process. If there is only God, then even the development of ego is ultimately a gift from God when seen as part of the evolutionary process. As Ken Wilber aptly puts it, there can be no transcendence of ego until there is first an ego. The development of ego is inevitable. The problematic character of human affairs is due to the fact that, first, many people have not even reached that state and, second, of those who have, many are "stuck" there because the nature of ego is to resist anything which calls for its surrender. I elaborate on this central point throughout the book.

Yet the universe has a way of kicking out the underpinnings of the egoic structure so that it collapses from sheer weight of its insatiable demands. The result is called suffering. And when that happens, the person (if he survives the pain of his dysfunctional behavior) is ready to open to higher dimensions of reality. That, too, is happening at an unprecedented rate, as I see it.

Consider, for example, the astonishing proliferation of self-help groups which have arisen in the last three decades from the Alcoholics Anonymous model for recovery from alcoholism. There are now support groups for dealing with drug abuse, sexual and emotional addiction, schizophrenia, overeating, gambling, shoplifting, credit card abuse, the problems of adult children of alcoholics, and many other forms of dysfunctional behavior—those very forms of behavior which some commentators see destroying the roots of society. I see in all the turbulence of current affairs a healing process, which, in my judgment, can be described as *global*, even though such groups are still rare in the Soviet Union, China, and Third World countries, and as *spiritual*, even though at a relatively low-level stage in the spiritual process. In the sweep of human history, not only has such a thing never happened before; nothing even remotely similar to it has ever happened, let alone so rapidly.

Yes, the masses of humanity are still largely immature, with less than fully formed egos. And, of course, self-transcendence should not be confused with simply developing a mature ego, which is about where the AA model of growth takes people (although it also offers a perspective which points beyond the ego and the means—fellowship and spiritual practices—to move there). But these changes are occurring all around the world at a pace which is blinding compared to the pace of evolution prior to, say, 3000 B.C. If we measure that process by the half-life of rock stars or TV sets, it is very slow, of course. But by applying the yardstick of geologic time, it is obvious that something absolutely unprecedented in human history is now happening at an accelerating pace. I can't quantify it precisely; my vision of it is qualitative and defies exact description. But my gut feeling is that within two or three centuries, the changes in world society resulting from a fundamental shift in the human sense of identity will be well enough established to demark the beginning of a new era in which spiritual concerns characterize the time.

Call that the beginning of the New Age. Yet, there will continue to be large numbers (perhaps, for a time, the majority of the world's population) who have not truly grasped the transpersonal. That may go on for hundreds or even thousands of years, just as the majority of people today are not at the level of fully functional ego—2000 years after Jesus made the Christic demonstration, 2500 years after the Buddha exposed the illusion of egoic self-identity.

The defining characteristics are psychological: changes in consciousness. For the first time in human history, a society—roughly speaking, Euro-America—has fulfilled its physical-material needs so well, despite unfortunate pockets of poverty, that an entire industry is built on diet and exercise, losing weight and keeping fit through means other than the grinding drudgery of daily toil. The spiritual import is this: the fulfillment, even surfeit, of material needs is producing a sated society in which people are being forced to reckon with their inherent higher-level needs. Now, it is true that the next higher level beyond the physiological is sexual-emotional, so the immediate result of filling that need is the flood of drugs, pornography, liquor, and other cheap thrills people resort to—along with such problems as crime and inadequate rehabilitation facilities generated by them. But survivors are already moving beyond that level and meeting their needs in social concerns such as those I have mentioned. These efforts are global precisely because information communication is global, but they are also spiritual even though they utilize material means such as ships and planes to transport food, radio and TV to reach out for donations, and so on.

However, the extent and influence of these trends and developments should not lead to any facile notions of overnight transformation. Retarding forces are still deeply entrenched. Moreover, distinct differences in the degree of transpersonality are embodied in the developments just noted. As Georg Feuerstein, author of *Jean Gebser: What Color Is Your Consciousness?*, points out in his study of psychohistorian Jean Gebser, "There are cultural pockets in the United States and Europe where personal growth, self-actualization, or consciousness expansion are pursued as new values. Overall, this is promising simply because it is more benign than the defunct and degrading values of a materialistic mass culture. Yet in many ways it is also perilous because, despite all good intentions, it still betrays a lack of real understanding of the spiritual aspect of human existence. Personal growth, which is the hallmark of the New Age ideology, is clearly a desirable pursuit in a culture that, notwithstanding its great humanistic ideals, fails to encourage real creativity and genuine individualism. Nonetheless, personal transformation, as commonly practiced, does not amount to profound self-transcendence, which is the central spiritual value that *really* matters at this critical juncture in human history."[3] In "The New Age: Progression or Possibility?" in *Spectrum Review* (Spring 1988), Feuerstein calls for "a healthy measure of clarity, in which both reason and faith (rather than mere belief) have their rightful function." Amen!

If the New Age movement is successful—a big "if"—the world will put on a profoundly different face. But growth to higher consciousness, the sole qualification for true membership in the New Age, is not a quick and easy "Ten Weeks to Enlightenment" course and certainly cannot be attained by sending in a coupon, buying a book, or joining a group. You may *begin* there, but, as I point out in Chapter 2, enlightenment is ultimately a gift of grace. (Grace is for everyone, however!)

The New Age is not here yet to any significant degree. Evolution takes time. Nevertheless, a great awakening is under way at a quickening pace. It is an awakening in which you are called to have a role. The aim of the New Age movement is to create a unified planetary culture in which you and everyone else can fulfill your deepest nature and realize your greatest longing. It aims at creating a global society which transcends the perennial divisions of race, creed, gender, caste, nation, ethnic origin, political ideology, affectional orientation, and so forth. So, if you've ever despaired about the meaning of life and your place in the cosmos, know there is hope. HOPE is an acronym for Help Our Planet Evolve. You can help by actualizing your incredible potential for self-directed growth in body, mind, and spirit and then sharing that lovingly with others, whatever your circumstances. Do that and you'll be carrying out your part to welcome the New Age.

There will never be a better world until there are better people in it, and the place to start building better people is within yourself. To begin, I suggest you include in your own New Age orientation this pledge of allegiance or at least its spirit and attitude:

> I pledge allegiance to Humanity
> And the planet on which we live,
> One world, under God, indivisible,
> With peace and enlightenment for all.

PART I

SCIENCE—THE ASCENT OF HUMANITY

Commentary

In the early 1970s, while researching a book about the brain and consciousness, I was deeply impressed by scientific findings demonstrating human capacities well beyond our idea of "the norm." At that time the social implications of this research were essentially unexamined in science and unknown to the public. The research was specialized, scattered through many disciplines, technically written, and published two or three years after the fact in journals that circulate primarily to specialty libraries.

While science, in its objective fashion, was generating surprising data about human nature and the nature of reality, I saw that hundreds of thousands of individuals were coming upon subjective surprises of their own. Through systematic explorations of conscious experience, using a variety of methods, they were discovering such phenomena of mind as accelerated learning, expanded awareness, the power of internal imagery for healing and problem solving, and the capacity to recover buried memories; insights from these explorations changed their values and relationships. They were reaching out now for any information that would help them make sense of their experiences.

These words from the introduction to Marilyn Ferguson's famous 1980 best-seller, *The Aquarian Conspiracy: Personal and Social Transformation in Our Time,* succinctly show that science is at the leading edge of the transformation happening around the world. Science is there probing it, describing it, and even, because of its influence on societal affairs, guiding it to some extent. However, if what is happening is not merely technological, but deeper than that—as deep as the minds which produce technology—then the transformation is essentially an evolutionary advance manifesting the Divine, and science is in fact demonstrating the presence of God amid human affairs and human destiny.

Most scientists probably would not accept that as a description of their work or that of the scientific community in general, but from the perspective I'm offering here, it makes perfect sense. There is only God. Thus, everything is an expression of God, albeit often in forms which are seemingly far removed from, and even horrible distortions of, the one great Being. At the heart of all things, however, is a spark, an impulse, a sense of the Divine.

And now, around the globe, that unconscious awareness of humanity's sacred essence is coming forth in people as conscious knowing and active seeking for a higher state of being.

The long evolutionary ascent of the human species can be described thus far as a journey from a state of unconscious ignorance to conscious knowing, from nescience to science. At this point in our history humanity is characterized by a state of consciousness called ego. But if evolution is still going on, what might come next in our journey? From a spiritual perspective, the answer is clear: The purpose of the human journey is to regain heaven, our lost estate. Heaven is union with God. Its opposite, hell, is separation from God—or, since everything is a form of God and nothing is ever truly separate from God, the illusion of separateness. The difference between heaven and hell is measured not in units of distance but in degrees of self-transcendence.

The self to be transcended is ego. What is ego? It is essentially *bound* consciousness. It is the notion of separate selfhood, personal autonomy, independence from the nurturing matrix of society and environment which support individualized life. It is limited identity. It is self-conceived as being apart from God or Ultimate Reality or Cosmic Wholeness. Thus, the ego—the illusion of separate self—is hell. And thus, also, if the egoic state of consciousness characterizes present human affairs, it is not inaccurate to say that Earth is a living hell created by ourselves—our separate selves, our self-separation from God. The illusion of separate selfhood is precisely what has brought humanity to its present predicament. Every aspect of society is tainted, corrupted, and fallen from grace, from the natural state of harmony and nonsuffering which plants and animals demonstrate. The threats to life on the planet are all direct expressions of Man's ego.

But society per se, society in itself as an evolutionary development, is not evil or corrupt. Rather, it is the consciousness of people who create and constitute society which is the ultimate source of our living hell. Earth could be a living heaven if the consciousness of people were transformed.

That is where science can be most beneficial. Although ego is not the ultimate state of self-identity for people, it is nevertheless an all-important one. It is the critical point at which we, as an evolutionary experiment in operation of things which were now perceived as being apart from people, outside their own sphere of consciousness.

The fruition of that tendency to act upon nature, coupled with the faculty of ratiocination, became, over millennia, science.

Science is therefore a powerful expression of the ego. The hallmark of ego is the desire for self-aggrandizement, the desire to play God and create the cosmos in its image rather than recognize the prior existence of God as its very source of being. It is the familiar pursuit of domination and control over all others. The scientific urge for omniscience and omnipotence is all too obvious. But the inherent limitations of ego-based power and understanding bring it to conditions beyond its control and understanding, and thus suffering arises. Suffering is the means by which consciousness becomes aware of its egoically conceived identity and sees through the illusion of separate self.

Precisely that process has been at work in science. The hallmark of science is the urge to dominate and control nature. Technology, the principal expression of science, is essentially an extension of human powers. But that extension, despite its awesome achievements, has now begun to rebound upon us in the form of critical world conditions— military and ecological—which threaten our very existence and promise not happiness but suffering in the extreme.

The situation has forced science to step outside its limited purview and take a larger look at itself and the universe. Science in its best form is a powerful means of probing the universe and testing the nature of reality. That in turn feeds back into the processes by which we humans seek to know ourselves and the world, thereby clarifying our understanding and refining our awareness. As we examine our existence ever more deeply, gaining knowledge and power, the scientific process helps take us beyond ourselves—our limited, egoic selves.

Rightly understood, then, science is part of the process by which Spirit is shaping humanity and helping it ascend to godhood. Science is both an expression of evolution and a means for furthering the evolutionary process. That process has now reached a point where, for the first time, Man has the power to begin directing it. As evolutionary anthropologist Pierre Teilhard de Chardin phrases it, "the psychic temperature is coming to a boiling point." Science can buffer nature's influence on evolution while enhancing our own capabilities and choices. Yet science is a mixed blessing. It offers tremendous potential for human betterment but is not consistently used for that purpose. As always, it is consciousness which is of primary influence. If the consciousness of scientists and those who apply science were expanded beyond ego, the world situation would change radically. The power of science would remain, but its use would be purified.

the great theater of Nature, may self-destruct or move forwa
transegoic condition which fulfills the cosmic calling we humans
we, as a species, can transcend ego, every aspect of human life
transformed through the recognition of its inner, hidden nature
form of God.

Science, too, is a form of God. At the moment, it is an egoic
which means it has the potential for self-unfoldment and transforr
but is presently not acting in accord with that potential. It is "go
because its philosophy allows no place for morality or theological (
tion. It is also "materialistic" because its perspective is by defii
focused on the physical nature of the universe.

Now, it is a feature of the spiritual process that ego-transcenc
cannot occur until there is first an ego to be transcended. In the prc
of ego formation, certain powers and abilities emerge. Ego is the anc
the fixed point to which latent abilities become tied in place for act
Considered that way, ego is ultimately a gift from God for our spiri
development. But its value becomes understandable only from
far side of the process, only beyond ego. In the words of transp
sonal psychologist Dane Rudhyar, author of *The Planetarization*
Consciousness:

> The process of formation of the ego is . . . a very necessary feature in the full
> development of man's potentialities; but the ego is a means to an end, and not the
> end in itself. . . . The role of the ego could be at least partially illustrated by
> considering this ego as the "scaffolding" needed to build, say, a soaring temple.
> This scaffolding is necessary for the adequate, timely, and efficient transportation
> of the building materials to where they belong . . . but once the temple is
> completed, the scaffolding should be dismantled and its materials used for other
> purposes.

Prior to the emergence of the egoic state of consciousness in humanity,
people were still embedded in nature. They functioned with a sense of
identity which was essentially defined by the tribe, clan, or social group.
This is seen clearly in so-called primitive peoples today. At the time of
humanity's ego-emergence, however, the feeling of identity with the
naturic realm disappeared. As the individualized self-sense solidified in
humanity, people developed a sense of personal autonomy—a power to
function for themselves rather than the group. A tendency developed to
act *upon* nature rather than *in* nature or in harmony with nature.

With the development of egoic consciousness also came new mental
faculties, notably ratiocination or the ability to think in analytical-
conceptual terms which "stood on their own" free from the need to be
referred to "the gods" or some external authority for validation. People
began to think for themselves. A tendency developed to question the

The essays in this part are intended to show the usefulness of science for consciousness expansion-evolution. I am not a scientist—only a student of science. As such, however, I have deep regard for the value of science in helping humanity to understand reality—the world around us, our own mind's operations, the origins of humanity. I have tried to use science as much as possible in my explorations of consciousness. So this section presents some of my findings and speculations based on use by scientific data and thinking. The subjects of my explorations, however, have been largely beyond the pale of official science. There is no great rush to fund research into UFOs, firewalking, kundalini experiences, pole shift predictions or yogic powers. However, all these subjects and the others covered here have import for higher human development and expanded understanding of the cosmos. They caught my attention, demanding comprehension. When I felt I had attained it, I wrote about it, offering my comments as "information for transformation."

The Great Awakening now under way around the planet is behind these essays. Although the bulk of humanity is largely ignorant of the Divine hidden within, the "imprisoned splendor," that interior divinity is identical with consciousness as ultimate reality. All our knowledge and discoveries are events in which we learn ever more deeply that all is one, that the deepest aspect of ourselves is intimately related to the foundations of the cosmos. I see a meeting of science and spirit occuring which will remind us of that. It will re-mind us in the sense of helping us attain a "new" mind which sees through the illusion of separation between "I" and the universe. If that state of ignorance can be dispelled, the true dimensions of the self will be known by all and a New Age will have arrived.

I conclude this commentary with a quotation to balance the opening one. Paul Brunton, a modern master of wisdom, told us in his 1935 book, *The Secret Path:*

> When the truth about the hidden side of the universe and of man is once more unveiled, demonstrated so far as it can be in a scientific and rational manner, the new scientific findings will stagger the most powerful intellects. We shall then build a pillar of higher wisdom which shall rise up into a new and finer age, and we shall testify anew to those eternal spiritual truths which no advance of science, no progress of civilization, no lapse in human character, can ever render obsolete (p. 221).

1

Neuroscience and the New View of Mind

The relation between mind and brain is a centuries-old debate, never settled to the satisfaction of everyone. Philosophers and theologians have maintained, by and large, that mind and brain are separate entities (psyche and soma) which interact but nevertheless belong to distinctly different domains of existence, the physical and the metaphysical. However, scientists—including many psychologists—have for the most part taken an opposed view, arguing that mind is a byproduct or epiphenomenon of the brain and nervous system which ceases to exist when the brain stops functioning. The mind, they said, is wholly explainable in terms of the physics and chemistry of matter. The psyche is not necessary for psychology.

In recent years important findings and statements from neuroscientists in the forefront of brain research have challenged the materialist view of Man and support the ancient position that mind is real in and of itself.

One of the opening volleys was fired by neurophysiologist Sir John Eccles, whose work on the nervous system earned him a Nobel Prize for medicine in 1963. Eccles rejects the soulless view of Man, declaring that consciousness cannot be explained through science. "I believe that there is a fundamental mystery in my existence, transcending any biological account of the development of my body (including my brain) with its genetic inheritance and its evolutionary origin," he wrote in 1961 in *The Brain and the Unity of Conscious Experience*.[1] More recently he said in an interview: "The genetic code and natural selection explains quite a lot. But not how I came to exist. It doesn't explain even the origin of consciousness. If you look at the most modern texts on evolution you find nothing about mind and consciousness. They assume it just comes automatically with the development of the brain. But that's not the answer."[2]

Then what is? "If I say that the uniqueness of the human self is not derived from the genetic code, not derived from experience," Eccles told an interviewer, "then what is it derived from? My answer is this: from a divine creation. Each self is a divine creation."[3] In his 1985 book, *The Wonder of Being Human*,[4] Eccles summed up his life's work as a neuroscientist by declaring that each of us has a "divinely created psyche" which must be considered central to all questions of immortality and self-identity. Remarking on the book, he said that he believes in both a material world and a mental-spiritual world.

Eccles also says he has discovered the precise location in the brain where the mind interacts with it: the supplementary motor area. First there is motive, then intention, then action. Motive and intention are mental, nonmaterial; they are impressed onto the brain, which causes neural action leading to behavior: "Mind 'scans' and 'probes' and 'gently influences' the brain in a 'selective and unifying manner.' with physical and metaphysical implications."

One such implication is free will: "I want to insist that we do have this moral responsibility stemming from free-will, from the ability of the mind to work on the brain."[5]

Canadian neurosurgeon Wilder Penfield, famed for his discovery of evoked memories and new mental experiences through electrical stimulation of the brain, likewise challenged the notion that mind can be explained in terms of brain mechanisms. Although he had first thought that his discovery provided a physical "window" into the psyche through which it could be observed and measured, experience proved otherwise. In *The Mystery of the Mind*, written after four decades of brain research, he stated that the mind will always be quite impossible to explain on the basis of electrochemical action in the brain and nervous system: ". . . the mind is peculiar," Penfield wrote. "It has energy. The form of that energy is different from that of neuronal potentials [electrochemical activity] that travel the axone [nerve] pathways. I am forced to choose the proposition that our being is to be explained on the basis of two fundamental elements."[6]

Those elements are mind and matter. A few days before his death the following year, Penfield said in an interview "The mind is independent of the brain. . . . The brain is a computer. . . . But it is programmed by something that is outside itself, the mind."[7]

Dr. Roger W. Sperry of the California Institute of Technology is another top-ranked neuroscientist whose work suggests a new view of mind. Sperry was awarded the Nobel Prize in 1981 for his split-brain studies, which led to the discovery of hemispheric functioning and dominance. He showed that neurological activities accompanying mental processes are assigned either primarily to the brain's left or right hemisphere. Thus, a person whose corpus callosum joining the hemispheres has been severed can, for example, visually recognize an object (a right-hemisphere function) but cannot say the word for it (a left-hemisphere function).

Like Penfield, Sperry had originally (in the early 1950s) thought that consciousness was derived from brain activity. Also like Penfield, he was forced by his research to abandon that position. In trying to account for the paradoxical unity-and-duality of conscious experience in split-brain experiments, he had to recognize mental events as having equal status with brain function.

Today, although he does not go so far as Eccles and Penfield in his view of mind, Sperry states that mind has causal power in its own right. It emerges, he says, via hierarchically organized physical systems of brain components, yet it nevertheless somehow supersedes activity of the brain and nervous system. Although Sperry does not claim to understand how the mind emerges from the body and then transcends it to attain primary status, he says it is nevertheless "the crowning achievement of evolution." He points out in *Science and Moral Priority* that the power of the whole (in this case, the mind) is greater than the sum of its parts (brain mechanisms and components) just as water is an emergent property of hydrogen and oxygen.

"Current concepts of the mind–brain relation involve a direct break with the long-established materialist and behaviorist doctrine that has dominated neuroscience for many decades," writes Sperry. "Instead of renouncing or ignoring consciousness, the new interpretation gives full recognition to the primacy of inner conscious awareness as a causal reality."[8]

Neuroscientist Dr. Karl Pribram of Stanford University also has contributed to the ferment in mind–brain research. In his book *The Language of the Brain* (1971) he drew on holography, a lensless photographic process which produces 3-D images, to explain brain function and mental experience. The brain's "deep structure," he said, is essentially holographic. The brain seems to Pribram a hologram interpreting a holographic universe. This conception has delighted people interested in mysticism and other topics usually considered to belong to religion and philosophy because it suggests the convergence of "inner space" and "outer space," psychology and physics.

Thus, the research of these authoritative brain scientists is undermining the chemical-neurological model of mind which denies the reality of a nonmaterial realm. This "new" view of mind offers experimental evidence pointing to a metaphysical domain which interacts with the physical and works into brain processes, yet nevertheless retains its own character as psyche, soul, mind.

The implications are vast. Briefly stated: Mind which can *function* independent of brain processes provides a scientific rationale for psychic abilities, and mind which can *exist* independent of brain provides a scientific rationale for life after death. At the very least, the research restores the psyche to psychology and provides a rational basis for religious faith.

It also underscores the humor in the joke "The materialist view of Man is mindless."

2

Enlightenment and the Brain

An article in *The New York Times* headlined "New Evidence Points to Growth of the Brain Even Late in Life" (July 30, 1985) noted that the traditional view of brain development is changing. That view says development is complete by late childhood due to innate genetic design. However, new research indicates that even in old age, the neural cells of the cerebral cortex respond to an enriched environment by forging new connections to other cells. (The cerebral cortex is the "thinking" or "intellectual" part of the brain.) In other words, the brain can grow nerve cells at almost any age in response to novelty and challenge. A study of rats showed that neurons increased in dimension and activity, glial cells (which support neurons) multiplied, and the dendrites of neurons (branches of neurons which receive messages from other cells) lengthened. The dendritic increase allows for more, and presumably better, communication with other cells.

Another *Times* article (Sunday magazine, July 28, 1985) about brain research focused on "The Stuff of Genius." It reported that the brain of Albert Einstein was investigated recently by neuroanatomists who likewise counted the neuronal and glial cells. They found that parts of Einstein's brain used in mathematical thinking had significantly more glial cells for each neuronal cell than the brains of people not known to have been geniuses.

There is nothing firmly conclusive in this intriguing research, but it reminded me of something I wrote in the introduction to *The Highest*

13

State of Consciousness (1972). There I suggested that enlightenment involves a repatterning of the brain's neural networks. Integration or unification is a primary aspect of the mindstate called enlightenment. Since mind and brain are obviously closely related, it seems clear that whereas before enlightenment the brain's nervous system had unconnected or "compartmentalized" areas (the neurological analog of a "fragmented" understanding), in enlightenment there is a breakthrough resulting in an integration of the nerve pathways through which we think and feel. Our multiple "brains" become one brain. The neocortex (the "thinking–intellectual" part), the limbic system and thalamus (the "feeling– emotional" part), and the medulla oblongata (the "instinct–unconscious" part, at least according to Carl Jung) attain a previously nonexistent but always possible mode of intercellular communication. A threshold is passed, probably explainable in terms of both cellular electrochemical change and growth of new nerve-ending connections. However it may be accomplished in neurophysiological terms, the result is intimately associated with a new state of consciousness, a new mode of perception and feeling associated with the discovery of nonrational (but not irrational) forms of logic—forms which are multilevel/integrated/simultaneous rather than linear/sequential/either–or.

What does this have to do with spiritual disciplines, you may ask. And isn't enlightenment ultimately a matter of grace? After all, God can't be commanded and heaven can't be taken by storm.

Theologically speaking, grace is an inscrutable experience, wholly beyond human knowledge and control, defined by Webster as "unmerited divine assistance given man for his regeneration or sanctification." Yet, if there is a relationship between the brain and enlightenment, grace must be accounted for in some way, to some degree. What in the body of scientific knowledge has the characteristics theologians ascribe to grace? Answer: a cosmic ray. I suggest that a partial description of the event called grace can be made in terms of physics and physiology.

As explained in Chapter 20, grace falls like rain on everyone but, also like rain, it can only be received by a vessel properly prepared to catch it. The preparation involves a change of readiness brought about through spiritual discipline and self-purification. Without preparation we are merely rough stones on which the rain of grace slides off; with it, we become worked stones hollowed into urns or chalices which can retain what falls from heaven. The entire process is a paradoxical mixture of effort and effortlessness. The effort is spiritual practice, our own ascent toward heaven; the effortlessness is grace, which perpetually descends from heaven for our benefit. I suggest the following is a partial description of what occurs upon one's first entry into *turiya*, the Sanskrit term for the ultimate state of consciousness.

What has been happening physiologically in a person practicing a spiritual discipline in order to realize God or experience enlightenment? In neurological terms, that person has been altering the structure, efficiency, and quality of his nervous system. He might be quite unaware of this aspect of his effort. Nevertheless, by directing his consciousness godward he has been growing new dendrites in the brain so that better, more efficient neuronal connections may be made, just as the *Times* articles suggest. Body follows where consciousness goes; matter is directed by intention of mind (this is one of the laws of noetics). Thus the spiritual aspirant has also been subtly altering the electrochemical composition of his neurons so they can pass on information better. He has also been eliminating the effects of stress which lower the efficiency of the nervous system. Altogether, he has been undergoing a holistic process of purification necessary for unification of body, mind, and spirit.

All this has been going on below the threshold of personal awareness, building up a condition in the brain and cerebrospinal system which is at a critical point at the moment of grace. The person's physiological condition is subtly altered. It is just on the borderline, the threshold, the point of shift to making that quantum leap accompanying a major consciousness change. But it still needs a little something more. It is in a necessary condition but not a sufficient condition.

Then, *wham!* The person is struck by something so subtle, so unpredictable, so swift and so strong that it triggers a psychophysical transformation process within him. The trigger could be almost anything, even a cosmic ray. A cosmic ray—who can tell it's coming or going? But it's all that I needed, I suspect, to turn that alchemical vessel, the human body, from lead to gold. That is all that's needed to precipitate or catalyze the essential ingredients together into a new and stable element.

A cosmic ray may be God's grace-full tool for inducing cosmic consciousness. And we are constantly bombarded by them, drenched by them, immersed in them like the rain! That little packet of energy probably hits the person between the eyes—in the "third eye"—and goes into the pineal gland, the master gland, which controls hormonal production and balance. We know from physics that when a cosmic ray enters the charged (i.e., ready) chamber of a geiger-counter tube and strikes a molecule, it sets off a cascade effect which develops into an avalanche of molecules. This avalanche in turn becomes one of the "clicks" from the geiger counter. Similarly, a "chance" cosmic ray entering the pineal gland may be all that is needed for the ready vessel-person to start a quantum mechanical chain of events which quickly escalates up to the molecular level and sets off a change in the hormonal balance of the body, which in turn is all that is needed to issue a command to the nervous system: Okay, neurons, repattern yourselves; connect up those loose ends, shift to the new support processes, *change your ways.*

And in the flash of an "I," there the person is: caught up in visionary experience, looking on the universe in *samadhi,* cosmic consciousness, in *satori,* enlightenment. Not final enlightenment, to be sure, because enlightenment is an endless process. What I've described is just the entry stage through which we access turiya, but it nevertheless marks a major shift in the mind–brain relation and its attendant physiology.

A cosmic ray is not God's only tool, of course. Enlightenment doesn't care how you get there and God is everywhere, using every means at His[1] command (and they are considerable!) to awaken us to divinity. So this speculative description of the psychophysiology of enlightenment is by no means definitive. On the other hand, I don't think it detracts from God's glory to try to extend science ever farther into the metaphysical realm. After all, God is always the root of our exploration and the fruit of our discovery, science included. So sometimes a cosmic ray is God's tool and sometimes God's tool is something less gentle and elegant, like the slap in the face Tilopa gave to Naropa centuries ago in Tibet, inducing Naropa's enlightenment. Sometimes it's a blow on the head from the Zen master's slapping stick as we sit in meditation, just as Hakuin, the Zen master, was liberated when a housewife who resented his monkish rice-begging hit him on the head with a broom. And sometimes it's the blow to the heart given us by someone's treachery, someone's unexpected death, someone's "chance" remark, someone's kindness in the face of our own stupidity or brutish behavior. Grace surrounds us. The entire universe is conspiring to awaken us, to release us, to enlighten us. God doesn't care how we get there.

3

Meditation
and Evolution

Life on Planet Earth is threatened from many directions; many responsible sources warn of this. There is the possibility of nuclear, chemical, and biological warfare by the superpowers. There is worldwide pollution of the air, land, and sea by all nations. Nonrenewable resources—topsoil, water, minerals, tropical rain forest, and the ozone layer among them—are being wasted or destroyed. Overpopulation is straining the biosphere, bringing drought and pestilence.

All these threats to life are manmade; all of them originate in the minds of people. Our behavior is a manifestation of our thinking and emotions, and in turn our thoughts and feelings are dependent upon our state of consciousness. Our present world situation, then, is one in which we exhibit much irrational behavior. That, in turn, is due to what we might call "a crisis of consciousness." If so, the solution to the problem presented by these threats can be stated very simply: Change consciousness.

Survival demands a change of consciousness. Not just survival, but evolution as well. As I read the history of nature, I see evolution as a record of ever-more-complex forms of life coming into being in order to express more fully the consciousness behind life. The history of evolution is a story of creating ever-more-complex forms of consciousness.

Evolution is always at work. That means now, today. And what I see today, in addition to the threats to life, are signs that the life force itself is mobilizing its resources to resist extinction. How will it resist? The

17

answer is simple: By evolving forms of life suited to the new conditions on Earth—forms of life which know how to live in harmony with the planet and its creatures. They will know how to live this way because their consciousness will have changed.

They-in-the-making is us. If we have seen the enemy—human irrationality—we also have seen the possibility of participating in the evolutionary process and changing ourselves in a conscious, self-directed fashion. Meditation is one of the means to help ourselves make the necessary change of consciousness a New Age demands. Meditation is a means of personal and transpersonal growth. Meditators claim that the best way for people to change is by "working on yourself" from within via meditation. It is a time-honored technique (perhaps humanity's oldest spiritual discipline) for helping people release their potential for expanded consciousness and fuller living. As a technique for assisting in the enlightenment process of knowing God or ultimate reality, meditation appears in some form in nearly every major religious tradition. The entranced yogi in a lotus posture, the Zen Buddhist sitting in zazen, the Christian contemplative kneeling in adoration of Jesus, the Sufi dervish whirling in an ecstasy-inducing trance: all can be properly described as practicing meditation. Although the cultural or religious trappings may vary, meditation's core experience is an altered state of consciousness in which the ordinary sense of I—the ego—is diminished, while a larger sense of self-existence-merged-with-the-cosmos comes into awareness.

Meditation Research

Meditation works on all levels of our being: physical, psychological, and social as well as spiritual. Research shows that it improves general health and stamina; it decreases tension, anxiety, and aggressiveness; it increases self-control and self-knowledge. Drug use and abuse are usually curbed and sometimes stopped. Psychotherapy progresses faster than usual. Personal and family relations tend to improve. And except for borderline psychotics, meditation is safe, harmless, extremely easy to learn, beautifully portable, available in endless supply, and completely legal.

Meditation research has been reviewed by Michael Murphy and Steven Donovan in their very valuable book *The Physical and Psychological Effects of Meditation*.[1] It covers scientific research from the first meditation study in 1931 through 1988 and summarizes what has been found to happen, physiologically and psychologically, during and after meditation sessions. Murphy and Donovan show that most claims for meditation are valid so far as the first stages of meditative activity go. Although they say more and finer research is needed to look at the "greater heights and depths of transformative experience," research to date corresponds with traditional accounts by meditators sufficiently to suggest that "the ancient paths toward enlightenment produced the kinds of integration and illumination they claimed."

Gains from Meditation

There will never be a better world until there are better people in it. Meditators claim that meditation changes their lives for the better. Edgar Cayce described meditation as an emptying "of all that hinders the creative forces from rising along the natural channels of the physical man to be disseminated through those centers and sources that create the activities of the physical, the mental, the spiritual man; properly done [this] must make one stronger mentally, physically" (Reading 281–13). Dr. Haridas Chaudhuri, philosopher and author of many works on spiritual development, defined meditation as "the art of bringing to full flowering the hidden spiritual potential of man's psychophysical system.

"Although enlightenment is the ultimate goal, many (perhaps most) meditators will not reach this fulfillment. Nevertheless, if you begin meditating, you can be reasonably certain that you will still find many worthwhile benefits in your life. These are likely to include:

1. Freedom from the feeling of pressure in day-to-day affairs.
2. Avoidance of what is generally called "that tired feeling".
3. Minimal recurrence of chronic nagging pains such as headache, arthritis, indigestion, and colitis.
4. Reduction of insomnia, caffeine and nicotine dependence, and general use of drugs.
5. Greater tolerance and love for others.
6. Greater satisfaction from your religious affiliation, if you have one.
7. Greater desire to be helpful, either in public service or in your own private life.

In the more advanced states of meditation, mental and physical stillness is complete. The meditator is totally absorbed in a blissful state of awareness having no particular object. His consciousness is without any thoughts or other contents; he is simply conscious of consciousness. In yoga, this emptiness of consciousness without loss of consciousness is called *samadhi.* In Zen it is *satori.* In the West it is best known as cosmic consciousness or enlightenment. In this there is a paradox. In the emptiness comes a fullness—unity with divinity, knowledge of humanity's true nature, and (to use a phrase from St. Paul) "the peace of God which passeth all understanding." Lama Anagarika Govinda, a German who became a Tibetan Buddhist lama, said that meditation is "the means to reconnect the individual with the whole—i.e., to make the individual conscious of his universal origin. This is the only positive way to overcome the ego-complex, the illusion of separateness, which no amount of preaching and moral exhortation will achieve. To give up the smaller for the bigger is not felt as a sacrifice but as a joyous release from oppression and narrowness. The 'selflessness' resulting from this experience is not due to moral considerations or pressures, but a natural attitude, free from the feeling of moral superiority; and the compassion which flows from it is the natural expression of solidarity with all forms of sentient life."

Definitions and Techniques

That experience of peace and unity is difficult to attain, however, because the mind is always wandering. Meditation might be described as a technique for developing attention control so that worry, fear, anger, and all other anxieties gradually dissipate. The dictionary definition of meditation, based on Western psychology, is inadequate to describe this experience. To contemplate or to ponder is not synonymous with meditation as a spiritual practice. Going further in the dictionary, we find a better sense in which it may be understood: "a form of private devotion consisting of deep, continued reflection on some religious theme." This is closer to the true meaning but still is not completely adequate to explain meditation.

In physiological terms, meditation is neither ordinary waking, sleeping, nor dreaming but rather what has been described as a "wakeful hypometabolic condition." Brainwaves, heartbeat rate, blood pressure, respiration, galvanic skin resistance, and other body functions are altered in meditation. They slow to the point achieved in deep sleep and sometimes beyond, yet the meditator remains awake and emerges from meditation with a feeling of rest and loss of stress and tension. All this certainly is not included in the dictionary definition of meditation.

The common core of all meditation experiences is an altered state of consciousness which leads to a diminishing (and, hopefully, a total abolition) of ego, the self-centered sense of I. This core experience has been called "relaxed attention," "nonanxious attention," "detached alertness," and "passive volition."

To attain this state, many forms and techniques of meditation have been developed. Some are passive—as when a yogi sits cross-legged in a lotus asana with so little motion that even his breathing is hard to detect. Other forms of meditation, such as tai chi, involve graceful body movements. Sometimes the eyes are open; sometimes they are closed. Sometimes other sense organs than the eyes are emphasized, as when beginners in Zen pay attention to their nasal breathing. In other traditions, however, sensory withdrawal is dominant; attention is taken away from the senses. Some meditative techniques are silent; some are vocal. Transcendental Meditation is an example of the silent form while the Krishna Consciousness Society uses the *Hare Krishna* ("Hail, Lord Krishna") chant. Some meditations are private and some, such as Quaker meetings, are public. And, although most forms of meditation are self-directed, sometimes they are guided by a group leader.

Silent Forms of Meditation

The silent forms of meditation center on three techniques: concentration, contemplation, and the mental repetition of a sound. The sound, called a *mantra,* may be a single syllable such as *om.* It may be a word, phrase, or verse from a holy scripture. The Tibetan Buddhist *Om mani padme hum* ("the jewel in the lotus," or enlightenment) is an example. So is the simple prayer in the book called *The Way of a Pilgrim* which goes "Lord Jesus Christ, have mercy on me." Many Christians use the Lord's Prayer as a basis for meditation. Saying the decades of the Rosary is likewise mantric meditation. The Indian sage Kirpal Singh taught his followers to silently repeat five names of God which he gave them in a ceremony. Likewise, Maharishi Mahesh Yogi and his teachers of Transcendental Meditation initiate people into TM with various Sanskrit mantras; the meditator then uses his mantra during his meditations. Zen Buddhism has a variety of meditative techniques, some of which involve use of a *koan,* an apparently unsolvable riddle which the meditator silently examines. A widely known koan asks "What is the sound of one hand clapping?" Another inquires more directly about the basic nature of self-identity: "Who am I?"

In contemplative forms of meditation, the eyes are open so that the meditator sees what is called in Sanskrit a *yantra,* a form on which he centers his attention. The focus of attention may be a religious object such as a crucifix, statue, or picture. It might be an inscription, a candle flame, a flower. (All serve the same purpose.) Or the meditator may use a *mandala,* a painting or drawing, typically a square-in-a-circle design of many colors, which symbolizes the unity of microcosm and macrocosm.

Concentration is generally considered the most difficult form of meditation. In concentration techniques, an image is visualized steadily in the mind. It could be the thousand-petaled lotus of the Hindu and Buddhist traditions or the crescent moon of Islam. It could also be Judaism's Star of David or Christianity's mystic rose. Alternatively, the mind may be held free of all imagery and "mental chatter"—a clearing away of all thought. Or the attention might be focused upon some part of the body. For example, the mystical "third eye" at a point midway between the eyebrows (said to coincide with the pineal gland) is often used. Also common is the so-called concentration on the navel. This is actually a misunderstanding of the process of directing attention to the abdominal areas about two inches below the navel and simply becoming one with your breathing. The meditator flows into awareness of the rhythmical, cyclical body process by which life is sustained and united with the universe.

Some disciplines combine different aspects of several meditative techniques. For example, some styles of the martial arts use meditation in their training regimen. The Russian mystic Georges I. Gurdjieff taught his students to combine movements and meditation. Psychotherapist-author Ira Progoff of New York City guides people through therapeutic sessions using a technique he developed called process meditation. It is usually performed in a group, and Dr. Progoff speaks in order to guide the meditators into exploration of whatever imagery appears in their minds.

Meditation cannot be defined in a sentence or two. The term means many things to many people, varying in this or that aspect, depending upon culture, religious traditions, psychological orientation, individual purpose, and other factors.

Experience Is What Matters

In meditation, it is not really the definition but the *experience* which matters. Historically, the goal of meditation has been a transformation of the whole person. Research data dramatically validate many of the claims meditators make. Traditionally, these behavioral changes are reinforced through voluntary conformity with the meditative ethos and lifestyle—an aspect still little examined by science. Throughout history, teachers of meditation and spiritual masters have emphasized "right living" to support one's meditation. By that they mean a healthy diet; an honest means of income; association with virtuous and sympathetic people; truthful speech; kindness and humility in relations with others; a social conscience; giving up egotistical desire for power, fame, prestige, wealth, psychic powers, and so forth. As psychiatrist Arthur Deikman points out, "Probably the importance of meditation lies in its changing a person's orientation toward living, not in its ability to produce dramatic changes in states of consciousness. It's fairly easy for a normal person to have 'unnormal' experiences, but people meditating without the supporting philosophy are less likely to be involved long enough for some of the subtle changes to occur or to change their orientation from doing to allowing things to happen spontaneously."

This does not mean, however, that successful meditation requires extreme asceticism and withdrawal from society. The true aim of meditation is to bring the meditator more fully into the world, not to retreat from it. A religious retreat may be appropriate for some in the course of their meditative training and discipline. This is an honorable tradition— the way of the anchorite, monk, nun, and religious devotee. Yet even renunciate monks and nuns living reclusive lives often undertake efforts of a social nature: feeding and clothing the poor, for example, or offering spiritual sustenance to the ignorant and uneducated.

Here it is also important to note that meditation does not require abandonment of the intellect. It is true that in meditation the intellect's limitations become apparent, and other (usually unsuspected) modes of creative problem-solving and insight emerge. However, enlightened teachers, even illiterates like Ramakrishna, have always been recognized as brilliant people with finely honed intellectual powers who have enhanced their meditation "research" through study which cultivates the mind. Their writings and discourses display clear logic, a keen analytic discrimination, and a knowledge of tradition. It is no accident, then, that students frequently report improvement in their grades and ability to study after beginning meditation.

The greatest possible result of meditation is enlightenment. Spiritual masters of all ages have unanimously declared that through meditation people can come to know God. Through direct experience (not through intellectual conceptualization) people can reach a state of conscious union with ultimate reality and the divine dimension of the universe. In that state, all the long-sought answers to life's basic questions are given, along with peace of mind and heart. There are other paths to God-knowledge, of course, but this is one path easily available to many and the chief reason for the worldwide interest and enduring value placed on meditation. It is a tool for learning spiritual psychology, a technique for expanding consciousness.

The highest development in meditation, regardless of the school or "path," brings technique and daily life together. When learning and living are integrated in spontaneous practice moment to moment, the meditator becomes what has been called "meditation in action." Meditation is no longer just a tool or device or mental exercise, no longer just a "visit" to that state in which the larger sense of self-as-cosmos emerges. The gains from meditation become integrated in a manner of living best described as enlightenment. The meditator has so completely mastered the lessons of meditation that his entire life is a demonstration of the higher consciousness which can be experienced if sincerely sought.

People who attain this state have been recognized through the ages as special persons for whom attention and reverence is proper. For them the alteration of consciousness called meditation has led to a transformation of consciousness. Changing consciousness changes thought; changing thought changes behavior; and changing behavior changes society. Thus the changed ones live as inspiring examples for others who are on their way to personal transformation and who seek a viable, benign means of effecting planetary transformation.

This is the fullest development of meditation. Personal evolution becomes social revolution. By changing yourself, you help to change the world. This is the value of meditation.

4

Pole Shift Update: Consciousness Research and Planetary Transformation

In the early 1970s, there was a widespread rumor that the West Coast would experience a terrible earthquake and a large portion would slide into the sea. At that time, I was director of education at the Institute of Noetic Sciences in California. The institute had been set up by Apollo 14 astronaut Edgar Mitchell to study consciousness and human potential and to apply the findings to planetary problems. Because we were highly visible in the media, we began to receive communications from many people who felt they had psychic information about impending global disasters.

This rumor was probably due to the psychic readings of Edgar Cayce, the "sleeping prophet." In the 1930s Cayce had foretold certain global processes he called "earth changes." These changes were to include terrible earthquakes, volcanic eruptions, and the rise and fall of land masses. They would begin in the second half of this century and increase in intensity, culminating at the end of the century in what Cayce described as "the shifting of the poles." Cayce indicated that this shift of polar positions would be devastating. These predictions had permeated the

25

psychic community over the years and had set up the expectation of terrible global destruction.

Some people came to the Institute with messages of that sort. These people were well-intentioned and simply wanted us to alert the world. I listened sincerely to all such warnings, but it wasn't our function to warn the public (civil officials do that), so I turned down all requests for help in publicizing forecasts of earthquakes, UFO landings, and so forth. It proved to be the best policy, because in all cases the predictions were wrong.

Nevertheless my interest in precognition and psychic forecasting remained high, especially with regard to "pole shift." According to theory, a pole shift is a sudden and cataclysmic movement of the planet in which it flips end over end in space (as much as 180°) or—in the view of some pole shift theorists—the crust of the planet slips around the molten core (up to 90°). In either case, the result is said to be worldwide destruction.

One of the people who contracted the Institute was Jeffrey Goodman, author of *We Are the Earthquake Generation*. Both a geologist and an anthropologist, Dr. Goodman was researching the subject of earth changes by using a team of psychics to compile data about geophysical and societal changes over the next several decades. Goodman's purpose in contacting the Institute was not to make a warning but just to share some of his research findings.

The composite picture which emerged from his analysis of the psychic predictions was startling in three ways. First, there was a surprising amount of agreement among the psychics, even though they didn't know each other or what each had said to Goodman. Second, the composite picture foretold worldwide changes in the geography and climatic zones of the globe which would be almost instantaneous, geologically speaking, and thus would be catastrophic. (Imagine a tropical climate imposed overnight on the Arctic and vice versa.) Third, Goodman found that the predictions could be scientifically supported to some degree.

These changes, his psychic forecast said, would begin in the late 1970s and would build in intensity and frequency. There would be increasingly erratic freakish weather. There would be great loss of land in some areas through submergence and inundation, while in other areas new land masses would rise above sea level from the vast expanse of the world's oceans. All this would coincide with radical economic and political changes in society, population shifts, and a period of disorientation and suffering for civilization which would include terrible loss of life.

The final event in this scenario of earth changes would be a pole shift. According to some of the predictions, within a single day's time the entire planet or its crust would change position in space so that the polar positions would be shifted and relocated.

What would result from a pole shift? Global cataclysm. Enormous tidal waves would roll across the land as the oceans became displaced from their basins. Hurricane winds of hundreds of miles per hour would sweep over the planet. Earthquakes greater than have ever been measured would wrack the land. Volcanic activity would pour out huge lava flows along with poisonous gas and choking ash. Climates would change almost instantly. Land masses would rise and fall, altering the face of the globe. And if the shift were less than 180°, the polar ice sheets, moved into the temperate or tropic zones, would melt within a few hundred years while new ice sheets would begin to build at the new polar locations. Finally, large numbers of organisms, including humans, would be decimated or even exterminated, with signs of their existence hidden under thick layers of debris and sediment or at the bottom of newly established seas.

Has this ever happened? Might it happen again? That's what I became interested in exploring. Goodman seemed to have earth changes research well in hand, except that the question of pole shifts needed much deeper study and no one seemed to be doing that. So, out of intellectual curiosity and humanitarian concern, I decided to take on the job.

During six years of research I gathered a large amount of data which pointed strongly toward an affirmative answer to the questions above. The data came from three sources: ancient prophecies, contemporary psychics, and scientifically oriented researchers. Although their predictions and prophecies about a pole shift had many points of difference and even disagreement, they were almost unanimous in declaring that Planet Earth was going to experience a pole shift in the near future, about the end of this century. In 1980 I published *Pole Shift*, an examination of predictions and prophecies of "the ultimate disaster."

What are the sources of the predictions and prophecies?

First are the ancient prophecies I identified. These include the Bible, Hopi Indian and other Native American prophecies, Nostradamus, and several occult traditions claiming to have their roots in the lost civilizations of Atlantis and Lemuria.

Second are the contemporary psychics and others who claimed to have independently foreseen a pole shift. Edgar Cayce seems to have set the baseline for this topic in the psychic community. Among the others are Jeane Dixon; Ruth Montgomery; Paul Solomon, founder of the Fellowship of the Inner Light; and Aron Abrahamsen, a psychic who lives near Seattle.

Last is a handful of scientifically oriented researchers who claimed that pole shifts have happened before and that another is nearing. Immanuel Velikovsky was the most notable, although he did not predict another one. (When I interviewed him, he told me he was skeptical of those who do, although I was surprised to learn that he accepted the reality of ESP.) Albert Einstein also endorsed the idea of pole shifts, both past and future, in his introduction to a book on the subject by Charles Hapgood, *Earth's Shifting Crust*. Shortly before my book went to press, the prestigious *Journal of Physics* carried a long article by Peter Warlow, a British theoretical physicist, who discussed the evidence for previous pole shifts and proposed a mechanism to explain them. (He did not predict one in the future.)

The evidence suggesting previous pole shifts is dramatic but controversial. It comes from geology, astronomy, archeology, and physics. It includes frozen mammoths in Siberia and Alaska, including the famous Berezovka mammoth, which was found with undigested summer vegetation in its mouth and stomach. The evidence also includes coral reefs in Alaska; fossils of jellyfish and raindrops; well-preserved trees, thousands of years old, frozen under the treeless Arctic tundra, some with fruit and leaves still on them; glacial striations in rocks near the Equator which show a movement *toward* the poles; sudden reversals of the earth's magnetic field; animal extinctions correlated with ice ages; and ancient maps of Antarctica, apparently showing it free of ice, drawn hundreds of years before it was officially discovered in 1820. Still further suggestions of pole shifts are found in myths and legends from cultures around the world which tell of global floods, lost civilizations, and reversed celestial orientation of the earth. To some catastrophists, the pole shift concept appears to offer a unifying explanation of these diverse and enigmatic data, along with geological puzzles such as the question of the driving force behind continental drift and what caused abrupt climatic changes in prehistory.

In the ten years since I wrote *Pole Shift*, many new data have come to light which bear on the two principal questions I raised: Have there been previous pole shifts? Might there be one in the near future? Here I will briefly survey the new data and offer my assessment of their significance. I will also describe some of the events surrounding *Pole Shift*.

First, however, I will anticipate my conclusion. I offer this at the outset to alleviate the anxiety many people have expressed over humanity's future because of the pole shift predictions and prophecies I reported.

On the basis of a decade's hindsight, I think that the possibility of a catastrophic pole shift at the end of this century is increasingly unlikely. To be more precise, *I do not think a pole shift will occur as predicted.*

Why I Wrote *Pole Shift*

When I began my investigation of the pole shift questions, I neither believed nor disbelieved the various claims and forecasts. My stance was that of a journalist asking questions, not a scientist giving answers. When I had finished my investigation, I still neither believed nor disbelieved. There were too many unanswered questions, too many vaguely defined possibilities. My stance was still that of a journalist, skeptical and curious but convinced that a case for pole shifts could be legitimately made. However, as I said in the book, I am also aware that *presenting* the case for pole shifts is not the same as *proving* it. Personal conviction is not the same as public demonstration. Moreover, there was a strong case *against* pole shifts. I presented that also in the book, although only briefly because it was the point from which I began: the widespread assumption that our planet has not undergone any pole shifts and, by the "laws of nature," cannot. Therefore I also advocated an open-minded investigation by the scientific community into the *possibility* of a certain type of Doomsday event.

I did so for two reasons. The first was intellectual curiosity. My research had uncovered indications that a pole shift is theoretically possible and that one or more shifts may have occurred in the past. The pole shift concept appeared to offer a unifying explanation for a wide range of scientific anomalies and mysteries detailed in the book. Thus the explanation, if validated, would amount to a potential revolution in many fields of knowledge. On scientific grounds, therefore, a pole shift investigation seemed justified.

The second reason was humanitarian. The psychic and prophetic traditions pointed to various "earth changes" preceding a pole shift. Among them are increasing seismic activity in the form of earthquakes and volcanic eruptions; increasingly erratic weather; dramatically changing climatic patterns; shifts in oceanic currents; and societal instability marked by political, military, and economic forces, leading to cultural breakdown and population migrations. Events in the news during that time indicated that all those precursors were occurring to some degree. Such signposts caused anxiety among some people who were aware of the earth change and pole-shift predictions. On humanitarian grounds, therefore, a pole shift investigation also seemed justified.

New Data About Pole Shifts

When I wrote *Pole Shift* I was well aware that every generation has had its predictions of Doomsday—predictions which were obviously wrong. Moreover, I had no desire to be an alarmist. Rather, I sought through rigorous, thorough research to resolve various questions about pole shifts. Answering those questions could, I felt, help humanity take prudent action to avoid, or at least reduce, loss of lives and property if research seemed to confirm the predictions. On the other hand, if the questions were answered so as to disprove the pole shift concept and to refute the predictions, public fears could be allayed and attention could be turned to *real* problems.

What new data bearing on these topics have emerged since *Pole Shift* was published? Here are the principal categories of evidence supporting the pole shift concept, an explanation of why they do, and a summary of new developments. Some of the questions which prompted me to present the case for pole shifts are still unanswered. But enough has come to light to refute the pole shift theorists in two of these categories (the frozen mammoths and the ancient maps of Antarctica). In a third category, new theoretical support for sudden axis reversals has also come forth; at the same time, however, counterarguments have refuted one pole shift theoretician.

1. Anomalous Glacial Striations. Continental drift does not explain all anomalous glacial striations, pole shift theorists say. Those in South Africa, for example, show a direction of movement toward, not away from, the South Pole. Tectonic-plate theory indicates nothing to explain them. However, no further evidence or commentary on this subject has come to my attention. These data continue to defy the conventional notion that ice sheets have always spread out from the present polar locations. (For a relevant datum to the contrary, however, see the end of the next section.)

2. Ice Ages. Pole shift theorists ask this question: If slow and regular changes in the orbital geometry of Earth, reinforced by changes in the climate cycle, are the cause of ice ages, as conventionally claimed, what explains (1) the extremely rapid appearance and disappearance of continental-size ice sheets; (2) the vast epochs—each several hundred million years long, far exceeding the alleged periodicity of the ice ages—in which the planet was free of polar ice sheets; and (3) the fact that the North American ice sheet during the last age was centered in Hudson Bay while the present north polar area was virtually ice-free?

In 1982 Peter Warlow, to whom I had devoted a chapter, presented his position at length in a book, *The Reversing Earth*. Warlow proposes an extraterrestrial source as the trigger mechanism for pole shifts. He also proposes that planets are born as ejected cores of some larger bodies, which lead to a sequence of disturbances in a solar system. He states that it is possible for a celestial body "to exert a torque on the Earth even though it does not come into direct contact. We thus have the means of turning the Earth over."

After discussing the characteristics of such a body and the forces involved, Warlow calculates that a pole shift could occur "on a time scale of days rather than weeks, months, or years" but he does not predict that such an event will occur. In fact, he specifically rejects predictions and prophecies of "the Earth's axis tilting." Asserting that there is nothing special about the year 2000, Warlow concludes:

> I do not know when the next event is likely to occur. If the idea of planet birth is correct, it may well be a long time before another is born to disturb the Solar System . . . it may be many millions, or tens of millions of years. . . . In any case, it is likely that we will have as much time to build our arks and our stone circles, or their equivalent, as our ancestors had. In all probability, we will have plenty of forewarning—but from astronomical sightings rather than from any psychic insights.[1]

Warlow's presentation resulted in a number of papers examining his assumptions and mathematics. Dr. Victor J. Slabinski, an astronomer in the Intelsat Physics Department in Washington, D.C., challenged Warlow in a *Journal of Physics* article entitled "A Dynamical Objection to the Inversion of the Earth on its Spin Axis" (September 1981), in which he demonstrated that Warlow's explanation was mathematically unsound. In a further comment in *Kronos* (Winter 1982), he noted that Warlow had miscalculated the necessary torque for flipping the Earth, adding "Cosmic bodies large enough to invert the Earth act for a period much less than the 24 hours assumed by Warlow. . . . Not even confining the inversion to a thin crustal shell yields a practical solution."

Further refutation of Warlow's position was offered in the same issue of *Kronos* by C. Leroy Ellenberger, a long-time investigator of the pole shift question. He began as an advocate of Velikovsky's work. However, the weight of evidence in his continuing research has led him to conclude that Velikovsky was thoroughly wrong. Greenland ice cores, bristlecone-pine rings, and ocean sediments show that Velikovsky's version of our solar system history did not happen, he asserts. Ellenberger reviewed Warlow's argument and mathematics, noting various errors, and concluded: "For the entire Earth or its crust to flip over solely under the gravitational influence of a passing cosmic body of any size seems impossible."

In a long technical letter submitted for publication by the Society for Interdisciplinary Study's *Workshop* (1988:2), Ellenberger wrote

> There simply is no physical evidence for a geographical inversion ever having happened. Warlow's book discusses four lines of physical evidence that supposedly support their occurrence: geomagnetic reversals, ice ages, sea-level changes, and mass extinctions. Perhaps Warlow . . . now realizes that these events are inadequate as evidence since they can be readily explained by other less extravagant processes. . . . I believe the best physical evidence would be uniquely related to an inversion, e.g., formations on Earth reminiscent of the tidally-induced bulge, or some other mass concentration, that enabled a torque to flip Earth or systematic worldwide coastal destruction caused by the accompanying ocean floods. I am unaware of any evidence for the former presence of such a bulge or mass concentration.

About the time Warlow's book appeared, a Swedish theoretical physicist, Dr. Stig Flodmark, presented a long paper, "The Earth's Rotation," at the European Geophysical Society's annual meeting in Uppsala in which he proposes a mechanism for explaining pole shifts. Flodmark is associated with the Institute of Theoretical Physics at the University of Stockholm. In August 1981 he offered a new model of polar shifts which also accounts for ice ages and their anomalous (rather than regular) appearance in Earth's history. He proposed a "double-top" model of the planet in which the solid inner core is separable from the solid mantle and viscous part of the core. Frictional forces normally keep the "tops" rotating in unison or nearly so, but there is a slight differential which can explain observed small polar motions known as the annual wobble and the Chandler wobble. The double-top model, Flodmark asserts, also can explain glacial ages, magnetic role reversals, faunal extinctions, and other enigmatic topics in Earth's history and geology. Unlike Warlow, Flodmark predicts that Earth *is* nearing the moment when another pole shift will occur within the space of a single day and that "some perturbance of the smooth rotation of the earth could be expected shortly."

In subsequent papers Flodmark modified his model to a triple-top. With that he also proposes explanations for the end of ice ages through frictional heat from mantle wobbling, the necessary power for geomagnetism, and the cause of earthquakes, volcanism, and mountains.

The only commentary on Flodmark I've found was offered by Ellenberger in the *Kronos* article noted above, in which he wrote "In light of the unsolved and apparently unsolvable problems attending the solid body tippe top model, Flordmark's double-top model, at this same, seems a viable replacement. . . . However, a high priority should be placed on validating the double-top model." As already noted, Flodmark himself revised the model. I am not aware of any further commentary or criticism of Flodmark's work.

That work may provide the mechanism sought by Dr. Michael Herron, research assistant professor at the State University of New York at Buffalo, who, at about the time of Warlow's and Flodmark's pronouncements, offered the results of a ten-year drilling project completed in Greenland. A 7000-foot core from the Greenland ice sheet revealed climatic data on a year-by-year basis as far back as 10,000 years ago, when the last great glaciation—the Wisconsin glaciation—ended.

According to Herron, the data show that the change between "normal" and ice age conditions on Earth has been surprisingly and dramatically abrupt. In fact, Herron said, climatic change may have been so sudden at the end of the last glaciation that he has no idea what mechanism might account for such a quick change.

In a related matter—the fact that the last north polar ice sheet was centered in Hudson Bay—C. Covey's *Scientific American* article "The Earth's Orbit and the Ice Ages" (February 1984) points out that recent advances in climatic modeling (the Milankovitch theory connecting ice ages and Earth's orbit) show that no pole shift or axial tilt is required to explain that fact. Rather, Covey says, the eccentric location with respect to the pole is a natural consequence of land-water distribution.

Altogether, then, the latest evidence in this category weighs against pole shifts, although the onset of deglaciation is unexplained and the theoretical work of Flodmark warrants consideration.

3. **The Frozen Mammoths.** The evidence in this category, as interpreted by pole shift proponents, suggests that the famed Berezovka mammoth died suddenly by asphyxiation in late summer in a temperate climate and that it was frozen by the imposition of temperatures in excess of $-150°$ F in ten hours or less. Contrary to popular belief, they claim, the mammoth was not an Arctic mammal because it lacked the sebaceous oil glands cold-adapted land animals have to lubricate their skin and thereby avoid death by dehydration. Moreover, the Arctic could not possibly supply enough vegetation to support vast herds of these herbivores, who required several hundred pounds of vegetation daily for each member. Yet their skeletons litter the tundra by the hundreds of thousands.

This has been a topic of lively debate among some of my correspondents. William White of England, an opponent of the flash-freeze school of thinking, wrote a critique in which he makes these points: (1) The findings of the new science of taphonomy, the study of all the processes an animal goes through from the time it starts to die until its remains are finally embedded in a geological stratum, demonstrates that mammoths died not as a result of disastrous temperature change but from asphyxia (e.g., drowning in an icy stream, suffocating in a landslide, etc.). (2) Other studies demonstrate that mammoth flesh is not so well preserved as has been claimed, but rather the flesh had begun to putrefy *before* being frozen in permafrost. (3) Sebaceous glands, which are said by pole shift theorists to be necessary in all Arctic mammals to tolerate extreme cold, are missing in mammoths but present in woolly rhinoceroses. Since rhinoceroses are often found frozen in company with mammoths, how can the internment together of the two (supposedly living in widely separated locations at the time of a catastrophic pole shift) be accounted for?

Dwardu Cardona of Canada, a catastrophist who defends a sudden freezing of mammoths, rebutted White's position in "The Mammoth Controversy" in *Kronos* (VII:4) 1981/Summer.

Despite White's statement to the contrary . . . the commencement of putrefaction *prior* to freezing has never been satisfactorily proven. Eyeballs are among the first parts of the body to rot after death, yet some of the mammoths discovered in Siberia had their eyeballs intact.

Dima [a baby mammoth found in Siberia in 1978] is the only specimen so far to have been discovered in an unthawed condition. I might be wrong but, to my knowledge, it showed no signs of putrefaction. Yet even if it did it would not much matter, for there is nothing in prevalent catastrophic theories which excludes interim, even if minimal, thawing between catastrophes.

The fact remains that where mammoth carcasses, in whole or in part, have been discovered, decomposition has been minimal. They did not decompose away . . . [If] climatic conditions have not changed since the mammoths roamed, why is it that only extinct species are ever discovered entombed in ice?

What I do grant William White is that the direct cause of the Berezovka mammoth's death was asphyxia *before* freezing. That has always been known and admitted by catastrophists. Suffocation, however, is not necessarily the result of drowning and/or landslide burial as White and others would have us believe. Ivan Sanderson, Immanuel Velikovsky, and Charles Hapgood have all described extraordinary, but *possible,* atmospheric conditions which *could* have asphyxiated the mammoths just prior to freezing. While not necessarily correct in the details these investigators have supplied, it is a fact that, both in Alaska and Siberia, mammoth remains are associated with evidence of atmospheric tempests of unprecedented dimensions. *And it is this overall picture, not the hair-splitting issues we have been debating, that is the crux of the matter.*

The "young but powerful science of taphonomy," upon which White relies, has shown that the carcass of an African elephant decays in about three weeks, leaving nothing but the tough skin covering the bones. In temperatures which, according to Farrand, were higher than the present 90–100° F of the Siberian summer, the Berezovka mammoth should have likewise decomposed. The position in which this beast was found clearly indicates that it could neither have been drowned nor crushed beneath a slide. Its stance suggests that it was felled on its haunches, that it attempted to regain its feet, that it was then somehow asphyxiated, and that it froze in this animated position. It did not even keel over.

The latest word on the mammoth controversy comes from White's rejoinder to Cardona and Ellenberger in a three-part *Kronos* statement (Fall 1985 to Summer 1986). White effectively countered nearly all their arguments, convincing Ellenberger, at least, that processes and mechanisms less extravagant than a pole shift can account for the frozen mammoths.

White shows, first, that prevailing Arctic conditions (blizzards whose low temperatures are compounded by high winds, producing wind-chill factors equivalent to −150° F) are sufficient to freeze a mammoth, including its stomach contents, into the state in which they are presently found. "It is therefore glaringly apparent that the allegedly compulsory rapid chilling of a dead mammoth, including its stomach, would have been readily accessible under known conditions."

The Berezovka mammoth died in late summer, according to the analysis of Pfitzenmeyer, who dissected the mammoth in 1901 and noted the vegetable contents of its stomach and mouth. White points out that it would have been possible to preserve the animal even in a Siberian August because sufficient meteorological conditions occasionally prevail.

What about the amount of vegetable biomass needed to support "truly vast herds" of mammoths? White writes:

> Where is the evidence for such a large population and herd-size? Neither of the living species of elephant move in herds more than a fraction of this number. He is on firmer ground when he speaks of "untold numbers of mammoths *in the past.*" Few would care to dispute this, given that their skeletal remains run into tens of thousands of individuals! Yet, such numbers are unremarkable considering the ideal conditions for the preservation of skeletons in the cold ground plus the fact that the woolly mammoth flourished from the penultimate glaciation of Europe (240,000 years before the present?) until circa 10,000 years B.P.—or later still, according to my critics. Thus, in 200,000 years or so, the death and preservation of only *one mammoth per year* would be adequate to account for all those tusks found. This makes it obvious that the Mammuthus primigenius population was much smaller than certain writers have chosen to presume and/or that only a small proportion of their remains have been preserved (in any form).

Another argument in favor of flash-freezing of mammoths has been their relatively good state of preservation. White states that "putrefactive degradation [of tissues] is solely under the control of bacterial enzymes and, *when these are absent, decomposition does not ensue* . . . the available evidence dictates that decay upon thawing was *very slow* indeed. So low was the ambient temperature and bacterial population that some of the mammoths in question were substantially complete when examined years after the initial re-exposure of the carcasses."

He goes on to point out that rare photographic views of Dima's right profile reveal a large hole, with exposed ribs and thoracic cavity. "Moreover, decomposition was much more extensive than was claimed initially, such that microstructural studies of the brain and muscles have had to be abandoned while the analysis of albumin was marred by the general decay of tissue proteins that was evident. Thus, Dima was not "perfectly preserved" as some claimed and I reported.

Even the survival of eyes, while remarkable, is not miraculous, White notes. Eyes are often present in Peruvian and Egyptian mummies. Hence, preserved mammoth eyeballs are not prima facie evidence of a pole shift. Moreover, if the woolly mammoths were the victims of a widespread calamity, why are so few found? "It is the paucity of their complete bodies in a frozen state that is remarkable. . . . Human agents were, in fact, responsible for many of the vast caches of mammoth bones which seem to cause so much consternation." (White, XI:2 Winter 1986, p. 86)

White demolishes the oil-gland dispute with a number of morphological arguments. Mammoths were adapted to cold conditions, he demonstrates, not only because of the morphological evidence but also because of evidence from paleontology, which shows mammoth bones in association with cold-loving species, and archeology, where paleolithic cave art shows the same thing.

White's final argument is radiocarbon dating of frozen mammoth remains. The dates allotted to mammoth carcasses "have too wide a spread to be consistent with the theory of mammoth extinction in a single cataclysm."

Concluding his statement, White emphasizes that the known complete mammoth remains have been found in "fossil traps, which were responsible for both the demise and the preservation of the individual beasts." He acknowledges that no categorical solution to the problem of the frozen mammoths has yet been given because the evidence presented by the preservation of the animals is equivocal in that it can be used in support of a wide range of hypotheses, some even diametrically opposed. "My chief concern," he writes, "has been that frozen mammoths alone provide but a flimsy basis upon which to build a theory."

4. The Ancient Maps of Antarctica. Charles Hapgood, who died at seventy-eight in 1982, summarized this subject in his 1979 revision of *Maps of the Ancient Sea Kings:* "The maps in this book show that an ancient advanced culture mapped virtually the whole earth [about 15,000 years ago or more, and] that its cartographers mapped a mostly deglacial Anarctica."[2] And in *Catastrophism and Ancient History* in 1980 he wrote: "Our best indication of a warm Antarctica is an authentic map [the Oronteus Finaeus map of 1531] showing Antarctica free of ice." At the time of *Pole Shift*'s publication, this research had never been refuted; it had only been ignored.

Since then, Hapgood's work has been challenged by researchers who claim that his interpretation of the ancient maps was wrong. In the words of one critic, David C. Jolly, "I do not think that Hapgood was intellectually dishonest—merely that he uncritically accepted any evidence supporting his views and did not try very hard to come up with alternative explanations. Ultimately, he became a victim of his own enthusiasm." (*Skeptical Inquirer,* XI:1, Fall, 1986, p. 37)

In 1980, a journalist-scholar team concluded that Hapgood's work was open to serious question, although certain moot factors could weigh in his favor. Paul F. Hoye, editor of the Aramco Oil Company's magazine, and Paul Lunde, a graduate of London's School of Oriental and African Studies working on Arabic manuscripts in the Vatican Library in Rome, examined Hapgood's work in an article entitled "Piri Re'is and the Hapgood Hypotheses" in *Aramco World Magazine* (January–February 1980). They pointed to "serious weaknesses in Hapgood's case."

First, they say, Hapgood's theses depend entirely on mathematical projections and logic; there are no examples of "advanced" source maps such as he postulates, nor can he display a single artifact from the "lost" civilization which supposedly mapped the Americas and Antarctica. Also, his postulate of an ice-free Antarctica conflicts totally with accepted geological theory, which says the Antarctic ice cap has been in place for millions of years. Among other objections to Hapgood's work, the most compelling arguments in their opinion, concern the Andes mountains and Antarctica. "Is the chain of mountains to the left of the map really the Andes? Is the coastline at the bottom really Antarctica? Are there any mountains shown there? And is Antarctica free of ice?"

> To put it more simply, Piri Re'is, or the scribe who copied his work, may have realized, as he came to the Rio de la Plata, that he was going to run off the edge of his valuable parchment if he continued south. So he did the logical thing and turned the coastline to the east, marking the turn with a semicircle of crenelations, so that he could fit the entire coastline on his page. If that was the case, then the elaborate Hapgood hypotheses—or at least those based entirely on the Piri Re'is map—would have no foundation whatsoever.

Hoye and Lunde find that the Oronteus Finaeus map, in which Hapgood puts so much store, is more reliable but also open to question. After discussing various possibilities, they conclude that simpler and more prosaic explanations are possible. Nevertheless, they acknowledge that Hapgood's belief that an advanced source map will be found might one day be fulfilled, since there are massive collections of documents crammed into museums and archives in Istanbul, many still unexamined. They also acknowledge that their criticism of Hapgood's work might itself be questioned. "Major historical and cartographical problems . . . remain unsolved. The mystery is still there."

David Jolly disagrees. He feels Hapgood's work is completely flawed and unacceptable and that there is no mystery. Jolly, who publishes an annual handbook for the rare-map trade, asked in *The Skeptical Inquirer* (Fall 1986), "Was Antarctica Mapped by the Ancients?" He examined Hapgood's sources and reasoning. On both grounds, he faulted Hapgood. With regard to the Piri Re'is map, Hapgood assumed that a portion of the South American coast was really a misplaced section of Antarctica. Jolly shows that to be most unlikely, based on comparison with other ancient maps and mapmaking techniques of the time. Likewise, Jolly argues, Hapgood's assumptions about the Oronteus Finaeus map, so important to his position, were not well founded. Again, Jolly surveys other ancient maps and concludes that "the Finaeus map may be a blend of imagination and fact." The simplest theory, he writes, "is that Finaeus drew an asymmetrical, bi-lobate blob of no special shape to conform to ancient belief in a southern continent and to Magellan's discovery. The blob-theory is consistent with the varying shape of Terra

Australis on maps both before and after the Finaeus map. If there were actual observations or maps of the coastline, one would expect a more consistent representation."

Jolly also cites M. M. du Jourdin and M. de La Roncière's recent book *Sea Charts of the Early Explorers,* which shows that "the so-called portolan charts of the Meditarranean evolved from crude prototypes and were not derived from ancient sources as Hapgood claimed." He concludes his examination of Hapgood's work by saying that Hapgood's ideas were rightly rejected in scholarly circles "not because of animus but because he had not proved his case. Too many leaps of faith were needed to establish his thesis."

It therefore appears that Hapgood's thesis that the Earth was mapped by a prehistoric civilization thousands of years ago and that these maps show an Antarctica free of ice has been refuted.

5. **The Case Against Velikovsky.** Although the work of Immanuel Velikovsky is contained by three of the four categories of evidence for pole shifts (he does not refer to ancient maps of Antartica), it is so well known that it deserves special attention. I single it out here because of Velikovsky's prominence in the pole shift debate.

A major critique of Velikovsky appeared in 1984 entitled *Beyond Velikovsky.* The author, Henry Bauer, gives an account of the Velikovsky controversy up to that time.

The most comprehensive, although succinct, refutation of Velikovsky's position was offered by C. Leroy Ellenberger. In a two-part *Kronos* article, "Still Facing Many Problems" (November 1984 and July 1985), he commented on a wide range of topics bearing on Velikovsky's hypothesis, ranging from orbital changes, geomagnetism, and the cooling of Venus to plate tectonics, ice-age dynamics, and sea-level changes. For each topic he shows that Velikovsky's data were wrong or that his use of those data was wrong, and sometimes both.

In a letter to *The Skeptical Inquirer* (Summer 1986), Ellenberger further sealed the case against Velikovsky: ". . . the Terminal Cretaceous Event 65 million years ago, whatever it was, left unambiguous worldwide signatures of iridium and soot. The catastrophes Velikovsky conjectured within the past 3,500 years left no similar signatures according to Greenland ice cores, bristlecone pine rings, Swedish clay varves, and ocean sediments. All provide accurately datable sequences covering the relevant period and preserve no signs of having experienced a Velikovskian catastrophe. Although Velikovsky believes *Earth in Upheaval* proved his scenario happened, his evidence can be explained without invoking cosmic catastrophes."

Two letters by Ellenberger in *The New York Times* complete this summary of the case against Velikovsky. On May 16, 1987, his letter to the editor stated:

Velikovsky . . . does not deserve to be taken seriously for two reasons: (1) his use of mythohistorical sources was discredited by Sean Mewhinney in the winter 1986 issue of Kronos . . . and by Bob Forrest in the winter 1983–84 issue of The Skeptical Inquirer . . . and (2) no physical evidence exists to support recent catastrophes of the magnitude described in "Worlds in Collision." . . . That Velikovsky's catastrophes did not happen is proved by the Greenland ice cores. Their annual layers can be counted back 7,000 years. The ice contains no trace of the cometary debris that Velikovsky said caused 40 years of darkness following the bibilical Exodus.

And on August 29, 1987, *The Times* published this statement by Ellenberger:

. . . your August 6 article about the redating of the Minoan eruption of [the Agean volcanic island] Thera from 1500 B.C. to 1645 B.C., using Greenland's Dye 3 ice core . . . should be the final evidence needed to end the Velikovsky controversy.

According to the revised chronology of Velikovsky's "Ages in Chaos" books, the date for Thera's eruption [whose remains are now called Santorini] is required to be about 950 B.C. With this keystone removed, Velikovsky's revised chronology collapses utterly. The absence of copious cometary debris in the cores further proves that the catastrophes . . . never happened.

The ice cores have thus repudiated both Velikovsky's catastrophes and his chronology.

So where are we in the debate about pole shifts? From the *scientific* perspective, the question of previous pole shifts appears resolved in favor of a noncapsizing planet with stationary poles. Velikovsky's case has been demolished; the evidence he offers for recent catastrophes can be explained by noncatastrophic processes. The theoretical support for pole shifts offered by the work of Warlow appears disproved, although Flodmark remains in need of thorough examination. When disproof of Hapgood's cartographic contentions is added to the mundane explanation for frozen mammoths, the case for pole shifts is seemingly beyond recovery. In addition, although the question of ice ages remains open insofar as the absence of ice sheets over long periods is not explained by the conventional explanation, those absences in and of themselves are not evidence of pole shifts. So with these refutations of the major categories of evidence for the pole shift concept, the case for pole shifts is now virtually nonexistent.

The Psychics Were Wrong

If the data from science regarding the existence of previous pole shifts and the theoretical possibility of such an event remain ambiguous to any degree, the predictions from psychics regarding future pole shifts do not.

A number of signposts or precursors of a pole shift were predicted which never came to pass. The period from 1982 to 1984, for example, was to be a time of major seismic activity around the globe. Some psychics went on record as saying that the "Jupiter Effect" would be devastating.

The 1982–1984 period passed without significant seismic events, at least not significant enough to fulfill even remotely the various psychic predictions for that time.

Paul Solomon had stated that Japan would disappear beneath the sea, the Great Lakes would empty into the Gulf of Mexico, new continents would begin to rise in the Atlantic and Pacific oceans, much of the West Coast of North America would disappear, the North American continent would be split in half down the center, and other disasters of similar magnitude would occur in a general scenario of global seismic upheaval.

Likewise, Aron Abrahamsen stated that by 1981 the point of no return would have been reached. At that point, he said, "people will have improved or the momentum will be so great that it will be difficult to induce a change in the events which are to follow." I noted in *Pole Shift* that some of Abrahamsen's predictions for previous years had not been accurate. In light of world events during the years following 1981, which are notably lacking in geophysical events of the sort he forecast, I conclude either that human consciousness and behavior has radically improved, thereby offsetting geophysical disaster through the mind–matter linkage psychics identify, or Abrahamsen's earth-change predictions were incorrect. The latter seems more likely, although I'll discuss the mind–matter linkage concept because it may also explain the situation.

What about Edgar Cayce, whose readings had set the baseline in the psychic community regarding earth changes? I pointed out in *Pole Shift* that Cayce's readings about earthquakes striking the West Coast of America, even when interpreted in the broadest possible fashion, would have reached their limit of reliability by the end of 1982. That in turn would bear directly on the accuracy of his pole shift predictions.

The old saying "Time will tell" has proved true. Time *has* told us that the psychic predictions for events to date (1989) were wrong. They were wrong with regard to both type and magnitude of events. For example, while it is true that there have been volcanic eruptions in the Cascade Range along the West Coast of North America—notably, Mt. Saint Helens in Oregon in 1980—and a major earthquake in the San Francisco area in 1989, there has been nothing even remotely resembling the loss of the the West Coast, with the Pacific Ocean flowing inland through many states. In fact, as one professional geologist said to me in personal correspondence, "There has been no significant change from the normal and anticipated geological pattern." The geologist, who is also a student of metaphysics and the Cayce predictions, noted that geologists are expecting some large and damaging earthquakes on the West Coast in the next twenty years, but they are not at all likely to destroy the coastline in the manner Cayce foresaw.

The psychics were wrong. Why? A plausible explanation can be found in the near-death experience (NDE) research of Dr. Kenneth Ring, professor of psychology at the University of Connecticut and author of the 1984 book *Heading Toward Omega,* a study of the meaning of NDEs. One chapter surveys what Ring calls prophetic visions (PVs), which are particular sequences of imagery perceived during an NDE which have to do with earth changes and a pole shift.

Ring found about two dozen persons who reported PVs as part of their close approach to death. Several other American and British investigators have likewise noted the feature as part of the NDE and have confirmed Ring's description of the general scenario, which he summarized in an *Anabiosis* article, "Precognitive and Prophetic Visions in Near-Death Experiences" (1982):

> There is, first of all, a sense of having total knowledge, but specifically one is aware of seeing the entirety of the earth's evolution and history, from the beginning to the end of time. The future scenario, however, is usually of short duration, seldom extending much beyond the beginning of the twenty-first century. The individual reports that in this decade there will be an increasing incidence of earthquakes, volcanic activity and generally massive geophysical changes. There will be resultant disturbances in weather patterns and food supplies. The world economic system will collapse, and the possibility of nuclear war or accident is very great (respondents are not agreed on *whether* a nuclear catastrophe will occur). All of these events are transitional rather than ultimate, however, and they will be followed by a new era in human history, marked by human brotherhood, universal love and world peace. Though many will die, the earth will live. While agreeing that the dates for these events are not fixed, most individuals feel that they are likely to take place during the 1980s.

In "Prophetic Visions in 1988: A Critical Reappraisal," which appeared in the *Journal of Near-Death Studies* (1988), Ring noted that the PVs' forecast of cataclysmic destruction tended to converge on a single year—1988—as the critical time. Writing toward the end of that year, Ring reviewed the six interpretations of PVs he offered in his book. The most obvious fact, of course, is that the PVs did not come to pass in a literal sense. From that point of view, they were totally wrong.

The central lesson for us, Ring concludes, is that modern NDE-inspired PVs are "not the literal forecast of planetary doom, but rather the foreshadowing of the need for a new myth of cultural regeneration." This conclusion forced itself on Ring for two reasons. First, the critical period passed safely. Second, he learned from others that such PVs have a long history. The first PV to come to his attention from a source outside his data base stated that planetary upheaval was imminent; that PV was recorded in 1892! In 1987 Ring read John Perry's *The Heart of History*, which argues that many such PVs can be found throughout history, particularly in sensitive individuals whose cultures were undergoing a period of deep crisis. Perry states that "the horrific vision of world destruction is part and parcel of the mythic imagery of rapid culture change and world views in transition. . . . Beholding the world coming to its end amid storm, earthquake, flood and fire we have found to be a typical experience of a prophet whose psyche is registering the emotional impact of the end of an era." Ring, agreeing with Perry, concludes that such prophets arise during times of cultural crisis and bring a messianic message of the need for cultural renewal:

> What I am asserting is that whereas PVs are indeed prophetic utterances, they should not, in my opinion, be regarded as truly precognitive or taken literally. Rather they seem to be reflections of the collective psyche of our time, which is generating its own images of planetary death and regeneration for which the sensitive souls of our era serve as carriers.

Ring cautions, on the basis of his research and the lessons of history, that images of general apocalypse should not be taken literally. Rather, they should be seen as "harbingers of hope that point to the possibilities of human regeneration and planetary transformation."

Conclusion: Spiritual Advice

I think that is the most sensible—and spiritual—note on which to conclude this update on the pole shift issue. From a scientific perspective, pole shifts are nothing to worry about because there is almost no scientific basis to the concept. But even if there were, according to the predictions and prophecies, a pole shift is not inevitable. Its possibility is influenceable by our manner of living and thinking. Human consciousness, the predictions and prophecies say, will be of critical importance in triggering or preventing a pole shift. In essence, they say, the state of consciousness among people will determine the outcome of an approaching global crisis. This will be the final factor which influences the matrix of geophysical and astrophysical factors operating to stabilize Earth in space.

Some people fearfully watch the poles to detect the slightest movement. But that is self-defeating, the psychics and prophets say. We should be soul watchers rather than pole watchers. In other words, if there are people changes for the better, earth changes for the better will follow.

Let's consider the situation in more detail to see what the relationship between planetary safety and human consciousness is said to be, as described by esoteric psychology.

All the world's major spiritual traditions tell us that free will operates in human affairs and that we can influence the outcome of events through the application of our physical, mental, and spiritual resources. The predictions and prophecies described in *Pole Shift* largely agree with this, although a few have said that a pole shift is inevitable.

From the esoteric point of view, the purpose of prophecy is to warn people against the consequences of certain kinds of action. Dire prophetic words are spoken by a prophet to awaken people to their erring thought and behavior. By setting people into a new course of action, the prophet either diffuses the disaster-in-the-making or else causes people to prepare for it sufficiently far in advance that death and destruction are minimized. The people's new mode of behavior eventually proves the prophecy wrong—which is exactly what the prophet wanted in the first place!

The mechanism by which consciousness modifies a set of circumstances has been described by some of the psychics as "thought forms." The term and the concept behind it come from esoteric psychology and metaphysics. The concept says there is mental or psychic energy as an intermediate substance between matter and consciousness. From this perspective, thoughts are things—real but nonphysical energy configurations, produced by human consciousness—and exist objectively in space outside the human beings who produce them. A thought form is the energetic embodiment of the idea on which a person dwells, consciously or otherwise, and it takes on an existence external to and independent of the thinker. By a process of which official science knows little, our thoughts, as a poet put it, "take wings."

In other words, when we think or focus our attention in a goal-directed way, the experience of thinking is not simply electrical activity within the neural pathways of the brain or confined to the limits of the cranium. Research into extrasensory perception suggests a fifth force in nature beyond the four known physical forces. It is a metaphysical or mental force—a psychic force. The question then arises: What becomes of a thought *after* it has been thought? Does it simply disappear, vanish?

Apparently not. From the point of view of psychics, metaphysicians, occultists, true magicians, shamans, and so on, thought activity extends beyond the physical body, partaking of a "field of mind" surrounding the planet and extending into space for an unspecified distance. The mind field is composed of the collective experience of the human race. That is, our thoughts, feelings, and actions are somehow impressed or encoded into the field of mind energy, creating thought forms. Untold numbers of thought forms over millions of years have been contributed by the human race to the planetary field of mind.

Moreover, thoughts of a similar nature tend to coalesce over time and gather into what would be called "thought fields." These thought fields are equivalent to what psychologist Carl Jung called an archetype, which is a nonspatial, nontemporal repository of a certain basic human experience. The totality of thought fields, or archetypes, constitute an "atmosphere" of thought energy which extends through our planet's physical atmosphere but goes beyond it and can be understood as what Jung called the collective unconscious. The concept I am presenting here can explain in quasi-scientific terms how it is that people everywhere have access to archetypal experience, as Jungians and other schools of psychology claim. This is simply because we are all immersed in the collective unconscious mind field, which is suprapersonal. (I elaborate on this in chapter 7.)

Mind energy interacts with the physical energy matrix sustaining the planet in space and can influence it, subtly but directly, in either a positive or a negative fashion, depending on the vibratory quality of thoughts arising from the human level. Harmonious, loving mental states are said to produce a stabilizing effect on the planetary matrix of physical energies; disharmonious, hateful thoughts result in a destabilized matrix.

This mind–matter interaction is a two-way process. People can "receive" from the planetary mind field or collective unconscious, as well as "give" to it. For example, certain universal or primordial images and symbols have been perceived by people in dreams, meditation, and other altered states of consciousness regardless of race, sex, or culture. As another example, consider how a new idea or discovery often appears almost simultaneously in several separated locations, apparently as "fallout" or "precipitation" from nonphysical levels of reality to the physical.

Goodman coined a term for the psychokinetic process by which human thought forms influence the total energy pattern of earthly life: *biorelativity,* the interaction of people with their physical environment via psychic, or mind, energy. The Hopi rain dance is an example. In *We Are the Earthquake Generation,* he says, "Since energy can be neither created nor destroyed, the energy of thought, psychics say, is still in existence as a sort of atmosphere or field surrounding the planet, recording all the experience of humanity. This is the so-called akashic record which Cayce and other psychics claim to 'read' when they obtain paranormal information about the past."[3]

Thus, from the point of view of the psychics on Goodman's research team, the influence of our minds and our basic state of consciousness is there all the time, inevitably affecting the total Earth-organism, for better or for worse. The important question, then, is not *whether* we are going to affect it but *how* we are going to affect it.

In that regard, the predictions and prophecies say, virtuous living and respect for the planet will infuse Earth's energy matrix with powerful stabilizing influences. Prayer is a familiar form of this influence. It is no coincidence that psychic and spiritual traditions declare the efficacy of selfless prayer as a psychospiritual tool or resource. Prayer adds constructively to the mind field of Earth.

Even better still would be the development among people of a steadily focused consciousness which recognizes the mutual dependence humanity and the cosmos have upon each other as co-creators of our joint destiny. Such a loving state of consciousness (which can properly be called a sense of conscience) would constantly govern our thoughts and acts in a life-enhancing way.

Spiritual traditions warn that we shall reap what we sow. Esoteric traditions and psychical research offer an explanation of how and why this must be. Hatred, anger, greed, fear, and other negative character traits and qualities of mind can affect the total process of energy activity on and around the planet. The many "crimes against nature" which people are perpetrating—including overpopulation, environmental pollution, wasting of nonrenewable resources, and nuclear testing—along with "crimes against humanity" such as war, economic exploitation, and the imposition of inhumane living conditions, religious persecution, political abridgement of human rights, intolerance, and bigotry toward minorities, and so forth are pouring negative thought forms into our planet's energetic foundations. The result, the predictions and prophecies say, will be geophysical cataclysm in the form of violent earth changes and a pole shift as the Earth-organism seeks to restore balance in the system.

Thus, from the point of view of psychic, prophetic, and spiritual traditions, rather than saying we will be punished *for* our sins, it would be more accurate to say we will be punished *by* our sins. The law of karma or cause and effect is a stern one, so if there is global devastation in the future, we will have no one to blame but ourselves.

If a pole shift destroys civilization some people will survive, according to the predictions and prophecies. The great loss of life will open up niches in the environment where new life forms can emerge. Those most deeply attuned to cosmic processes will become the seedbed from which, it is said, a new race, a higher humanity will evolve in accelerated fashion. The new breed will know from firsthand experience the terrible consequences for failing to "walk in balance on the Earth Mother," as Native Americans say. The new ones will know how to live in harmony with cosmic processes and will inherit the Earth.

Predictions of pole shift serve to point out that we must change our consciousness from ego-centered to God-centered living and recognize that there is a benevolent wisdom governing the universe, including us.

From a spiritual perspective, there are no problems—only situations. Problems don't exist in nature. Only situations do, only sets of circumstances. It is the human mind which projects attitudes and values onto those situations and then labels them problems. But that label doesn't describe what nature is doing. It describes the state of mind of the human who labeled the situation.

Problems are a reflection of your state of mind, a state based on self-centeredness and fear and an unwillingness to face new experiences. But change your attitude and, suddenly, there are no problems. The set of circumstances remains, but the situation now becomes an exciting challenge in which to learn and deepen your understanding, your familiarity with the unknown. New values come into mind and are projected onto the situation so that what was once seen as a problem becomes a fortunate opportunity for growth and discovery.

A pole shift probably will not occur in the near future, but even if it does, we need not dwell upon it as a source of fear and destruction. Our primary task as citizens of Earth is to attune ourselves spiritually with Life—with the processes of the planet and the cosmos—and thereby understand that, if we are at the end of a cycle, we are being given an occasion to grow, to evolve, to transform ourselves on the basis of deeper understanding and wider vision.

Spiritually speaking, we should remember the words of Jesus not to be anxious about the morrow, but rather to consider the lilies of the field, which are arrayed in glory and are tended by a loving Providence who tends us every bit as well. To the awakened mind, every experience is a blessing, even situations commonly labeled misfortunate or even tragedy, disaster, catastrophe, cataclysm. The attuned consciousness will receive all it needs, and more, from a loving universe whose whole purpose is to nurture the evolution of organisms like us to a higher state of being.

This can be likened to the birth of a baby. In such a situation, we don't focus all our attention and preparation on a few brief moments of birth pains. Rather, we joyfully look ahead to the presence among ourselves of a new child. We prepare to receive another into the family. We don't cower in a corner because there will be some degree of suffering during delivery. The mother prepares for delivery to ease the birth passage, knowing that the hours spent in delivery are worth the years to be spent in company with the child.

I'll conclude with a brief story given to me by a wise man from India who read *Pole Shift*. One day Mr. Plague was talking to the Keeper of the Akashic Records when he remembered that he had an appointment at a distant city. So he broke off conversation and rushed to keep his appointment. Now, the Akashic Records are a kind of metaphysical account of everything which happens to humanity, so when Mr. Plague returned from the distant city, the Keeper of the Akashic Records asked him how many people had died on his mission. Mr. Plague, recognizing the need for accuracy, replied, "Five thousand died due to me and ten thousand due to fear."

Think about that. According to the predictions and prophecies, humanity is approaching one of the most critical junctures in the history of our planet. It seems clear that the significance of those predictions and prophecies is in offering not geophysical data but psychological guidance. Will there be global destruction or planetary transformation to a new world order—a New Age—based on love and wisdom? The choice, they say, is ours. The proper choice, the wise choice, is to shift our consciousness from the pole of egotism to the pole of enlightened living. We must realize that from the standpoint of God-realization, pole shifts are merely an exotic way to die. The *real* question is: Are we ready to die? Are we living lives surrendered to God under all circumstances, even our own inevitable demise? Since the immortality pill hasn't been invented, none of us will get out of here alive. Pondering our mortality is the beginning of wisdom. If we do that, the pole shift predictions and prophecies will have served humanity and the planet alike by proving themselves wrong in the best manner possible.

5

Firewalking: The Hottest Thing in Town

Then Nebuchadnezzar came near to the mouth of the fiery furnace, and spake, and said, Shadrach, Meshach and Abednego, ye servants of the most high God, come forth, and come hither. Then Shadrach, Meshach and Abednego came forth of the midst of the fire. And the princes, governors and captains and the king's counsellors, being gathered together, saw these men upon whose bodies the fire had no power. [Daniel 3:26–27]

The flyer received in the mail invited me to a four-hour seminar on firewalking. "Everyone participating will be taught how to walk barefoot on hot coals without burning their feet," it proclaimed. To a long-time investigator of the paranormal like me, it was an irresistible challenge. So I made a deposit toward the $75 registration fee to reserve my place, and looked forward eagerly to the event.

I didn't doubt the reality of firewalking, a feat well documented for centuries. Firewalking has almost always been done in a religious context, as part of a ceremony. The phenomenon was recorded as far back as Pliny the Elder in the first century A.D., who told of the practice by an ancient Roman family which performed it at an annual sacrifice to Apollo. Anthropologists have observed it today in India, Greece, Spain, Japan, China, Bulgaria, Sri Lanka, Tibet, Thailand, Fiji, and Brazil.

I'd personally witnessed firewalking in 1974 at a California festival of religious, spiritual and metaphysical organizations; it had been done by a Japanese priest who demonstrated it as part of his sect's worship.

Several years later a friend of mine had spent three days meditating and chanting at a yoga center in Canada as preparation for his own successful firewalk with others at the center. About that time I became friends with Komar the Hindu Fakir, who holds the *Guinness Book of World Records* distinction of having walked on hotter coals than anyone else. Komar (the stage name for Wooster, Ohio, cheesemaker Vernon Craig) casually strolls over coalbeds wearing Hindu type clothing and a turban but with no more preparation than perhaps smoking a cigarette and sipping a Coke. And I knew that firewalking had been done by thousands of ordinary Americans in the last few years as a veritable craze, sweeping the West Coast thanks to a California teacher named Tolly Burkan, originator of the firewalking movement, and those he had trained. Burkan demonstrated it on *The Phil Donahue Show* in 1984; a Burkan student, Tony Robbins, demonstrated firewalking on *The Merv Griffin Show*. Another friend of mine, Russian emigré and psychic researcher Larissa Vilenskaya, was writing a book entitled *Firewalking*, which tells of her experiences as a Burkan-trained teacher and as a scientific researcher into the paranormal.

Could it be done? I had no doubt whatsoever. But could it be done by *me*? That was the question.

Now, I've dealt with fears of many kinds, from physical to metaphysical. As a teenager I had a near-death experience through drowning; I spent four years as a naval officer in antisubmarine warfare and nuclear weapons, with time on the Cuban blockade and in Vietnam. Later, in 1967, I risked a prison sentence when I took on the Pentagon by giving the media classified information to show that the U.S. Government's version of the Gulf of Tonkin events was false. After military service I'd gotten into consciousness research more intensively and investigated such paranormal phenomena as hauntings, demonic possession, black magic, and UFO contact. (That's not to brag—just to say that I've been in some unusual situations where I had to deal with fear, and did.) Nevertheless, as I contemplated treading on the coals, I sometimes felt apprehension. After all, their pyrometer-measured temperature would be nearly 1300° F, higher than the melting point of the cast aluminum used for the engine block in my car. Would I walk or chicken out? Several friends whom I'd told of the firewalk also signed up, and we casually discussed the question, each for himself. My answer: I'll decide when I face the coalbed.

So at 7:00 P.M. on a bitterly cold evening in January 1985, two dozen people and I met at a private home in West Hartford, Connecticut, for the firewalking seminar. It was the first time for all of us. We'd come for various reasons: curiosity, to deal with fear, to explore our human potential, to say we'd done it, to extend professional counseling and training skills. And we were a diverse group: housewives, businessmen, astrologers, holistic health practitioners, karate instructors, an author (me), a dentist, a postal worker, an elementary-school teacher, and who knows what else. A reporter and a photographer from *The Hartford Courant* were also present to record the event.

Our instructor was a thirty-two-year-old, slightly built, bearded Connecticut resident with the self-conferred name of Shoshame (pronounced as three syllables: Show-*shah*-mee). He told us he had taken the name five years earlier for spiritual reasons, but didn't explain why or what it means. Shoshame's business card identified him as a firewalking instructor, researcher, lecturer, masseur, holistic health practitioner, nutritional and herbal consultant, and a multilevel marketing trainer and distributor of flower pollen, freeze-dried algae, wheatgrass powder, ion generators, and metabolic enzymes. He received his certification from Burkan after completing a three-week training course. Since his first firewalk he'd been on the coals seventeen times.

The seminar began with songs—simple, easy songs intended to build group spirit and enthusiasm and "get the energy going." There was a firewalking version of "Row, Row, Row Your Boat" done in rounds, and "I've Got Shoes." ("You may not have feet after tonight," Shoshame kidded us, "but at least you'll be able to say you have shoes.") We sang some songs written by Tolly Burkan, accompanied by him on tape. We heard a little from Shoshame about the firewalking movement and why he had named his seminar "Fear into Joy: Creating Your Own Reality." ("This seminar isn't about firewalking. It's about overcoming fear and limiting beliefs.") The reporter sat quietly and observed, taking notes. The photographer snapped a shot of Shoshame and the group and then went outside to set up his strobe equipment.

By eight o'clock we were ready to build the fire. Bundled up in our coats and gloves, we filed outside in silence to the frigid backyard, following Shoshame's instructions to take logs from a nearby woodpile and, one by one, create the pyre. A large area, lit by a spotlight on the house, had been shoveled nearly free of snow. We laid the hardwood logs in a five-foot circle, built it up several feet like a wall, and then filled in the center. When we finished in silence ten minutes later, it was waist-high and solid with half a cord of oak and maple. Next we crumpled sheets of newspaper and stuck them into the pile. Then we formed a circle around it, holding hands, while Shoshame doused it with several gallons of kerosene. He offered a prayer to God and to the spirit of the fire-to-be, and then lit the paper. We stood quietly as the flames quickly warmed us. When the fire was well lit, we went back inside single file and in silence.

Now the seminar became more academic. Shoshame resorted to colored pens and a marking board to present some of the key concepts through simple diagrams. His first point used FEAR as an acronym:

False Evidence Appearing Real. We are programmed from infancy, he said, to believe that reality works a certain way, and any experiences we have to the contrary are generally dismissed as crazy or hallucinations. We're trained to accept limiting beliefs; we're indoctrinated to remain within conventional boundaries of what's possible and impossible. All our fears come down to "What if?" What if this or that happens—what if, what if? We go out of our way to place limitations on ourselves by imagining things and by accepting the cultural party line on what reality is all about.

"But what if you walk on those coals tonight?" he asked. "What if you step on thirteen-hundred-degree coals and don't get burned? What does that mean about reality? What does that mean about the way you let fear control your life?"

He passed out paper and had us all write down our worst fears and then share them with the group. There were all kinds of fears: fear of height, fear of failure, fear of speaking before an audience, fear of success, fear of rejection, fear of death. "It doesn't matter what kind of fear you have," Shoshame declared. "You can build your own reality, you can change your programming instantly"—he snapped his fingers—"just like that. This seminar isn't about firewalking. It's about overcoming fear. The firewalk is merely symbolic of fear in general. If you can break through that membrane of fear and take that first step onto the coalbed, you can learn to overcome fear and limiting beliefs in every part of your life."

He paused, then continued. "But the firewalk is purely voluntary. You don't have to walk, and if you choose not to, that's okay. Trust your inner guidance, listen to your inner voice. If it tells you to walk, then walk. If it tells you not to walk, then don't. You don't have to impress anyone. For some people it can take more courage *not* to walk. But even if you don't go over the coals, you'll have a powerful learning experience. You'll learn how to turn your fear into joy."

The lessons were punctuated with a variety of jokes, stage-magic tricks, more songs, mantras, decrees, chanting, and Shoshame's eclectic philosophy. He referred to the Findhorn Community in Scotland, where respect for nature and nature spirits is a central theme. He had us concentrate on tasting a single raisin. He had us chant a mantra from an unidentified metaphysical school's teaching. He told of Norman Cousins healing himself of a terminal illness through laughter. He gave a mini-lesson in brain physiology back-to-back with a brief discourse on such esoteric subjects as the nature of the Great Pyramid and the Hundredth Monkey Effect.

The mixed metaphysics could have been stronger; the positive mental attitude rap could have been better grounded in psychology and brain studies. No matter; I was there to experience firewalking, and in that department Shoshame had what it takes.

By 11:00 P.M. the wood had burned to embers and we were ready to walk. Outside we went, pantlegs rolled up, socks off, shoes loose and ready to be removed instantly. Shoshame had us hold hands and sing a song, over and over, while he raked out the coals to a bed about six feet wide by ten feet long. The heat was intense. When he pulled the rake out and rested it on the ground, it hissed and steamed through the thin cover of snow. With a shovel he patted the embers into a solid mass. It glowed brilliant red-orange in the moonless night, with flames rising from some partly consumed logs resting along the edges forming a small alley of fire. At the end of the coalbed where we would step off, Shoshame had the ground soaked with water from a nearby hose, which he would use to douse the embers when the walk was over. We were to step into the wet soil, in case any embers clung to our feet. Then we could wipe off our soles on a nearby blanket, return to our place in the circle, and put on our shoes.

Everything was ready. We had been warned inside to walk straight and steady through the coals—no gazellelike bounds, no running, no mincing steps, no hot-dogging. We'd signed a release form which waived "all rights to compensation in case of injury," and there was no doubt in our minds there could be injury because Shoshame had said he'd heard of five cases where people were burned. One case was attributed to loss of concentration when a flashbulb went off in the person's face. Therefore, he'd told us, no one could take pictures except the photographer, and then only of Shoshame.

We were ready. I felt clear and calm—no apprehension whatsoever. I'd decided I would go, no matter what. Would I be burned? No way to find out but to walk. Would the coals feel cool, as some firewalkers had experienced, or would they feel warm, even hot, as they had to others? Would they feel like beach sand on a summer day or like peanut shells? These were all part of the description Shoshame had given us.

And then he was walking across the coals. It took perhaps five strides and five seconds. Midway across, the strobe light flashed. He repeated the walk at the end of the evening to give the photographer another chance.

Shoshame had hardly gotten off the coalbed before the first participant had his shoes off and was striding magnificently across the embers. The man next to him in the circle followed in rapid succession, and then half a dozen others went, all walking properly as instructed. I stepped out of my shoes and walked to the short line of waiting people. My mind was Zenlike: free from thought and mental chatter, focused clearly on the physical aspects of the event, observing without comment, performing without fear. Because of my years in consciousness research, I can say I wasn't in trance or anything like it. No one else reported being in trance, so far as I heard later. Inasmuch as there was an altered state of consciousness in me, it was simply pristine mental clarity, backed by a willingness—a positive mental attitude—to flow with the experience, no matter what.

Perhaps nine or ten people had crossed the coals. There was now one woman between me and the fire. She walked purposefully up to the coals, hesitated just a moment, and then turned away almost without breaking stride, returning to her place in the line.

Now it was my turn. Without hesitation or expectation, I walked forward onto the coals. My first step felt quite neutral—neither hot nor cool—except for the crunching sensation and noise as the coals subsided under my weight. The second step was the same. On the third step I felt a slight sensation of heat. The fourth and fifth steps were almost unnoticeable. And then I was off the coalbed, wetting my feet briefly before returning to my place in the circle. My feet felt unharmed as I stood there, watching others walk or not walk. If anything, they began to feel cold and numb from the frozen ground, but I decided to leave my shoes off anyway until I returned to the house.

Shoshame gave a one-minute warning: those who hadn't walked still could, but only if they did so within the next sixty seconds. Five had chosen not to go on the coals; none changed his mind.

And then it was over, with a prayer of thanks to God and a hallelujah for allowing us to experience the firewalk as a lesson in overcoming fear and expanding our sense of personal power. Shoshame turned on the hose, causing great billowing clouds of steam to roll over me on the downwind side of the fire. I stood there enveloped in whiteness, momentarily invisible to everyone, with everyone likewise invisible to me, feeling mildly euphoric.

Once inside, we shared our thoughts and feelings briefly, after which Shoshame had us write on a notecard. Those who didn't walk wrote "I can always trust my inner guidance!" The rest of us wrote "I walk on fire. I can do anything I choose!" We were advised to carry the card with us or place it somewhere at home as a constant reminder that we can create our own experience of reality through the infinite potential of our minds. No one was burned; one man had a blister.

The evening ended about midnight with health-food beverages and cookies and a feeling of great exhilaration. As I drove home, however, I noticed a slight sensation at two points on my left sole. I hadn't examined my feet closely after the firewalk; they'd seemed okay, so I'd just brushed them off and donned my footwear, feeling fine. When I got home, I reexamined them and discovered two slightly reddened spots, each about a quarter of an inch in diameter. Apparently I'd picked up some embers on that third step. But the discoloration was barely visible, and the next day had almost disappeared. There was no pain at any time, only a slight sensation that something wasn't quite right at those points. A few days later a small blister appeared at one spot.

And that was it. To put it in perspective, consider firewalking from the medical-scientific view: there is no explanation for it. Shoshame quoted medical authorities, who uniformly declare that subjecting human flesh to the conditions of the coalbed would leave the firewalker with CBS— charred bloody stumps. He consulted Bruce Fichandler, a physician's assistant at Yale-New Haven Hospital's burn center for twelve years, who warned that firewalk participants would be seriously burned. The next day Fichandler told the *Courant:* "I don't know how to explain how they are able to do that. At 1,300 degrees, that ought to burn your feet and burn them good. It would require skin grafting and four to six weeks' hospitalization, depending on how you recovered." Yet an estimated 30,000 people have successfully completed the firewalking seminars.

Some physicists have proposed the Leidenfrost Effect as an explanation—the effect seen when you sprinkle water on a hot griddle. The water droplets seem to dance around because their surface has vaporized, creating an insulating layer which protects the rest of the drop. The same thing, these physicists say, happens to your feet because of perspiration, so if you don't leave your feet on the coalbed for long—only a second or so—you can get away with it. The only trouble with that explanation is that it doesn't work for well-observed instances, reported by anthropologists, in which firewalkers have remained standing still in the coals for up to twenty seconds. In at least one case observed in Greece, the firewalkers kneeled down in the white-hot coals for *several minutes!* Speaking personally, I have to say that I don't buy the Leidenfrost-Effect explanation either because the sides and arches of my feet were quite dry, so they should have been burned.

Consider firewalking also from a psychological perspective. Making it across the coalbed performs heavy-duty therapy for some participants. An Arizona woman described it as the equivalent of a four-day est seminar in five minutes. A senior editor of *Parents* magazine said it helped him to do all kinds of things he was afraid of. Shoshame relates firewalking to therapy by saying that even those who choose not to walk receive valuable tools and methods they can use to overcome all the negative programming, fears, and limiting beliefs in their lives. It fosters personal growth and a sense of responsibility for creating a better world, he says. Who can argue with that?

Do I feel I'm a better person for firewalking? No, not in a moral or spiritual sense—but, yes in a cognitive sense. There's no substitute for firsthand experience, especially when investigating mysterious phenomena. The power of the human body-mind was shown to me dramatically.

Would I do it again? Absolutely. Would I recommend it to others? Absolutely. But not for purposes of showmanship. And like Shoshame, I warn you not to try it by yourself.

Firewalking is not what I'd do for a living, but it is what anyone can do for better living if fear is limiting him. When fears and belief-based limitations incapacitate you or reduce your happiness, the thing to do is face them. Walk through those fears as if you were walking through fire. Overcome limitations based on belief systems.

Finally, consider firewalking form a spiritual perspective. Crossing the coals, is, strictly speaking, a symoblic physical event of no special importance in and of itself. Rather, it signifies a metaphysical act: self-sacrifice to God. It signifies a willingness to surrender the ego, the sense of separate selfhood which is the ultimate illusion separating us from the Divine. In religious ceremonies, the sacrificial fire symbolically consumes all vestiges of self-centeredness, all bad karma, leaving the individual to realize his oneness with creation and the Creator. From a spiritual point of view, therefore, walking on coals is nothing less than stepping forward into the unknown in faith that there is a power greater than your own which sustains and protects you if you attune to it.

As you wake up to the ultimate limitation—ego—you can overcome that limitation by letting yourself "die" in the sacrificial fire. You die by yielding yourself utterly to the Divine. You don't have to actually walk the coals to do that. The fire of daily living which tests your love, integrity, and patience offers sufficient circumstances to purify yourself, to burn off the dross. And in that ego-death, in that surrender to God you will learn self-transcendence and freedom from fear. You will learn that fear is what separates you from your true self and the kingdom of heaven. Fear is what blinds you to the light of God shining in all things. / AMEN

When the coalbed becomes your moment-to-moment condition, when the sacred flame burns in all circumstances of your existence, there is only the clear, calm walk through life in selfless surrender to God, with the divine fire of Love awake in your heart, shining brightly.

> When thou passest through the waters, I will be with thee; and through the rivers, they shall not overflow thee: when thou walkest through the fire, thou shalt not be burned; neither shall the flame kindle upon thee.
> For I am the Lord thy God. [Isaiah 43:2]

6

UFOs and the Search for Higher Consciousness

our decades ago insurance salesman-pilot Kenneth Arnold saw nine unidentified objects in the sky near Mount Rainier, Washington, an event that caused the term *flying saucer* to enter our vocabulary. Immediate speculation was that Earth is being visited by extraterrestrials. The media and public alike responded to the phenomenon with deep attraction. Since then, the term *unidentified flying object* or UFO has gained general usage instead, as a large variety of shapes other than saucers have been sighted.

Since then also, the subject has been widely investigated, hotly debated, and eagerly watched. People around the globe have thrilled to the adventure of *ET, Cocoon, Star Trek,* and the *Star Wars* series; they've also been scared out of their wits by *Aliens.* Skeptics such as astronomer Carl Sagan and aerospace journalist Philip Klass deny that there is any evidence for UFOs; ufologists Lawrence Fawcett and Barry Greenwood show definitively in their 1984 book *Clear Intent* (now retitled *The UFO Cover-up*) that, despite repeated denials, the U.S. government and military have known for four decades that UFOs are real and represent a technology beyond human capability.[1]

If UFOs don't exist, then neither do stars. Some of the same types of evidence which long ago convinced us stars exist suggest that UFOs are a reality as well: visual sightings around the world by competent witnesses,

56

photographs and films of their appearance in the sky (pronounced genuine by many reputable experts), and observable secondary effects such as skin burns (equivalent to sunburn) and other radiational effects seen on those who claim to have had UFO encounters.

Additional physical evidence is available in the form of inexplicably broken tree branches, matted vegetation, imprints in the ground allegedly made by landing gear, soil samples which show unusual characteristics not seen in control samples, and frightened animals in the vicinity of the claimed sightings.

Add to this the fact that UFOs have been confirmed by multiple military and civilian radar sightings; by testimony from top military officials such as Gen. George S. Brown, who told a congressional subcommittee in 1974 that "[UFOs] caused us a lot of trouble in Vietnam"; and even by the former head of the FBI, J. Edgar Hoover, in a now-declassified memo stating that the Army took possession of a crashed flying saucer.

Consider also that in some alleged UFO abduction cases, hypnotic regression by competent professionals has verified that the abductees are not consciously lying. In still other cases, medical findings document the occurrence of burns, eye inflammations or temporary blindness, and other physiological effects—and even rapid or instant healings of previous conditions. These are attributed by the affected people to encounters with UFOs, and often no other cause can be found by medical examiners.

Many paranormal phenomena have been documented in connection with UFOs, such as telepathy, levitation, and materialization/dematerialization.

Classifying the Evidence

The evidence is in: UFOs are real. Enough data exist to suggest six classifications (devised by the dean of UFO researchers, the late Dr. J. Allen Hynek): nocturnal lights; daylight disks; radar visuals; close encounters of the first kind (observation of any UFO which comes within 500 feet of the witness); close encounters of the second kind (in addition to a nearby UFO, there are various forms of interaction between the UFO and the environment, such as impressions or burn marks on the ground, interference with auto ignition systems, or physical effects on humans); and the term used by Steven Spielberg for his movie on the subject, close encounters of the third kind (involving humanlike creatures in association with a UFO).

All things considered—and we do have to consider all things in coming to grips with the UFO experience—there is a mountain of evidence demonstrating that UFOs are real and constitute a multilevel phenomenon. The questions at this point are: What are they? Where do they come from? What do they want? The evidence indicates that no single explanation can cover all the experiences and events lumped together under the label "UFO problem." Little green men in spacecraft with Martian license plates are only one piece of the puzzle. In my judgment, the evidence falls into three major categories, and thus there are three "answers" to the UFO problem: terrestrial, extraterrestrial, and metaterrestrial. Let's start with the most familiar.

Extraterrestrial. Some UFO experiences are best understood, as the public widely does, as intelligently constructed physical vehicles occupied by ETs. Evidence of this is found in the Hill Star Map which contactee Betty Hill drew in 1964, during therapy for symptoms arising from the abduction aboard a UFO at Exeter, New Hampshire, in 1961. Her map was a reconstruction on paper—a drawing—of a three-dimensional hologramlike picture of space shown to her aboard the UFO. The map showed our sun and other stars from the perspective of the aliens' home star. When a model of space was constructed by Ohio schoolteacher Majorie Fish in an attempt to find the pattern of stars which matched Betty Hill's map, all her attempts at the time failed. Then, in 1969, revised astronomical data of the distance and position from Earth of local stars (within forty light-years) made it possible for Fish to construct a more accurate model of nearby space. Thereupon the home base was found to be the star Zeta Reticuli, in the constellation Reticulum, about thirty-seven light-years from Earth. Remember that the Hill Star Map, drawn in 1964, contained information unknown to anyone on Earth at the time. Thus the information on which Betty Hill based her map strongly suggests that it was of extraterrestrial origin.

Further evidence of ET contact is contained in *The Sirius Mystery* by Robert Temple, an astronomer. Temple says that the Dogon tribe in central Africa has had accurate information for several thousand years about the dark companion star of Sirius—information which was unknown to astronomers until this century.[2] The Dogon mythology says that ETs came to Earth millennia ago and revealed the Sirius information to the tribe. These accurate data about the dark companion's period of orbital rotation (indeed, the tribe's very knowledge of its presence) again indicate an extraterrestrial source. The Dogon further claim there is a *third* star in this stellar complex. While modern astronomy has not yet sighted such a companion to Sirius and its dark partner, the search is under way. If it proves correct, the Sirius mystery will be solved in favor of ET contact in the manner of the "ancient astronauts" theory of ufologist Erich von Daniken, who believes that primitive Man regarded such beings as "gods from outer space."

There are also persistant rumors, now chronicled in Charles Berlitz and William L. Moore's *The Roswell Incident* (1980) that a UFO crashed in New Mexico in 1947 and was recovered, along with the bodies of its occupants, by the U.S. Air Force, which spirited it away to Wright-Patterson Air Force Base in Dayton, Ohio. More recently, a set of controversial documents, referred to as the MJ-12 papers, were released to the public by Moore and his colleague Stanton Friedman as further evidence of the Roswell incident. Moore and Friedman claim the papers were "leaked" by a government source; the papers themselves purport to be a top secret account by President Harry S Truman and others who describe the retrieval of a crashed UFO and four deceased aliens. The government denies the authenticity of the incident, but Moore and Friedman have documented statements by several dozen military and civilian firsthand witnesses who attest to the reality of something extraordinary—and most probably of extraterrestrial origin—happening near Roswell, New Mexico.[3]

Terrestrial. Some other UFO experiences, however, may be best understood as originating from Earth itself, from an undersea civilization. Many UFO sightings have taken place at sea and involve craft which observers say burst through the surface and take off into the sky. Ivan Sanderson's *Invisible Residents* is the best description of this aspect of the UFO problem. (Some researchers think this ties in with the Bermuda Triangle mystery. I myself am not convinced such a mystery exists: I consider the Bermuda Triangle to be New Age nonsense, but that is another story.) Sanderson reasoned that since life began in the sea, when some organisms came ashore, it slowed their development; sea-living organisms continued to evolve, so today there may be advanced forms of sea life more intelligent and technologically capable than Man, living invisibly on Earth under the oceans. (Of course, ETs may have established undersea bases.)

Other UFO experiences in this category are best understood as human contact with a form of lower animal life native to Earth's upper atmosphere. The discovery of these strange aerial creatures is told in Trevor James Constable's *The Cosmic Pulse of Life*.[4] His text and photographs reveal a class of elemental fauna unknown to official science. Neither solid, liquid nor gas, these amoebalike aeroforms exist in the fourth state of matter—plasma—and are normally invisible for several reasons: (1) Their native habitat is far beyond discernibility by human gaze but well below the astronomers' usual telescopic focus. (2) They move at a very high speed—thousands of miles per hour. (3) Their usual condition is in the infrared portion of the electromagnetic spectrum. However, they have the capacity to change their density and thereby pass from one level of tangibility to another. Thus they sometimes do appear in the visible portion of the spectrum where, if seen by humans, they are quickly labeled UFOs (which, of course, they are). But they are not mechanical spacecraft; they are living creatures. They grow anywhere from the size of a coin (the World War II "foo fighters" sightings) to at least half a mile in diameter. They give a solid radar return even though invisible to the naked eye. They pulsate with a reddish-orange glow. They can change form but are generally discerned as discs or spheroids. Their diaphanous structure allows a limited view of the interior. Some have been seen close up on the ground in full physical density. (I give a full description of them and of the research objectifing their existence in Appendix 4.)

The term *earth lights* could provide another plausible explanation for some UFO sightings. As presented by Paul Devereux in his 1982 book of that title, and amplified in his 1989 *Earth Lights Revelations*,[5] strong evidence exists to show that geophysical activity deep in the Earth, especially along tetonic fault lines, produces a piezoelectric effect. Electromagnetic fields are generated which in turn produce luminous atmospheric phenomena—earth lights. These aerial luminosities have been noted around the world throughout history, but their origin has been attributed to supernatural causes and labeled "will-o'-the-wisp," *ignis fatuus,* ghost lights, etc. Dr. Michael Persinger, a psychologist at Laurentian University, Ontario, and Gyslaine F. Lafrenière, a research scientist there, demonstrated in their 1977 book *Space-Time Transients and Unusual Events* that such phenomena may have a terrestrial origin and be capable of inducing many effects in the minds of the human observers, depending on their distance from the geophysical luminosity, such as have been noted in UFO sightings and even abductions. Devereux and his colleagues' research, independent of Persinger and Lafrenière's, has enlarged upon the possibility that earth lights may account for some UFO sightings and mysterious ghostly figures. The generalized view of all these investigators is collectively known as Tectonic Stress Theory (TST).

Still another aspect of this category involves what psychologist Carl Jung (in his *Flying Saucers: A Modern Myth of Things Seen in the Sky)*[6] proposes are symbolic projections of deep human yearnings for wholeness and transformation in the collective psyche of humanity. Without denying their physical nature, Jung speculates that UFOs are either psychic projections perceived in objective space or the appearance of real objects that afford humans an opportunity to project mythological symbols from deep in the collective psyche. (I examine this topic more fully in the next chapter.)

This interaction between mind and matter, between the physical and the metaphysical, brings us to the last major category of UFO phenomena, a category that seems to arise at the hinterland of familiar space-time.

Metaterrestrial. The term *metaterrestrial* was coined by J. Allen Hynek to denote something which originates outside the familiar space-time framework in which we function. Also called extradimensional, interdimensional, ultraterrestrial, and supraphysical, this category provides evidence that some UFO experiences are due to nonphysical but real entities which come not from other locations in our universe but from other sets of dimensions which interpenetrate our space-time. Dr. Kenneth Ring describes this realm as the "imaginal" and emphasizes that it does not mean imaginary. Materialization/dematerialization and some other psychic or paranormal phenomena are best accounted for this way and are theoretically possible within modern physics' view of reality. In short, many UFO incidents appear to be contemporary versions of what was recorded long ago in mythology, religious scripture, and spiritual traditions as encounters with angels, demons, and the various inhabitants of other planes of existence. These metaterrestrial (MT) beings materialize into our space-time from other levels of reality—traditionally called heaven and hell in the Judeo-Christian world view but presently understood as hyperspatial dimensions or supersensible space-time frameworks with a wide range of beings native to them, just as ours has creatures ranging from viruses to whales.

The UFO phenomenon thus appears to be multifaceted. Evidence suggests that other life forms are present in the universe (the evidence from exobiology supports this idea, quite apart from the UFO data) and that they have contacted the human race throughout history and are still interacting with us in various ways. The interactions range from the benevolent, such as warnings from Space Brothers and Galactic Confederation emissaries about the threat of nuclear war, to the malevolent, such as the abduction of Whitley Strieber, who in his best-seller *Communion* told of being abducted, brain-probed with needles, anally examined with a rough instrument, and having his memory altered. (Strieber's experiences have continued, but he now believes the "visitors," as he calls them, are actually helping us to surmount deep-seated fears and to transform ourselves into "new" beings.)

What is the meaning of all this for humanity? In a recent comprehensive two-volume bibliography entitled *UFOs and the Extraterrestrial Contact Movement,* George M. Eberhart surveys the literature on UFOs and alleged contacts with ETs. It is significant that Eberhart describes the extraterrestrial contact phenomenon as a "movement." The movement is widespread, albeit unorganized. It goes far beyond mere public interest in flying saucers. In its deepest aspect, it represents a flowering of the human quest for God and growth to higher consciousness. There are *many* groups founded on the ET/MT-contact premise, often centering around a charismatic figure who claims to be in contact with UFO occupants and to have regular telepathic links with space or hyperspace.

These groups range from membership societies such as the Unarius Society (Escondido, California) and Mark-Age (Ft. Lauderdale, Florida) to communal/extended family situations such as that around David Michael the Cosmic Messiah (Berkeley, California) and "The Two," who preached a gospel called Human Individual Metamorphosis which promised followers would be removed from the planet by a flying saucer. All these groups extol the virtue of their unseen communicators and claim they have a mighty revelation to offer for the benefit of humanity. Many of them regard extraterrestrials and metaterrestrials as "gods from outer space." And many of them, such as "The Two," offer a program or prescription for higher human development and extension of human consciousness to godlike conditions if we will submit to "the gods."

But while their appeals to join the movement may be intriguing and enticing, remember that fools rush in where at least one form of ET/MT life—angels—fears to tread. The movement's appeal needs close and careful consideration. For the remainder of this chapter, therefore, I will offer a cautionary comment about the proper *attitude* toward UFOs and ET/MT contact.

From Outer Space to Inner Space

First consider the most intriguing aspect of the UFO experience: the convergence of psychology and physics. As the study of inner and outer space merges, consciousness becomes the key to understanding the situation. The UFO phenomenon actually leads us to still-larger questions. It is not enough to ask what are they, where they come from, and what they want. Our ultimate questions concern cosmology and ontology: What is reality and how can we know it?

These questions bring us slowly but surely to the realization that only by understanding the essence of ourselves can we understand the nature and structure of the cosmos, including the UFO phenomenon. It is a paradox recognized in all major religions, higher psychotechnologies, and sacred lifeways that the deeper we look inside ourselves, the more universal we become. Scientific and spiritual traditions—the objective and subjective aspects of our attempt to know reality—converge to reveal levels of consciousness far beyond what we ordinarily take for the limits of our awareness.

Conceptualizing these higher dimensions is difficult. Recent models of the cosmos by physicists, paraphysicists, and parapsychologists are resorting more and more to the esoteric, heremetic, metaphysical, and occult traditions, which claim to have long been aware of aspects of reality other than the physical material. These traditions use terminology such as the astral plane, the etheric plane, the plane of Mind, and so forth to denote hyperspaces—other space-time frameworks, other sets of dimensions—interpenetrating our own.

Where are these hyperspaces? All sources agree: They are within us, even while they seem to be outside; and at the same time, they are outside (the physical body) even though we arrive there by "going within."

The cosmos, then, may be conceived as having different but interpenetrating planes of existence which are space-time frameworks in their own right. The higher planes are the native realms of angels, spirit guides, ascended masters, and other evolutionarily advanced beings reported throughout history as interacting with humanity to guide and protect us.

Protect us from what? Malevolent inhabitants of the other planes. Outside the physical plane we humans inhabit not all is sweetness and light, according to these traditions. There are said to be objectively real but invisible intelligences which seek to penetrate human psyches in order to stop our evolution and enslave us to their will. It is said that these malignant entities can and do sometimes materialize into our plane of existence in various alluring ways to entice us off the evolutionary-spiritual path.

As a person evolves in consciousness and expands awareness, he passes through these different levels en route to the highest state of consciousness, cosmic consciousness or enlightenment. Those levels, in Judeo-Christian cosmology, are termed the heavens. In Hindu and Buddhist thought, they are called *lokas*. Though the terminology differs from culture to culture, the underlying unity of experience cannot be mistaken. Each level is said to have beings (presumably organized into some social structure) capable of materializing into other levels. As a person moves into those spaces through whatever spiritual discipline he practices to purify his consciousness and develop "organs of higher perception," the boundary between "inner" and "outer" events dissolves and a single, unified view of reality is perceived. This is why there has been unanimity of reports from "soul travelers" to the highest regions.

And what they report is this: We humans are confused about ultimate reality and our true identity. Both are something far greater than we ordinarily think, and both are actually one.

Next, consider what this means for human happiness and understanding. First, there *is* a core truth to which we can penetrate—an Ultimate Answer which alone gives purpose, meaning, and direction to our lives and our search. Second, that truth is accessible to each of us on the basis of direct experience, without need for intermediaries. Third, in order to attain that truth, we must ascend in consciousness; we must personally evolve through our own efforts. And, finally, if many individuals evolve, the result could well be a collective change of society, a transformation of the species, a radical change in human nature.

Evolution Beyond Man

Precisely such a change is now occurring, as I see things. Evolution has not stopped. A new race, a higher form of humanity, is now emerging on the planet. My reason, research, and personal experience lead me to this conclusion—and certainly it is not mine alone. As I point out more fully in Chapter 20, Nietzsche, Bergson, Teilhard de Chardin, Sri Aurobindo, Gopi Krishna, R. M. Bucke, L. L. Whyte, and others have proposed the same kind before me: Human beings are also human becomings.

The grand theme of history is the evolution of consciousness: a story of ever-more-complex forms of life coming into physical being in order to express more fully the consciousness behind existence itself. As this applies to the current world scene, I maintain, the many threats to life on this planet created by Homo sapiens' intellect-gone-wild have caused such pressure on nature that the life force—the intelligence governing creation—is mobilizing to resist the irrationality of Man.

How will it resist? As I remarked earlier, the life force will resist "the disease called Man" by bringing a higher form of life onto the planet, a form which will recognize the laws governing nature and live in accordance with them. The human race as we know it, in all its combative, divisive, exploitative, self-centered inhumanity-to-man will go the way of the dinosaur. The widespread signs of world unrest and cultural collapse around us indicate that a historical epoch, a world age, is ending.

Simultaneously, a great awakening is going on around the globe. It isn't merely a generation gap or a communications gap. A new species is awakening to its cosmic calling and is asserting—in the face of the threatening dominant species—its right to live. The planetwide uneasiness and societal upheaval seen today is fundamentally an expression of people straddling old and new worlds as they try to find out which species they belong to. The dominant species is ego-oriented, technology-mad, and unconsciously bent on self-destruction through its materialistic addictions and their unforeseen effects on the biosphere. The emerging species, on the other hand, is life-embracing. It seeks to live in harmony, create a unified planetary culture founded on love and wisdom, and (as Native Americans say) walk in balance on the Earth Mother. I have named the new species *Homo noeticus*.

In the course of people's effort to find their true identity, many errors and excesses will occur. The gods-from-outer-space concept is a notable example.

Now, there is nothing inherently implausible about the notion that more highly evolved life forms exist and have contacted us. Exobiology suggests that life will arise wherever conditions are not simply favorable but merely a little better than totally hostile. Since our sun is a relatively young star, there may be older star systems where organisms developed earlier than here and have become the more highly evolved inhabitants of supertechnological civilizations capable of space travel. They may even have come to Earth in UFOs, as the Hill Star Map and the Dogon oral history indicate.

The Danger of "Gods from Outer Space"

The immediate allure of contact with such civilizations is the possibility of learning new technologies from them. Imagine, for example, being given the means to build power sources such as those which propel UFOs. Some alien communications speak of "free energy devices" which tap space itself and could do away with the need for oil, coal, gas, and nuclear fuels. This is an exciting vision, promising—on the surface, at least—a new era of peace and prosperity such as people have dreamed of for millennia. Beneath the surface, however, this is more of the same narrow vision—the unquestioned faith in the power of science and technology to secure human happiness—which is endangering our species at this time.

Thus, inherent in the possibility of ET/MT encounters is a danger we must recognize beyond the mere idea of ferocious killers as expressed in *Aliens*. We *must* recognize this danger if we are ever to truly build a "heaven on earth." For such knowledge as we might obtain from extraterrestrial contact still does not give us the most important type of cosmic connection, the type we need in order to deal with the problems of daily living. Our endless accumulation of scientific facts simply does not add up to wisdom and understanding of the human situation in its cosmic aspect. Every new bit of information, every new answer we get raises a dozen new questions. Gathering scientific data is an endless process, and unless we are properly grounded in the *moral* foundations of the universe we will continue to find new ways of misusing science so that knowledge only leads to greater unhappiness, as we see most strongly in our present situation, a historically unprecedented threat to all life on the planet. As the recently deceased spiritual teacher Krishnamurti said in speaking of our Faustian quest, "Knowledge is only a part of life, not the totality, and when that part assumes all-consuming importance, as it is threatening to do now, then life becomes superficial. . . . More knowledge, however wide and cunningly put together, will not resolve our human problems; to assume that it will is to invite frustration and misery. Something much more profound is needed."

What is needed? A transformation of consciousness. Only a change in the state of human consciousness will allow us to find the knowledge and *wisdom* necessary to survive the threats facing Homo sapiens. For there is a type of knowledge beyond science—beyond even the science of supertechnological extraterrestrial civilization—which is nevertheless democratically available to every one of us. It is the core truth, the eternal message of all the world's sacred traditions. It is knowledge anyone can obtain directly from the cosmos, without intermediaries, without being dependent upon benevolent superior beings, whether they are angelic messengers, Space Brothers, spirit guides, ascended masters, walk-ins, or whatever. Call it God-knowledge, mystical union, attaining yoga, finding the Tao, or achieving enlightenment. These terms all refer to the same thing: the fundamental apprehension of Cosmic Wholeness transcending any and all parts of creation and its creatures. This is the knowledge which gives purpose, direction, and fulfillment to our lives by answering the ultimate questions spiritual traditions and science alike have tried to answer: Who am I and what is existence all about?

That is not to deprecate the value of whatever wise counsel or technical information humanity may be offered by extraterrestrials or meta-terrestrials in the matter of evolving to higher states of being. But in the last analysis, it is up to us to take responsibility for our own growth into higher consciousness. Nobody can do that for us—not through neurosurgery, genetic engineering, chemical implants, hypnosis, or any other forms of outside intervention such as various ancient astronaut theorists and UFO contactees are suggesting today. What is "out there" cannot save us. The impulse to grow must come from *within* as an organic expression of a person's total being.

The Meaning of *2001*

That is the unanimous advice from sages around the globe throughout history: Deep inside us, not far out in physical space, is the channel by which we can make the cosmic connection, the one which really counts. A powerful illustration of this is seen at the end of *2001: A Space Odyssey*. The film is a classic for many reasons, but the chief one is its insightful treatment of the grandest theme of all history: the evolution of consciousness and the growth of humanity to a godlike state. *2001's* "hero" is the astronaut Bowman. His technology-denoting name symbolizes an intermediate stage of human evolution which is still relatively crude but nevertheless well beyond the ape-man stage with which the film begins. At the end of the film, we see Bowman traveling on the (symbolically) sperm-shaped spaceship named *Discovery* through the atmosphere of Jupiter, preparing to land and begin searching for the advanced life forms who created the mysterious black obelisk. This is the famous psychedelic scene in which the audience goes through the streaming colors representing the atmosphere and surface of the planet. During the passage, an image of a human eye appears briefly now and then, filling the entire screen so that only the pupil and iris are seen. This is director-producer Stanley Kubrick's way of saying that the film's explicit journey to outer space is implicitly a journey to inner space, to the center of the mind. Because as the audience passes through Jupiter's atmosphere it also passes through the giant eye into the brain-mind behind it.

And there, in the center of the mind, is an amazing discovery, a startling revelation: *We ourselves are the real extraterrestrials* for whom Bowman has been searching. Humanity has gotten so "spaced out," so far from home, so out of touch with the Earth that we have forgotten our origins and lost our roots. We've become alienated to ourselves and the planet. And because of that, we are in danger of destroying life on the planet, and perhaps even the planet itself, just as some purported messages from space beings warn us.

In that alienated state of consciousness we are searching for advanced life in the universe—searching for higher consciousness—in outer space. Now, there undoubtedly are such life forms out there. But it is deep within ourselves, not out in astrophysical space, that the true cosmic connection exists. So long as we have not discovered our own potential for growth and further evolution we have become terminal, the dying old man Bowman is at the film's end. So long as we look for gods from outer space or any kind of saviors "out there," we are lost and alienated from Truth. But when we "look within" and find the power of consciousness directing our destiny and the destiny of all creatures, no matter how highly evolved, then we realize paradoxically that we are one with that consciousness, that cosmic intelligence, that transcendental reality.

The basic situation facing us today is a crisis of consciousness. Human consciousness is in a disturbed, unstable state and, through what could be called "extraterrestrial materialism," many people are making idols of UFOs and extraterrestrial life: false gods from outer space. But if we are ever to build paradise here, we must first heal ourselves, not rely on surrogate parents from the sky or wish for saviors from beyond the planet.

Depth psychology has shown that a child's parents are, its first gods. But growing up, maturing, requires relinquishing that illusion along with hopes and dreams of invoking magical powers and omnipotent forces to fulfill our desires and answer all our questions. Instead, we must do the slow, difficult, and often painful work of taking responsibility for our own actions and recognizing that if we are presently the real aliens, we are also potentially the gods we seek.

As Arthur Clarke, who wrote the novel and film script of *2001*, put it, humanity is near childhood's end. We stand ready to become what Carl Sagan calls "starfolk." We stand ready to join galactic society, through the mature form of the human race, the higher humanity I've designated *Homo noeticus*. That is the meaning of the Star Child floating in space at the end of *2001*, silently contemplating the Earth. *2001* is a mighty cinematic saga of human evolution from an apelike condition to a new stage of transhuman development. Star Child is Kubrick's symbol of the emergence of a new state of evolution: the development of the coming race—or the Son of Man, the offspring of humanity. Star Child is a citizen of the cosmos, no longer ego-centered or even Earth-centered but rather universally centered and cosmically conscious.

That godlike state beckons to us through many manifestations today. Although the manifestations are most often occulted, vague, and uncertain, the principal one has long been clearly recognized and revered. I refer to the true spiritual teachers of history such as Jesus, the Buddha, Krishna, Lao-Tse, Muhammad, Moses, Zoroaster, Guru Nanak, Saint Teresa, and other more recent figures such as Meher Baba, Sri Aurobindo, and the Mother, Mira Bai, and Da Love-Ananda. These illuminati, these godmen and godwomen are the people who most clearly demonstrate the future of human evolution. These enlightened ones are forerunners of the "new breed," specimens of an advanced humanity. Their lives have been dedicated to showing those lower on the ladder of evolution that they have within themselves the potential for self-directed growth to a higher state of being, and none has claimed to be extraterrestrial. They have, however, claimed to be universal and have said that all others can be also. How? To quote the Buddha's dying words: "by relying upon themselves only, and not relying upon any external help . . . not looking for assistance to anyone besides themselves." Or as Jesus put it, by seeking first the Kingdom of God.

That is why I caution against deluding ourselves with the glamour and mystery of UFOs and ET/MT contact. The two principal reasons can be stated thus:

First, the promise of such contact is tantalizing yet beyond our control. We are wholly at the mercy of whoever or whatever is out there, subject to their whims, unable to communicate except when they want to allow it, and unable to verify the information they give us about themselves. Some of them could prove hostile rather than benevolent, just as many abductees' experiences already indicate. The guidance and warnings of sacred traditions and spiritual teachers about this matter should not be lightly disregarded. Remember that the Bible describes demons as fallen angels, and Satan is said to disguise himself as an angel of light. We must *beware* of false gods.

Second, the greatest enemy and the greatest ally we have are still to be found in the depths of our own psyche. The proper attitude toward meetings with starfolk can only be the one which is proper for human teachers and helpers. When our attitude assumes the character of a master-servant relation or a deity-worshiper relation, our own evolutionary potential is discarded and our cosmic calling is unheard. Properly understood, however, ET/MT contact has value in the fashion the signs and wonders of Jesus had for the first Christians. They pointed to a still-higher source which is the creator of us all, and they demonstrated the reality of our own latent ability to become as Jesus was—and even more, as he himself acknowledged. The UFO experience can do the same thing for our time. We must *be aware* of True God.

We are rapidly entering the next phase of evolution. But evolution is essentially transcendence, and the source of all transcendence is the Transcendental. That is the source of our being as well as our becoming. Whether our meetings with advanced life forms seem to come from outer space or inner space, we must recognize that they principally reflect to us what we ourselves shall eventually become and that all time and space, all worlds and their inhabitants, arise from the Transcendental Source whose traditional name is God. Therefore, it is God alone to Whom we should aspire in our search, recognizing that the distant goal of our evolutionary journey is also the fountainhead of our existence moment by moment along the path, and that what is working itself out in cosmic space and eonic time is, beyond space and time, already so right now.

Paradoxically, our ultimate condition is a present fact: In Reality there is only God.

7

On Mind and the Physics of Paranormal Phenomena

The Occult Forces of Life

The reigning world view of the scientific community (or, to use more current jargon, the consensual reality) has been described as materialistic, reductionistic, and athiestic. As a formal philosophy which attempts to give *meaning* to its data, it has been called physicalism. The term denotes a widespread assumption in science, present from its beginning, that the secret of life is inherent in the properties of matter.

From the viewpoint of physicalism, life itself is the ultimate paranormal event. The universe is assumed to consist only of physical matter. It has no "spirit," no principle of vitality beyond the physical. In short, it has no metaphysics. The four basic forces modern science recognizes—electromagnetism, gravity, the weak and strong nuclear forces—are assumed to arise from properties of physical matter, albeit in its subtlest form. All phenomena, this philosophy says, including life and mental activity, will finally be reduced to an explanation in terms of these energies and physicochemical mechanisms acting in random fashion without purpose, meaning, or direction from any higher intelligence. If only we can get a fine enough analysis (the physicalist line of thinking goes), if only we can combine chemicals in the right way with the right amount of electricity, we can create life.

Mind is the hallmark of life and should therefore, from the physicalist point of view, be inherent in the properties of matter. But it isn't, as I showed in the first chapter. If mind is not to be found in the recognized forces of nature, we will have to look for it elsewhere.

Parapsychology and psychical research are doing precisely that. A century and a half of investigation into paranormal phenomena has established a wide range of events which clearly are *real* events. But what is the energy involved in these events? How can it be controlled and directed? What can we say with certainty and precision about the physics of these events?

The word *energy* comes from the Greek *energeia,* "active." It is generally understood as the capacity to do work or to be active. But in its original sense it means *vital* activity, that which can move or quicken inert matter. Energy means literally "of (itself) motivational-ness."

Thus, in earlier times, for many people there was a distinct and publicly acknowledged sense of a fundamental life force. This life force was self-evident to the ancients even though its nature was not readily understood. It was apprehended but not fully comprehended—recognized but not well explained. It was normally undetected, secret, hidden from sensory processes and from rational understanding. It was, in a word, occult.

In recent years, an increasing number of investigators seeking to understand paranormal phenomena have come to feel that science must recognize a new principle in nature: the same principle of vitality which ancient traditions considered primary. This principle introduces what may be called a *psychic* factor (from *psyche,* "soul" or "mind"). There has thus been a reawakening of interest in those ancient traditions which claim to have knowledge of the creative life force, what could be called a fifth force.

One researcher, electrical engineer Lawrence Beynam of Ankara, Turkey, summarized his views on the subject by saying there is an energy in living organisms which is weak and unpredictable but can be refracted, polarized, focused, and combined with other energies. It sometimes has effects similar to magnetism, electricity, heat, and luminous radiation, but it is none of these. Attempts to control and employ the energy have met with little success; investigators have not yet defined the laws governing its operation.

Addressing himself to the same topic, the fortean-naturalist Ivan Sanderson, founder of the Society to Investigate the Unexplained, editorialized in the society's journal *Pursuit* on the nature of the "new" force:

> This fifth force is certainly involved in various aspects of SSP [supersensory proclivities, Sanderson's term for psychic abilities] and it would now seem to be the major force operative in the true psychic field and possibly the only one acting therein. Its manifestations are in no way affected by any of the other known forces; and, while doubtless universal in nature, it can be observed, measured and investigated only in the biological field. The presence of a living thing is necessary to bring it to light. Although we have not yet defined it or its parameters, it has now been demonstrated that it, and it alone, can explain a whole raft of what were previously thought to be mysteries or pure imagination, such as mental telepathy, SSP [here meaning supersensory projection] and SSR [supersensory reception], the two PKs—psychokinesis and pyrokinesis—and possibly the whole group of things clustering around clairvoyance. It would explain all that has puzzled the psychologists about things like the so-called subconscious, hypnotism, and the like.[1]

Sanderson pointed out that psychics such as Peter Hurkos, who once demonstrated telepathy while inside a Faraday cage, show that these abilities do not function along electromagnetic lines. Uri Geller's performance of the same feat, reported by Stanford Research Institute scientists Harold Puthoff and Russell Targ in *Nature* (October 1974) reconfirms the phenomenon. Experiments in the Soviet Union by Leonid Vasiliev in the 1930s also indicated this hypothesized fifth force.

"Is it not time," Sanderson asked in his editorial, "that we stopped ignoring all these things, or blithely relegating them to that vague field of the psychic, and got the technicians to work, trying to define the nature of this force and, by both theory and experimentation, give us a set of laws for it such as govern the other four forces?" He pointed out that there is ample published material to begin with, so that a "basic pattern" might be assembled almost immediately. "There is then," he concluded, "the matter of seeking its parameters and fitting new observations into this pattern, rejecting them, or altering the pattern."

As I pointed out in my book *Future Science,* this fundamental force seems to have been recognized many times in history by various prescientific traditions; an appendix shows that accounts of a mysterious energy run through ancient occult and spiritual documents. For example in his book *Transcendental Magic* the eighteenth-century French magus Eliphas Levi described the properties of the magician's "astral light" this way: "There exists an agent which is natural and divine, material and spiritual, a universal plastic mediator, a common receptacle of the vibrations of motion and the images of form, a fluid and a force, which may be called in some way the Imagination of Nature. . . . The existence of this force is the great Arcanum of practical Magic."

More than 100 other names for this mysterious or X energy have been identified from various sources around the world. In the Orient, for example, the Chinese conception of *qi* or *chi* (*ki* in Japanese) was thought to be the intrinsic vital force throughout all creation. It is this life energy which acupuncture manipulates to maintain health and which can be concentrated through disciplines such as tai chi and aikido to perform paranormal acts. According to Confucianism and Taoism, without chi nothing can exist, and from it spring the yin and yang forces which in turn give rise to all things, including living organisms.

Paralleling this idea in the yogic tradition of India and Tibet is the notion of *prana*. The same concept can be found in practically every culture. Polynesians and Hawaiians call it *mana*. To the Sufis it is *baraka*. It is *yesod* in the Jewish cabalistic tradition. The Iroquois call it *orenda;* the Ituri pygmies *megbe*. In Christianity, it is the Holy Spirit. These and many other traditions claim to recognize and, in some cases, control a vital cosmic energy underlying paranormal phenomena.

Within modern times there have also been people who claim to have identified *through science* a fifth and fundamental force in nature. Wilhelm Reich is perhaps the most notable. His discovery of *orgone* energy is considered by orgonomists to be at the heart of sicence and life itself. In the Reichian view, orgone is the all-pervasive ocean of life energy—primordial, massless, and preatomic—from which all other forms of energy are derived. Some investigators see parallels between it and both Franz Anton Mesmer's *animal magnetism* and Karl von Reichenbach's *odic force*. There is a parallel, too, between it and the Soviet concept of biplasma.

Many traditions, both ancient and contemporary, claim to have identified the energy behind paranormal phenomena. I have felt it best to be all-inclusive rather than selective, yet it was apparent that the terms are not fully synonymous in all cases, with varying measures of overlap or convergence among some. Prana, for example, is said by yogic tradition to have a number of gradations. Likewise, there are various forms of chi. Rudolf Steiner's presentation of the etheric formative forces lists seven: the life ether, the chemical ether, the light ether, the warmth ether, and three "higher" ethers. The chemical ether seems equivalent to orgone. Orgone itself, however, is single-state. In general, however, the terms I have noted as forms of X-energy point toward the idea of a new principle in nature for science to recognize in the form of a spiritual but nonetheless real creative life force.

As I noted in *Future Science,* Lawrence Beynam examined this vast subject and reported the following characteristics of the X-energy:

1. It is observed in the operation of heat, light, electricity, magnetism, and chemical reactions, yet is different from all of them.
2. It fills all space, penetrating and permeating everything, yet denser materials conduct it better and faster, and metal refracts it while organic material absorbs it.

3. It is basically synergic. It has a basic negentropic, formative, and organizing effect even as heat increases, and thus is the opposite of entropy (that is, disorganization and disintegration) as set forth by the Second Law of Thermodynamics, which it thereby violates.

4. Changes in the energy precede physical (observable) changes, and it is supposed to create matter, energy, and life. This is also observed in certain psychic phenomena where metals continue bending long after the initiating agency/psychic has touched them.

5. It has its opposite number. Seen clairvoyantly by psychics as red and yellow, this energy is opposed to the life-giving energy outlined above. It can be seen when the life-giving energy is leaving instead of entering (emerging into) a region. (For example, in Kirlian color photographs of a psychic healer's finger, the finger is blue to begin with and then turns reddish-yellow when the healer transfers energy to a patient.) While the blue, synergic energy gives a cool, pleasant feeling to the sensitive, the yellow-red, entropic energy creates a feeling of heat and unpleasantness.

6. In any structure which is highly organized (e.g., crystals, plants, humans), there is a series of geometrical points at which the energy is highly concentrated (e.g., chakras in the yogic tradition, acupuncture points).

7. The energy will flow from one object to another. According to the Huna tradition, it is "sticky" so that an invisible stream of energy will always connect any two objects which have in any way been connected in the past (the basis of sympathetic magic). The energy is subject to exponential decay, radiating outward in the course of time from an inert material, but there is always a residue (since decay goes on to infinity). The density of this energy varies in inverse proportion to the distance; this ratio sets it apart from energies which obey electromagnetic and gravitational laws, but to this ratio a theory of potentials may be applicable.

8. The energy is observable in several ways: as isolated pulsating points, as spirals, as a cloud surrounding the body (aura), as a flame, as a tenuous web of lines (Don Juan's "lines of the world" and the occultist's "etheric web").

Research engineer James Beal of Huntsville, Alabama, independently arrived at the same conclusion as Beynam's first characteristic of the X-energy. In a talk to the American Anthropological Association's 1974 symposium on parapsychology and anthropology, Beal noted that the effects should not be construed as the cause behind unexplained psychic events. According to him, some bioelectric field effects noted by conventional science may actually be "weak indicators, precursors, or stimulators in regard to effects filtering down from a higher system."

Dr. Harold Saxton Burr of Yale University discovered such an indicator system. His electrodynamic theory of life, first announced in the 1930s but still largely unknown to the scientific establishment, offers a solid link between electromagnetics and the mind: a bridge between the physical and the prephysical foundations of life.

Burr's work, much of it done in collaboration with his student-colleague Dr. Leonard Ravitz, shows that there is a guiding field which performs a directive, organizing function on the physical structure of an organism. This guiding influence is generally termed the L-field, short for life field. Burr and Ravitz demonstrated that the state of health of an organism could be determined far in advance of the least observable physical sign by using a microvoltmeter to inspect its L-field. Ravitz later learned that the L-field as a whole disappears *before* physical death. Sensitivity to the L-field might explain in part how psychic healers function in diagnosis and cure.

It is clear, however, that L-fields are themselves affected by higher-level forces. Ravitz made the further discovery that the state of *mind* (in the form of unspoken thoughts and images) affects the voltage gradients of the L-field. In his book *Design for Destiny* Edward W. Russell refers to this power of thought as a T-field, meaning thought field. He notes that although L-fields are ordinary electromagnetic phenomena, not a new force in nature, they are nevertheless of immense importance for showing how mind or T-fields can *measurably* affect L-fields and thus the physical body. L-fields give science a clear opening into that mysterious area where physics and psychology come together—the mind.

The concept of morphogenetic fields proposed by British scientist Rupert Sheldrake in his 1981 book *A New Science of Life* presents a widely discussed hypothesis of "formative causation" postulating an invisible matrix or organizing field which regulates the structure, growth, and behavior of all kinds of things. These fields are causative, serving as blueprints or guiding patterns for form and behavior of entities across time. This capacity is called *morphic resonance*. "When any one thing forms (a crystal, say) or any animal learns a new behavior, it will influence the subsequent learning of formation of all other crystals or animals of the same kind," Sheldrake says. He denies that the morphogenetic fields have energy; their influence seems to operate ex nihilo. Nevertheless he proposes that psychic and paranormal events may be explicable by his hypothesis.

Although Sheldrake dispenses with all conventional forms of energy as the force behind forms, the data cited in this essay strongly suggest the reality of a new force in nature, which could be the missing link which saves the morphogenetic fields hypothesis from ex nihilo operation. In a personal communication to me, Sheldrake agreed: "When I say morphogenetic fields are non-energetic, I do so to avoid confusion with the kinds of energy known to physicists. I hope that further research will indeed enable these problems to be resolved."

A concerted investigation of the fifth force or X-energy seems a promising research avenue to pursue in developing what Sheldrake terms "a new science of life and mind." He echoes Princeton physicist Eugene Wigner, who once wrote that "the present laws of physics are at least incomplete without a translation into terms of mental phenomena. More likely, they are inaccurate, the inaccuracy increasing with the role life plays in the phenomena considered."

This brings us back to the metaphysics which physicalism has so long denied and tabooed. It brings us beyond the physical into the realm of mind and suggests a promising avenue of investigation. In their search for an explanation, investigators of the psychic and paranormal should, of course, consider everything conventional science has to offer. But it seems that conventional science and parapsychology alike are up against the wall in their efforts to explain the paranormal—or, in the case of physicalists, to explain them away. Real progress is going to occur only when psychic and paranormal events are acknowledged and approached in a fresh and imaginative way. As Einstein once said. "The mere formulation of a problem is far more essential than its solution, which may be merely a matter of mathematical or experimental skill. To raise new questions, new possibilities, to regard old problems from a new angle requires creative imagination and marks real advances in science."

In that spirit I have suggested the plausibility of a fifth force in nature and the need to investigate this hypothesized force which is, from my perspective, one of the keys to explaining paranormal phenomena. I will now consider two others: the structure of space and the possibility of higher life forms.

From Parapsychology to Transpersonal Psychology

It is well known that the Swiss psychiatrist Carl Jung, one of the pioneers of transpersonal psychology, had a deep interest in psychic phenomena and paranormal events. He himself experienced them, and his concept of synchronicity was developed in an attempt to make rational what otherwise defied all scientific notions of reason and cosmic orderliness at that time. In his later years Jung came to look upon physics as the field which could most profitably link with psychology to elaborate upon the concepts (such as synchronicity, archetypal experiences, and the collective unconscious) he himself had been unable to articulate adequately. In fact, it was Nobel laureate Wolfgang Pauli, one of the chief architects of quantum theory, who collaborated with Jung in his development of the synchronicity principle.

Explorers of the unknown since Jung have recognized paranormal phenomena as points of convergence between psychology and physics—between our investigations of inner and outer reality. The paranormal turns out to be an opening into the larger question: What is reality and how can I know it?

Another topic Jung pondered is UFOs or, as he called them, flying saucers. Although he felt their ultimate significance for people was psychological, he recognized their "psychoid" nature, meaning they have quasi-physical characteristics as well and exist objectively in astrophysical space, where they could be photographed, seen on radar, and create physical trace marks on the earth. I feel that Jung was advancing in the right direction with such formulations, but he did not go far enough in explaining the interaction of mind and matter. Here is the outline of what I think Jung, who died in 1961, would have concluded today in light of the data from parapsychology and ufology.

Exobiology suggests that life will begin almost anywhere in the universe, not just where conditions are favorable but also where they are only slightly better than totally hostile. That being the case, and since the sun is a relatively young star, there is a high probability that life exists in stellar systems older than ours. In other words, there probably are more highly evolved life forms in the universe: higher consciousness, if you will.

At the same time exobiology has been telling us this, the UFO scene has been intensifying. I have already pointed out that UFOs and contractees are one of the focal points for investigators of paranormal phenomena. Some UFO contactees describe meetings with nonphysical entities who materialize into our three-dimensional space-time continuum from other sets of dimensions or higher planes of existence. Call them what you will—Space Brothers, metaterrestrials, ultradimensionals—their existence is said to be on a scale enormously beyond the human, just as ours is beyond that of insects, which in turn are similarly beyond microbes. From their level of reality, it is said, these higher forms of life influence and even guide human affairs.

It is interesting to consider that these notions of more-highly evolved entities match many of the descriptions of higher beings which we have from ancient religious and spiritual traditions. Are they merely the same ideas dressed in contemporary garb or are the reports of such beings valid and independent of those ancient traditions?

As I pointed out in chapter 6, the Judeo-Christian cosmology tells us there are angels and archangels, cherubim and seraphim, inhabiting the heavens. And the term *heaven* is generally taken to denote a higher level of reality in the supersensible realm invisible to normal perception—a higher level of consciousness with its native life forms. In the Hindu and Buddhist traditions, the term for heaven is *loka*. Various entities inhabit the lokas also, notably the devas.

Deva means "shining one" or "radiant being" in Sanskrit. It is conceptually equivalent to "angel." Devas have been described as belonging to another kingdom of life. They are neither animal, vegetable, mineral, nor human. Rather, devas are a separately created order of life which has the role of supervising lower orders. Considered abstractly in scientifically oriented terms, devas can be described as conscious, formative principles which guide and regulate life forms below them in the ladder of creation or the great chain of being, irrespective of space–time coordinates.

What has such supernaturalism and mythology as devic beings to do with parapsychology? I have suggested the presence of a nonphysical force in nature as the energetic mechanism producing psychic phenomena. Various ancient traditions identify it as the motive power behind paranormal phenomena; I've designated it the X-energy. Conventional science does not recognize the X-energy, but occult science does.

Grant for the sake of discussion that the X-energy exists. That is not sufficient to explain paranormal phenomena. Energy must be directed and controlled by a higher-level intelligence. Can the human mind exert such an influence? Parapsychology answers yes. For parapsychologists, some poltergeist phenomena seem plausibly explained as unconscious psychokinesis by living persons. Healing through the laying-on of hands is an example of psychokinesis through conscious, willed direction of X-energy. However, other paranormal phenomena appear to be of such magnitude that any intelligence presumed to be producing and controlling the energetic situation would have to be of a stature surpassing humanity by many orders of magnitude. The events at Fatima, Portugal, in 1917 (popularly referred to as "the day the sun danced" but more soberly regarded as a spectacular UFO appearance) is such a situation.

Are there such beings? As I pointed out in the preceding essay, exobiology suggests there are. Ufology and various spiritual and occult traditions also point with some degree of overlap to the notion of more highly evolved life forms whose existence is much older and grander than ours. Tie that in with noetics—which suggests that where life is, consciousness is—and the mystics begin to make sense when they say there is a hierarchy of conscious life forms leading up the great chain of being to the source of consciousness, God. (One astrophysicist speculated recently that pulsating neutron stars, pulsars, are intelligent beings, which brought to mind Edgar Cayce's statement that the sun may be an angel in another dimension.)

Now let's see how these two hypotheses—admittedly undemonstrated in scientific terms—might offer some explanation of paranormal phenomena and their relation to the human mind.

Recall our consideration of the terms *archetype* and *collective unconscious* in Chapter 4. Jung describes them this way in *The Archetypes and the Collective Unconscious:*

> A more or less superficial layer of the unconscious is undoubtedly personal. I call it the *personal unconscious.* But this personal unconscious rests upon a deeper layer, which does not derive from personal experience and is not a personal acquisition but is inborn. This layer I call the *collective unconscious.* I have chosen the term "collective" because this part of the unconscious is not individual but universal; in contrast to the personal psyche, it has contents and modes of behavior that are more or less the same everywhere and in all individuals. It is, in other words, identical in all men and thus constitutes a common psychic substrate of a suprapersonal nature which is present in every one of us.
>
> The contents of the collective unconscious are known as *archetypes.*[2]

Jungian psychologist Ira Progoff elaborated on his mentor's work in *Jung, Synchronicity, and Human Destiny.* This passage is particularly relevant:

> The Self is the archetype of all the archetypes that the psyche contains, for it comprehends within itself the quintessential purpose behind the impersonal archetypes and the archetypal process by which the ego and consciousness emerge. The Self may be understood as the essence and aim and the living process by which the psyche lives out its inner nature. As such the Self can never be contained by the ego or by any of the specific archetypes. Rather, it contains them in a way that is not limited by space or time. The way the Self contains the various contents of the psyche is in a kind of "atmosphere," a state that is more than psychological, an "aura" that sets up the feeling of this situation in a manner that is neither psychological nor spatial nor temporal. It involves something that can be spoken of as a nonphysical continuum by means of which the correspondences within the cosmos, the microcosm and the macrocosm, can come together to form patterns, at once transcendent and immanent, and constelling situations that draw physical as well as psychological phenomena into their field.[3]

Progoff's statement has many levels of affinity with various religious and spiritual traditions. The concept of a higher Self which is simultaneously immanent and transcendent is an ancient one. But this paradoxical statement about Jung's work fails to cross the same language barrier which stopped Jung. It still doesn't integrate psychological concepts with physics as Jung hoped would be done. That is why Progoff had to put certain words in quotation marks. They indicate that the words are vague and imprecise. At best, the words are figurative and abstract, not literal and concrete. Where, for example, are archetypes stored in the brain? How are they transmitted from generation to generation? Saying they are encoded in the DNA molecule is unsatisfying because, even if finally proven so (and I doubt that it will), that materialistic position doesn't explain how *mental experiences* arise from *physical* combinations of atoms.

If we put aside the physicalist perspective and look in another direction, we see that parapsychology and ufology are beginning to offer some data with which to build a bridge between psychology and physics, between inner and outer space.

Kirlian photography, for example, shows that the corona discharge around a person (whatever the corona itself may finally prove to be) is subject to both the thoughts of the person himself and the thoughts of others, as in psychic healing. Photographing this energy through the Kirlian method shows dramatically that thoughts have immediate physical effects. In that regard, it is remarkably similar to the work of Burr and Ravitz.

In other words, there is an energetic dimension to thought or, as occultists and metaphysicians maintain, thoughts are things. the Burr–Ravitz data and Kirlian photography demonstrate the power of thought over physical matter and the visually observable level of reality.

Therefore I offer this speculation. If thought is energy (or at least has an energetic aspect) and if energy is neither created nor destroyed, then all the thoughts which have ever been thought are still in existence somewhere. Perhaps their form has changed; perhaps their energy content has dissipated. On the other hand, various esoteric traditions such as Tibetan Buddhism, Rosicrucianism, Huna, and true magick say that if the emotional component of a thought is sufficiently strong, or if the intellectual component is sufficiently prolonged and concentrated, it may impress itself upon the nonphysical X-energy continuum in such a way as to create a thoughtform. A thoughtform (called a *tulpa* in the Tibetan tradition) is an energetic embodiment of the idea on which the person focused or dwelled mentally. Somehow it becomes disembodied and takes on an independent existence in physical space for a time. Its form and character accord with the thoughts and emotions of the mind (human or otherwise) which called it into being. (It is said that when ascended masters appear physically in our level of reality, they "clothe" themselves in materialized thoughtforms drawn from the nonphysical X-energy continuum.) Dr. Gerald Langham of Fallbrook, California, a plant geneticist concerned with the relation between form and energy, coined the word *energysm* to denote phenomena of this sort. He says that an energysm is just as alive as an organism. If an organism is a being consisting of visible matter, he says, then an energysm is a being consisting of feelable energy which has not yet condensed to the state where it become visible to the naked eye.

An anecdote from Dilip Kumar Roy and Indira Devi's *Pilgrims of the Stars* illustrates this concept. The authors are yogis who recount their experiences on the yogic path. Indira possessed considerable psychic gifts, including clairvoyance. This gift enabled her to realize, she writes, "that many of the thoughts we take to be our own actually float in from the atmosphere and that it is our own free choice whether to accept or reject them." A vivid experience taught her this. She was meditating in her guru's temple hall in Poona, India, with a group of friends. She could see very clearly that most of them had an aura of tension around them. They were concentrating so hard to silence their minds that it only heightened their awareness of thoughts. Not one person in the group was completely relaxed, the first necessary condition for meditation.

> Suddenly she *saw* a sex thought floating in from without and touching one person who accepted it. He became restless, but the thought developed in his mind in the form of jealousy, which is one of the concomitants of sex. He played with the thought and was soon carried away on the wave of a grievance and anger against the guru, the world and God.
>
> The thought touched two other people but as they did not give it a fireside seat, it quickly turned away from them. Another friend accepted the thought as his own and felt terribly anxious about his health.
>
> It was fascinating, though the whole thing did not take more than a minute.[4]

If thoughts are real but nonphysical things, then perhaps human thoughts of a similar nature, or thoughts arising out of similar circumstances, may seek one another, coalesce, and become what could be called a thoughtfield. Especially intense thoughts arising out of powerful experience from the collective history of the human race could then generate what Jung called an archetype, a psychic entity and (when consciously perceived) symbolic event in which certain deep experiences of racial history are contained.

But notice: An archetype would then not be simply an idea in someone's mind. It would be a subtle repository of experience encoded in some energetic form *outside* the human brain/body. Its physical location would be the equivalent of an atmosphere around the Earth, not in the figurative sense Progoff uses but in a literal sense. The archetypes would be an energetic shell or envelope, composed of some nonphysical energy (the X-energy) which surrounds the planet and which people have access to during dreams, meditation, and other altered states of consciousness which lower our perceptual filters and allow our psychic senses to operate more fully.

Since archetypes are "universal" experiences, it would not be rational to conceptualize them as spatially limited to a geographic area. Rather, they would be coextensive with the planet's physical atmosphere. How far outward they might extend is a problem still to be solved, as is the problem of how information is encoded in such an energy envelope. But at least this conceptualization accounts for something neurophysiologists and conventional psychologists cannot explain: how and where an archetype or any other form of instinctive behavior is "stored" in the brain. From the point of view of archetypes as energy thoughtfields, the "storage" is outside the brain/body. Both Dr. Elmer Green of the Menninger Institute and his biofeedback research subject, Swami Rama, support this position when they declare that their findings and experience suggest that "the brain is in the mind but not all the mind is in the brain." Green himself suggests the possibility of a "field of mind" around the planet. (The implications this concept raises about the nature of memory are, of course, on the same order as what I've just described about archetypal experience.) Furthermore, this concept relates directly to my conclusion in Chapter 1.

What, then, is the collective unconscious? In terms of what I've developed here, it would be an energetic shell or envelope surrounding the planet, composed of all the archetypal thoughtfields created during human history, to which all people have access and which grows out of the historical experience of evolving humanity. (It might well include the collective unconscious or racial memories of any other civilizations existing on Earth prior to our own: Atlantean, Lemurian, the "root races" of Theosophical tradition, and so forth.)

This conceptualization does two things. First, it satisfies Jung's requirements that the collective unconscious be both transcendent and immanent—beyond the individual yet within him—and that it must contain various contents of the psyche in a manner neither psychological nor spatial nor temporal in the ordinary sense derived from physical science.

Second, this conceptualization supplements and supports the psi field theory of parapsychologist William Roll. It supports his theory by presenting a nonphysical but real means by which psychic sensitives may get extrasensory access to information about past human experiences.

Some psychics have given a description of how they operate in terms which parallel this conceptualization. Most notable was Mr. A, the anonymous but spectacular psychic healer (of Berkeley, California) whom journalist Ruth Montgomery wrote about in several books. Mr. A said he got his diagnostic information and healing energy from what he called "the ring"—something he described as a magnetic ring around the planet and apparently not the Van Allen radiation belts.

I have extended the ring into a sphere. Whether it finally proves to be a relatively localized sphere or some unlimited field extending throughout the universe, it at least presents a model of the occult concept termed "the Akashic record" which Edgar Cayce and other psychics have said they "read" in order to get psychic information. This model also agrees in part with the "cosmic computer" metaphor which some psychics and UFO contactees say is the source of their psychically derived data. And it ties in nicely with Sheldrake's hypothesis of morphic resonance and morphogenetic fields.

But two important questions arise at this point. First, if this speculation is valid, how can we explain the way in which psychics obtain knowledge about the future as well as the past? Second, does this conceptualization satisfy the requirements set down by spiritual traditions and transpersonal psychology for defining the nature of the higher Self?

It is clear that there must be more to the conception I've offered than just the foregoing if these questions are to be answered. At this point I suggest that the "something more" may include the notion of the noosphere proposed by Pierre Teilhard de Chardin (see his *The Phenomenon of Man*). It may also include devas and angels.

Remember that we have seen there may be more highly evolved life forms whose existence, occult and spiritual traditions maintain, is to some degree entwined with humanity's as they influence and guide human affairs in the interest of evolving us to a higher state of being. From that point of view, the future of humanity already exists to some unspecified degree. That is because devic/angelic consciousness is characterized, among other things, by knowledge of the future since in some way it guides and organizes the human future. We ordinarily think of time as flowing from the past through the present to the future, but from the perspective I'm developing here, we could say that time flows from the future to the past, in the sense of the potential becoming actual. And devas, existing in a nonphysical but real form magnitudes of cosmological order beyond the human level, are of a still subtler or more rarefied condition of being than the energy thoughtfields I've just called archetypes.

Devic/angelic consciousness thus interpenetrates the collective unconscious and is cospatial with it, just like water vapor and air. David Spangler, one of the early residents of Findhorn who claims to have channeled communications from devas and other forms of higher intelligence, told me that if the devas could be seen with unmediated vision, all that would be perceived would be a shifting pattern of color and form.

What I am hypothesizing here, then, is an energy field surrounding our planet which has different densities or planes to it. Those densities or planes may be based on different gradations or forms of the X-energy spectrum. It seems likely that the energy or energies from which the devic/angelic kingdom emanates are of a higher order than the X-energy composing thoughtforms.

Most probably, the energy field has both a static and a dynamic

aspect. In its static aspect, the collective unconscious grows infi-
nitesimally over millennia as the pool of human mentality adds new
psychic information, images, and concepts to it. In its dynamic aspect,
devic/angelic consciousness is in constant flux as it interacts with
humanity.

Taken as a single organism, the energy field or field of mind might
satisfy Teilhard de Chardin's description of the noosphere, which, he
said, in one sense is still to be built but in another sense already exists.
When he says "different senses," I feel I can specify them precisely. They
have to do with different points of view—the human and the devic/
angelic. From the latter point of view, the noosphere already exists
because the devas and angels have it "in mind" for us and guide us toward
its manifestation. From the human point of view, the noosphere is
abuilding as we ascend in consciousness and add our psychic contribu-
tions to the process which creates it.

Philosopher Oliver Reiser suggested there is a mutual induction
process going on by which higher consciousness reaches down to humanity, while humanity in turn reaches up to higher consciousness. This
conception of a two-way process for building Teilhard de Chardin's
"spiritual earth" or what Reiser called "the psychosphere" would, I feel,
adequately answer the two questions I raised about how psychics get
future knowledge and also about the nature of our higher Self. Of course,
the concept of the highest Self, God, is beyond all which I've set forth
here.

In this essay I have tried to show that physics and psychology (especially transpersonal psychology) come inexorably together in the
study of paranormal phenomena. The meeting ground of inner and outer
reality is consciousness, and paranormal phenomena turn out to be only
a wedge into the more fundamental question: What is reality and how
can I know it?

As I pointed out in Chapter 6, these questions about cosmology and
ontology bring us to the realization that only by understanding the
essence of ourselves—the "layers" of the psyche, including our higher Self
and our highest Self—can we understand the nature and structure of the
cosmos. And paradoxically, the deeper we look inside our personal self,
the more transpersonal we become. The split between mind and matter is
healed through transcendence. Scientific and spiritual traditions converge to reveal planes of consciousness or hyperspaces beyond ordinary
awareness.

Where are these other planes? They are within us, even though they
seem to be outside us in physical space; at the same time, they are indeed
out there, even though we arrive "there" by "going within" through
various psychotechnologies (such as meditation) for purifying personal

consciousness and "cleansing the doors of perception." In this way we learn, as Jungian psychologist Marie-Louise von Franz has put it, that matter and psyche are merely the outer and inner forms of the same ultimate reality, consciousness: "the ultimate components of matter present themselves to our consciousness in similar form-structures like the ultimate or primordial ground of our innermost being."

The cosmos can be conceived as different but interpenetrating levels of consciousness, just as I've conceptualized our local planetary space as having interpenetrating layers of psyche. As a person expands awareness, he passes through these different levels of consciousness en route to the highest state of consciousness.

As he grows in mindfulness and develops "organs of higher perception," the boundary between "inner" and "outer" space dissolves. The subjective becomes objective.

This is why great spiritual teachers have calmly accepted the paranormal as quite normal and have displayed psychic talents far beyond anything seen in the laboratory. Think of Jesus raising the dead and healing the sick. Think of Sai Baba of India materializing fresh fuit out of season to feed the hungry. Think of Emmanuel Swedenborg telling someone about a fire raging in his home town as it was actually happening 300 miles away. Think of Rudolf Steiner clairvoyantly penetrating Hitler's mad scheme (as told by Trevor Ravenscroft in *The Spear of Destiny*) and mobilizing forces which were significant in the eventual defeat of the occult Third Reich.

From their higher level of consciousness, the supernatural is perfectly natural and mythology's symbolism turns out to be literally true. Both are concrete realities originating in a supersensible world, nonphysical but real, long known to clairvoyants, seers, and sages.

Does this mean that spiritual seekers should abandon science? Quite the reverse. The word *science* means "to know." The essence of science is its method, not the world view built from a limited body of data obtained through the scientific method. The prevailing philosophy of science— mechanistic, reductionistic, and athiestic—can be set aside without sacrificing what is valuable: the scientific method. That method is an extremely powerful tool for investigating reality and has already begun to give us technological means for objectifying what until now has been imperceptible to normal human senses. (See, for example, Appendix 5.)

But the scientific method is not our only way of knowing reality, and history has shown that science is no more powerful than the vision and imagination of those who use it. Has a century and a half of parapsychological investigations brought us any nearer to understanding paranormal events than those pioneering investigators who founded the psychical research societies? Yes, insights abound—but comprehension eludes us. Perhaps it is time, then, to take a fresh, innovative approach to the physics of paranormal phenomena. Perhaps it is time to take a more comprehensive view of existence: one in which we tentatively adopt the perspectives of our spiritual teachers, our primitive and occult traditions, our superpsychics.

This does not mean that scientists and researchers should forsake their rational faculties and intellectual integrity. Nor does it mean they should spend all night on a hilltop praying to a spacecraft (except, perhaps, as an attempt to follow Dr. Charles Tart's strategy for investigating states of consciousness). That way madness lies.

But by adopting those world views as hypotheses for investigation, researchers into the paranormal will, I feel sure, navigate safely along that narrow, tricky path between having an open mind and having "a hole in the head." By remaining faithful to the scientific method without being bound by the world view prevailing among scientists, humanity will, I believe, see a flowering of the spirit of science leading to a science of the spirit.

And what would a science of the spirit be? Quite simply, it would be a commonly held higher level of knowing in which the nonphysical becomes objectified, empirical, and publicly demonstrable. It would answer our questions about the physics of paranormal phenomena in a way which integrates our intellectual knowledge with our deepest feelings and most honored values in a life-supporting, life-enhancing manner. And in doing so, it would help bring about a new social order which various spiritual and esoteric traditions envision: the New Age.

8

Karma, Reincarnation, and Evolution

I t is said that on the night he was enlightened, the Buddha recalled all his previous lives—some 900,000 of them. Don't ask me where that story comes from. I simply heard it and have no source reference. But if that is an accurate indication of how many past-life regressions a person would have to conduct to attain enlightenment and get off the wheel of death-and-rebirth, forget it! There isn't enough time in one's life to conduct that many past-life regressions, let alone contemplate and integrate them into one's psyche.

Fortunately for humanity, the Buddha and other sages have taught and demonstrated the "direct path" (sometimes called the short path or the steep path) to enlightenment, which goes directly beyond the entire space-time framework where reincarnation occurs. It is the path to the Source-condition which is the ground of the enlightened state *(nirvana)* and transcends the entire reincarnational realm *(samsara)*, yet includes it. The truth of existence *(dharma)* dispels the illusion of the separate self and shows that people can go beyond the mechanics of cause-and-effect *(karma)* to attain true spiritual freedom *(moksha)*. As the yogi Shankara put it a millennium ago: From the enlightened point of view, reincarnation does not mean that your ego moves through successive existences, but rather that the transcendent Self is "the one and only transmigrant." Or as Joseph S. Benner, author of the spiritual classic *The Impersonal Life* (1941) put it:

What have You, the Perfect, the Eternal, to do with past or future incarnations? Can the Perfect add to its perfection? Or the Eternal come out of or return
to eternity?

I AM, and You Are,—ONE with Me,—and always have been, and always will
be. The I AM of you dwells in and reincarnates in ALL bodies, for the one
purpose of expressing My Idea.

Humanity is My Body.[1]

Thus in a very real sense, the burgeoning interest in exploring past
lives can be self-defeating and a waste of time. The sensationalism and
glamour surrounding the subject is sadly misleading. All sacred traditions advise that here-and-now is what truly matters. Attend the present
moment. What's past is past; it doesn't have to be remembered in every
detail in order to transcend its effect in the present. The past is history;
the timeless present transcends history. All too often those who get
wrapped up in past-life recall are merely playing ego games of self-
glamorization. Even serious and humble spiritual seekers can get caught
up in trying to capture every little detail of a previous incarnation in the
hope that a full description of that lifetime will be the key to happiness
and understanding in this one, which is nonsense. What is necessary for
enlightenment is understanding the process of growth beyond the ego,
beyond that which reincarnates. Sacred traditions say it is possible,
through spiritual disciplines and purity of heart, to become free from the
wheel of death-and-rebirth by entering the timeless infinite from which
the entire scheme of nature, with its karmic operations, arises. There is
no karma in the Void of nirvana. Enlightenment is understanding one's
true self or original nature before the universe was born and after the
universe has been annihilated—that is, pure consciousness, the Void, the
suchness or "emptiness" of all things. It is most important to understand
the current moment, in which the ego-sense is constructed and used to
create the illusion of separateness which blocks perception of one's true
self.

Nevertheless, that is not to say past-life recall and reincarnation
research have no value. On the contrary, they can be extremely valuable
for certain stages of spiritual unfoldment and for scientific understanding
of Nature, especially the death experience. So, for example, past-life
regression therapist Florence McClain's transpersonal approach to past-
life recall (presented in her *Past Life Regression*) is useful because it is
both practical *and* spiritual. It offers detailed instructions for recalling
what may be past-life memories in a psychologically sound framework.
McClain's viewpoint is always focused on the here-and-now usefulness
for personal growth of whatever you may learn about your past lives. She
says that if it doesn't help you to function well in the world, if it doesn't
help you to become happier, saner, and more loving, then past-life recall
is merely a parlor game. I couldn't agree more.

As the Buddha taught, we do not need to recall all our previous lives to become enlightened. Nevertheless, since reincarnation *is* an aspect of born-existence, the transpersonal nature of personal growth through lifetime after lifetime must be examined and understood in the course of our rediscovery of the Self.

Scientific evidence of reincarnation is abundant, but it does not add up to incontrovertible proof. Dr. Ian Stevenson, a psychiatrist at the University of Virginia Medical School and perhaps the foremost investigator of reincarnation, takes that position. I think it is a sound one. The ability of our minds to play tricks on us is both vast and subtle. Stevenson and others have pointed this out, urging caution against accepting as fact the vivid impressions people get when undergoing guided past-life regressions. The mind, when in the relaxed and open state of hypnotic trance or similar states generated by guided regression, can react to the most minor cue or suggestion from the hypnotist/guide, resulting in dramatic imagery which is the result solely of the human faculty of imagination. Stevenson concludes that unless past-life memories arise *spontaneously* and are then verified through historical research, they are untrustworthy.

Even unarguable facts spontaneously brought to mind by someone and then validated through documents or other means acceptable to historians do not constitute proof of that individual's psyche passing from one lifetime to another. There are alternate and defensible explanations. One is possession or mediumship in which a discarnate entity (an earthbound spirit or a nonhuman entity) passes on information to a living person. A second is extrasensory perception of another person's life, technically called retrocognition, in which the past is seen, but not necessarily the person's own past; it might also be due to telepathically tapping into the mind of one or more living persons to gather information about someone deceased. Still another is genetic memory, the theory that memories are carried genetically from one person to another in the same way physical traits are carried through generations. Cryptomnesia is also a possibility—obtaining historically valid information through normal but subconscious means, as was demonstrated to be partly true about the famous case of Ruth Simmons (Virginia Tighe), about whom Morey Bernstein wrote in *The Search for Bridey Murphy*.

For those interested in truly scientific research of the subject, reincarnation is a rich and fascinating topic. Very promising work has been done by researchers such as Dr. Helen Wambach, reported in her books *Reliving Past Lifes: The Evidence Under Hypnosis* and *Life Before Life*. Remember that for the spiritual seeker, however, pursuing past-life memories can be a byway and a waste of time. The value of such memories, whether real or fabricated, is their therapeutic power, their potential for offering insight into the formation of personality, for healing trauma to the psyche, for resolving problems which may not yield to other therapies, and for release from the egoic dimension of mind so that the self beyond personality might emerge. In that respect, then, one would do far better to study spiritual traditions than psychic ones. As the sagely Manly Palmer Hall put it in his 1946 *Reincarnation—The Cycle of Necessity,* "The belief in reincarnation and karma is useless unless coupled with a reasonable doctrine concerning the ultimate state of man." (p. 198)

Among the spiritual giants of history who have contributed to our understanding of the mechanics and purpose of karma and reincarnation is the Indian yogi-mystic Sri Aurobindo, one of the small group who have ascended to the summit of self-realization. He is not widely known in the West, but the depths and comprehensiveness of his achievement is outstanding. It is one of the high points in contemporary spiritual efforts to probe ultimate reality and transform human life into what Aurobindo called, as the title of his masterwork, "the life divine." Although he did not use the term New Age, he was profoundly concerned with creating it, in the sense of bringing a divine force down to the Earth plane and anchoring it here, fixing it in the human sphere so that our consciousness and our very bodies are "divinized." His life and teachings offer a method of self-perfection well suited to modern times, especially to the spiritual seeker grappling with the problem of reincarnation. He is a luminous example of the meeting of science and spirit.

He was born Aurobindo Ghose in Calcutta on August 15, 1872. The title Sri, "revered," came later. His father, an agnostic and an Anglophile, sent Aurobindo to England for schooling when he was seven. Aurobindo did not see his native land against until 1893. In England he proved a superlative student but he grew up almost entirely ignorant of Indian culture and spiritual traditions.

When he returned to India, he later reported, a great peace descended on him as he stepped ashore. He began teaching English and French, and at the same time he threw himself into intense private study of his native languages, literature, and political life. Soon he was spearheading the drive to rid India of British rule. His fiery rhetoric and writings eventually landed him in prison. He spent a year in solitary confinement and during that time underwent a profound spiritual transformation, ignited by several progressive mystical experiences which unveiled new dimensions of reality and sent him in a direction other than political action. Human perfection, he now felt, would only come through a basic change in the consciousness of the world.

Toward that end he worked steadfastly for the next forty years. In 1910, a year after his release from prison, he settled in Pondicherry, on the east coast of India, and began teaching what he called Integral Yoga, a yoga of transformation which combined the best elements of the major traditional lines of yoga in a manner suited to the modern temperament. For four decades he hardly left his ashram, preferring to work quietly with his ever-growing number of students and disciples. In 1920 he was joined in his work by a French woman, Mira Richard, who came to be known as the Mother. Like Sri Aurobindo, she had experienced an ascent in consciousness to levels rarely attained, and she shared his vision of a world transformation. Eventually she took over the administration of the ashram, allowing Sri Aurobindo to withdraw even more from daily affairs and to produce more books, essays, and letters on various aspects of the human search for self-perfection. His output was prodigious.

Sri Aurobindo died in 1950; the Mother continued his work until her death in 1973. In the 1960s a world city, Auroville, was begun a few miles away from the ashram. Today both the Sri Aurobindo Ashram and Auroville are visited by thousands of people who, having been touched in some way by the legacy of Sri Aurobindo, seek to move further into the vision he held before the world. It is a compelling vision, supported by practical instruction and methods for attaining a mighty evolutionary advance in society—an advance which involves a transformation both of consciousness and of the physical body itself. It is, in short, a meaning for overcoming what Sri Aurobindo called "the problem of rebirth" and getting off the wheel of incarnation.

Central to Sri Aurobindo's teaching is "the descent of the Supermind." This concept involves a spiritual evolutionary process which began only recently as the culmination of Sri Aurobindo's years of concentrated yogic effort. Eventually, he says, the Supermind will penetrate the entire human race with its power, light, and truth, producing the Superman. Supermind is a previously unattained level of consciousness toward which the human race is tending as it returns to godhead. Unlike many earlier yogic endeavors, which directed people to "leap into nirvana" and thereby dissolve altogether out of the manifest universe of space-time, Sri Aurobindo sought to bring forth the divine potential of humanity in the realm of everyday life and to *embody* God in the material place of existence. Rather than turn away from Earth and Man, he sought to transform Earth and Man. Some people have found a profound correlation between his vision and that of Teilhard de Chardin, who wrote of Christogenesis and the human journey toward the Omega point.

The immense poverty and fatalism which pervades Indian culture, it has been said by various commentators, is due in large part to its spiritual heritage, which often denigrated earthly life, thereby preventing the sort of material and technological progress achieved in the West. Sri Aurobindo sought to redirect his country's impetus from a world-shunning, body-denying spirituality to one which sees God-realization as possible within earthly affairs. It will not happen overnight, he says, but in the course of our reincarnational progress Supermind will be embodied more and more by ever-greater numbers of people. Thus, the world of Matter will become pervaded by Spirit and humanity will be perfected. "The Supermind is the bridge between the higher and lower hemispheres of existence," he says.[2] Integral Yoga is a way of speeding up immensely one's evolutionary journey through the planes of consciousness and attaining Supermanhood, the life divine. His teachings on the subject are given comprehensively in his book *The Synthesis of Yoga*.

In the course of his inspection of the entire spectrum of human existence, Sri Aurobindo examined reincarnation and gave it new meaning, or at least lifted it above popular misconceptions and trivializations to reveal its true spiritual significance. He preferred to use the word *rebirth* and says in his principal book on the subject, *The Problem of Rebirth*, that this term better captured the fundamental idea of the ancient doctrine.

"Birth is the first spiritual mystery of the universe," he wrote in *The Life Divine*, "death is the second which gives its double point of perplexity to the mystery of birth; for life, which would otherwise be a self-evident fact of existence, becomes itself a mystery by virtue of these two which seem to be its beginning and its end and yet in a thousand ways betray themselves as neither of these things, but rather intermediate stages in an occult processus of life."[3]

When one becomes aware of the continuity of existence on either side of birth and death, then the notion of a succession of individual lives becomes problematic. Either they constitute a painful and futile existence from which it is necessary to liberate oneself by dissolving the process altogether (as do yogis who attain nirvanic release) or they constitute a growth of consciousness which culminates in a *terrestrial* fulfilment. The latter, of course, was Sri Aurobindo's experience. As Satprem put it in his study, *Sri Aurobindo or The Adventure of Consciousness*, "there is an evolution, an evolution of the consciousness behind the evolution of the species and . . . this spiritual evolution must end in a realization, individual and collective, on the earth."[4]

Seen from the point of view of the evolution of consciousness, Satprem remarks, reincarnation ceases to be the futile round some have seen in it or the "imaginative extravagance" others have made of it.

The human being, Sri Aurobindo says, is compounded from elements of the various realms or levels of being which constitute reality. The universe has differing gradations, ranging from the lowest form of insentient physical matter through the vital/bioenergetic and then the mental to the psychic-spiritual and, finally, the Supermind (and even beyond). All these planes of being are in actuality a continuum since they are ultimately none other than forms of God, the only reality. However, their nature is such that some take more permanent forms than others.

The physical constituents of the human being do not last beyond a single lifetime, Sri Aurobindo says. Likewise, at death, the vital/bioenergetic aspect of a human returns to the cosmic reservoir from which it was drawn. The mental—that which produces intellectual life and the ordinary psychological aspects of Man—may continue as part of the makeup of that which evolves from life to life, the "psychic being," Sri Aurobindo's term for soul. However, he says, the personality does not persist to any strong degree and, indeed, should not, since the evolutionary nature of life requires increasing refinement of character and intensification of consciousness, which necessarily brings change of personality, the facade or "frontal being" of the individual.

Who or what is it which evolves in consciousness, through birth after birth, and what is the goal of the evolutionary journey? Sri Aurobindo's answer: There is a supreme consciousness which has descended into matter and is gradually working itself back, through the multitude of life forms which inhabit the universe, to a state of realization of the Oneness which has been its condition all along. In *The Life Divine,* Sri Aurobindo says, "The universal Man, the cosmic Purusha in humanity, is developing in the human race the power that has grown into humanity from [the grades of life] below it and shall yet grow to Supermind and Spirit and become the Godhead in man who is aware of his true and integral self and the divine universality of his nature."[5] He continues:

> Our conception of the spirit is of something which is not constituted by name and form, but assumes various forms of body and mind according to the various manifestations of its soul-being. This it done here by a successive evolution; it evolves successive forms and successive strata of consciousness: for it is not bound always to assume one form and no other or to possess one kind of mentality which is its sole possible subjective manifestation. The soul is not bound by the formula of mental humanity: it did not begin with that and will not end with it; it had a prehuman past, it has a superhuman future.[6]

In other words, the popular conception of an "immortal soul" is not true. All things, even souls, are evolving into greater and greater degrees of wholeness, harmony, and awareness. Ultimately there cannot be a multitude of immortal souls because a soul's perfection will be to know itself as the One, in the realization that it has been none other than God all along the evolutionary journey, but God in hiding from itself, as a playful gesture of the Supreme, which chose to create the universe in the first place.

Reincarnation or rebirth, then, is not simply a process whereby certain memories, talents, or personality traits are carried over from one life to the next; those are merely the more superficial and ephemeral aspects of the process. "Nature develops from stage to stage and in each stage takes up its past and transforms it into stuff of its new development." Sooner or later the human will be transcended altogether into the superhuman, whose characteristics were boldly explored and recorded in their more notable outlines by Sri Aurobindo.

The soul does not slip back into animal form once it has reached the human level, according to Sri Aurobindo, nor does it continually cross over from one gender to another, but rather tends to remain either male or female in the course of its evolution. Likewise, the departed soul generally retains memory of its past experiences only in their essence, not in their form of detail.

The process of rebirth is governed by the lawful operation of the cosmos, a many-leveled process of cause-and-effect called karma. But it is not a process of inexorable determinism beyond our control and from which escape is impossible. Paradoxically, karma is the very means by which release, liberation, enlightenment is possible. As Jesse Roarke comments in his biography, *Sri Aurobindo:*

> Karma, inexorable though it may be at some times and in some ways, is a part of man's evolutionary freedom; he makes his own karma, and he is continually modifying it, making it anew. Absolute freedom is not to be had short of the divine consciousness; but the more one advances, the more spiritual and less egoistic he beomes, the more freedom he has, relatively; and, as one advances from level to level, karma changes its character, and becomes less a burden and more a help and collaborator; until in the spiritual liberation one is beyond karma altogether; at least, not bound by it.[7]

Sri Aurobindo explains it thus in *The Problem of Rebirth:*

> The idea of Karma has behind it two ideas that are its constituent factors, a law of Nature, of the energy or action of Nature, and a soul that lives under that law, puts out action into that energy and gets from it a return in accordance and measure with the character of its own activities. . . . As is [an individual's] use of the energy, so was and will be the return of the universal energy to him now and hereafter. This is the fundamental meaning of Karma.[8]

The conditions of one's future birth are determined at the time of birth. The psychic being chooses what it should work out in the next appearance and the conditions arrange themselves accordingly. It sloughs off the elements of the lower planes—the material, the vital, and the mental—and passes through the subtler worlds, eventually coming to abide in its native sphere, where it rests, assimilating the life just past and preparing for the future.

When the time for rebirth comes, Roarke explains, the psychic being or soul "takes, or in more advanced cases, makes new instruments for himself, with a new personality, and descends to the plane of evolution and takes birth in a new physical body. How long he remains out of incarnation, and when and where he returns, is by no means a mechanical thing, and depends on his development, his needs, and what he is to work out in his next life, what sort of experience he is to have for his further development; in which he may have more or less choice."[9]

From life to life, the soul or psychic being, acting under the law of karma, grows behind the frontal being which is the personality of each lifetime. "Each life," writes Satprem, "represents then one type of experience . . . and it is by an accumulation of innumerable types of experience that slowly the psychic being acquires an individuality, stronger and stronger, more and more conscious and more vast, as if it had not really begun to exist before it had run through the whole gamut of human experience."[10] He continues:

> And the more it grows, the more the consciousness-force individualizes itself in us, the more the psychic tension increases, pushes through, till one day it needs no longer its frontal chrysalis and springs up into full daylight. Then it can become directly aware of the world around; it becomes the master of the nature instead of being its sleeping prisoner; consciousness becomes the master of its force instead of being glued down in the force. Yoga is precisely the point of our development at which we pass from the interminable meanderings of natural evolution to an evolution that is conscious and self-directed; it is *a process of concentrated evolution.*[11]

According to Sri Aurobindo, then, rebirth "is an inevitable logical conclusion if there exists at the same time an evolutionary principle in the earth-Nature and a reality of the individual born into evolutionary Nature. . . . It is rebirth that gives the birth of an incomplete being in a body its promise of completeness and its spiritual significance."[12]

That completeness and significance should not be mistaken for ego games played in the name of reincarnation. It is not perfection of the ego which is the goal of the rebirth process, Sri Aurobindo says, but rather transcendence of the ego into the fullness and splendor of a God-conscious experience. As Roarke puts it:

> A yoga as large, complete, difficult and exacting as that of Sri Aurobindo may well require more than one life for its completion. In the process of rebirth nothing essential is lost, and one may take up where he left off, when the time comes. He may even make some advance on the inner, non-evolutionary planes themselves. But nevertheless the disciples of Sri Aurobindo and the Mother are urged to aspire and labor to the utmost, with the expectation or the hope or the goal of finishing now; not waiting for the next life, or entertaining an easy and too complacent reliance on the Eternal to get everything done eventually.[13]

This summary of Sri Aurobindo's view of reincarnation has neces-sarily been brief, but there is much in print from Sri Aurobindo himself and from various disciples and commentators. I've mentioned only a few of many works available.[14] To give another taste of the inspiring vistas of soul growth awaiting through the processes described by this titanic explorer of the universe, I quote Sri Aurobindo once again. In *The Problem of Rebirth* he says:

> Our humanity is the conscious meeting place of the finite and the infinite and to grow more and more toward that infinite even in this physical birth is our privilege. . . . To grow in knowledge, in power, in delight, love and oneness, towards the infinite light, capacity and bliss of spiritual existence, to universalise ourselves till we are one with all being, and to exceed constantly our present limited self till it opens fully to the transcendence in which the universal lives and to base upon it all our becoming, that is the full evolution of what now lives darkly wrapped or works half-evolved in Nature.[15]

That awesome perspective on the arc of human evolution should elevate your understanding above the common mentality which regards karma in accounting terms of "Well, if I just meditate fifteen minutes longer per day, I'll score an additional thirty karma points annually and knock off five incarnations per decade."

However, even Sri Aurobindo doesn't answer such technical questions as What determines the interval between lives? What is the average interval? What determines gender in each incarnation? And what is the process whereby a person chooses his or her parents, siblings, nation, etc.? These and other questions may legitimately be asked by the spiritual seeker, and they may eventually be answered by reincarnation research. A number of promising efforts are under way, such as the work described in Joel L. Whitton and Joe Fisher's *Life Between Life*. I also recommend a companion work in this Omega Books series, *Lifecycles* by Christopher Bache.

But don't fail to see the forest for the trees. There is only God; realize that and release yourself to it. The karmic process of rebirth will then occur for you from the dharmic perspective of "the one and only trans-migrant" and you will be released from anxiety and sorrow about the past and future. As M. C. (Mabel Collins) puts it in her short classic, *Light on the Path:*

> The operations of the actual laws of Karma are not to be studied until the disciple has reached the point at which they no longer affect himself. The initiate has a right to demand the secrets of nature and to know the rules which govern human life. He obtains his right by having escaped from the limits of nature and by having freed himself from the rules which govern human life. He has become a recognized portion of the divine element, and is no longer affected by that which is temporary. He then obtains the knowledge of the laws which govern temporary

conditions. Therefore you who desire to understand the laws of Karma, attempt first to free yourself from these laws; and this can only be done by fixing your attention on that which is unaffected by them.[16]

The thirteenth-century Persian poet Jalal ad-Din ar-Rumi, known today simply as Rumi the Poet, wrote one of the most beautiful statements of spiritual wisdom ever offered humanity, a succinct declaration which places reincarnation in the framework of God-realization and shows the way for people seeking enlightenment:

> I died a mineral and became a plant.
> I died a plant and rose an animal.
> I died an animal and I was man.
> Why should I fear? When was I less by dying?
> Yet once more I shall die as man, to soar
> With the blessed angels; but even from angelhood
> I must pass on. All except God perishes.
> When I have sacrificed my angel soul,
> I shall become that which no mind ever conceived.
> O, let me not exist! for Non-Existence proclaims,
> "To Him we shall return."

9

Healing Is Not
the Same as Cure

Because the dominant Western world view is based on materialism, people who reject that perspective sometimes indiscriminately reject anything having to do with material values, even though such values may be appropriate for certain situations. The attitude toward Western medicine of some members of the New Age movement demonstrates this.

Although the movement's critique of Western medicine is desirable, its rush to embrace non-Western medicine and alternative modes of healing nevertheless needs checks and balances to prevent malpractice by untrained people and to screen out misinformation and pseudoscience. (An example would be the claims for crystal healing, most of which, in my judgment, are founded on magical thinking and haven't a shred of evidence to support them. Any results are due solely to the placebo effect—a subject much more deserving of study than crystals.) All too often, naïve advocates of holistic healing simply reject Western medicine altogether, embracing unproved methods and approaches while failing to appreciate the true value of Western medicine, which is considerable. Such people make their own version of the mistake they intend to correct. While the Western materialistic perspective tends to explain all mental phenomena in physical terms (it reduces all mind to matter), indiscriminate advocates of holistic health try to explain all matter as mind. Neither perspective is wholly wrong. They are simply incomplete and therefore unbalanced.

This incompleteness and imbalance needs to be corrected; everyone can grow from it. Most of all, a philosophy of holistic medicine for the total human being needs to be articulated for guidance in all situations between physicians and patients, healers and clients, diagnosticians and the ill. It must recognize that conventional medicine knows a lot about the physical domain and that it deserves credit for what it has done with that knowledge to eliminate disease and pain. Polio, smallpox, yellow fever, bubonic plague, diphtheria, scurvy, rickets, and so forth—the medical establishment merits great respect for ridding the West, if not the world, of these scourges. Likewise, conventional medicine deserves credit for advances such as open heart surgery, prosthetic devices and artificial parts, CT-scan and magnetic resonance imaging, pharmaceuticals, and a host of other inventions and procedures which help restore and maintain health. Finally, a valid philosophy of holistic medicine must also recognize the unfairness of assuming conventional medicine, materia medica, to be accountable for things which simply are not part of its function. Toward that end I offer this contribution to developing an enlightened philosophy of health.

Healing is not always cure. Nor does cure always involve healing. Healing pertains to the spirit, cure pertains to the body-mind. Healing is awakening to God and the Transcendental Domain as Love. That is what the true healer does—and is.

Healing is not a panacea for every human illness and malady. Those conditions might be cured, but that is not the same as healing. Healing removes the state of consciousness which regards illness and malady as problematic—as the basis for suffering and self-contracted emotion and behavior.

Healing may or may not actually cure the physical condition in question; we simply do not know enough about the human body-mind complex to say with certainty what the outcome of Love/healing will be. On one hand, there have been miraculous cures as a consequence of a person awakening to, and as, Love. For example, when the Dutch psychic-spiritual teacher Jack Schwarz was in a Nazi concentration camp, he lost consciousness during a whipping. At that moment he had a vision of Christ and felt his radiant love. Upon awakening, Jack said to the guard, "*ich liebe dich*," I love you. The guard was shocked, even more so when he saw the wounds of Jack's body begin to heal immediately. Jack describes that event as a "re-birthday" for him. He claims he left the camp whole and healthy.

Remarkable as that is, there have been far more instances where awakening to Love has not had noticeable effect upon physical illness. Saint Bernadette of Lourdes—of the healing grotto—had a painful lingering, and fatal case of consumption. Ramana Maharshi, a great yogi-mystic of India, died of cancer; so did another, Ramakrishna. Both yogis were reputed to show such a high degree of divine love that on occasion they literally caused others to swoon in ecstasy. That did not prevent their terminal illness in middle age.

Why hasn't Love been all-protecting in these instances? Sri Aurobindo, provides the answer. He once broke his knee after a fall. The physician who attended him asked, "How is it that you, a mahatma, could not foresee and prevent this accident?" Aurobindo replied: "I still have to carry this human body about me and it is subject to ordinary human limitations and physical laws."

On the other hand, there have been miraculous cures due to the operation of Love through a healer which nevertheless left the "cured" person unchanged in consciousness. The story in Luke 17:12ff illustrates this:

> And as [Jesus] entered a village, he was met by ten lepers, who stood at a distance and lifted up their voices and said, "Jesus, Master, have mercy on us." When he saw them he said to them, "Go and show yourselves to the priests." And as they went they were cleansed. Then one of them, when he saw that he was healed, turned back, praising God with a loud voice; and he fell on his face at Jesus' feet, giving him thanks. Now he was a Samaritan. Then said Jesus, "Were not ten cleansed? Where are the nine? Was no one found to return and give praise to God except this foreigner?" And he said to him, "Rise and go your way; your faith has made you well."

Ten lepers were cured, but only one was healed. That is, only one took the treatment to heart; only one responded to the healer with gratitude and changed behavior. The other nine went their way physically cleansed but still in the self-centered state of awareness which blocks mental and spiritual development and which sullies relationships. Insofar as leprosy is a manifestation of a spiritual condition (for such was Jesus' and the biblical view) the nine would probably develop other kinds of disease because their spiritual malaise still festered.

All too often the practice of medicine is, as was taught in many medical schools, to "aggressively treat the body in the bed." That is fine as far as it goes, but it doesn't go far enough. It is not so much wrong as incomplete, and that incompleteness is based on a view of the human being as simply a body. Mind and spirit are unrecognized or ignored, to the detriment of patient and medical practitioner alike, and to society at large.

In simplest terms: Cure removes illness; healing promotes health. *Heal* comes from the Old English *hal*, meaning "whole." From it also comes "hale" (as in "hale and hearty") and "health." (It's a delightful irony that the name of the crazy computer in *2001* is Hal.) But wholeness is not to be found in the physical realm by itself. Humans are compound individuals, as transpersonal psychologist Ken Wilber phrases it—compounded from the mental and spiritual realms as well as the physical. All realms are aspects or manifestations of the One which is Ultimate Wholeness. The One transcends all creation and is prior to all creation, yet paradoxically also is all creation. Transcendence does not merely negate; it includes that which is transcended in a larger context, correcting imbalances and bringing completeness. Thus, healing practice which focuses simply on one realm or another and ignores the rest is incomplete practice.

To state the situation generally, each of the three great realms of manifest existence has its lawful operations which we must learn and adapt to as we ascend in consciousness to the Transcendental Domain. The mental realm is "higher" than the physical and the spiritual realm is "higher" than the mental. Although there is interchange between and among them, it is clear that physical medications are inherently incapable of curing mental and/or spiritual maladies because the latter are senior to the physical realm. The higher contains the lower but cannot be reduced to the lower. Healing, rooted in the Transcendental Domain which enfolds all creation, must be understood first to recognize the reality of the lower realms it embraces and then to include the curative principles and practices inherent to them.

Some materialists may object to this perspective on grounds of the evidence of psychosomatic medicine, claiming that it shows an equivalence of body and mind. So I hasten to clarify: *Symptoms* can indeed be treated through physical means, usually quite effectively, but *causes* are another condition altogether. It is clear, of course, that physical malfunctions can have physical causes and thus should be treated physically. A broken leg doesn't require psychotherapy; poisoning calls for a stomach pump, not meditation; and kwashiakor indicates the need for proper nutrition, not laying-on of hands. Some chemical compounds (psychoactive drugs) are useful for restoring the mentally disturbed to relatively normal psychophysical functioning by relieving or suppressing symptoms, but only effective therapy can uncover the life-situations which stressfully generated the biochemical imbalance in the first place. On the other hand, no amount of vitamin B_{12}, trace elements, or special diets will make such a person more compassionate or even more rational. They may bring that person's nervous system to finer functioning and boost his energy level, but they are not capable of opening the mental "eye of reason," let alone the spiritual "eye of contemplation," which are founded in domains beyond the reach of nutrition, medication, andjuany other physical, electrochemical, or "energy medicine" means of treatment.

At present, we in the West have health specialists to whom society conventionally assigns the research and development functions for the three great realms of existence. The specialists are called physicians (for the physical realm), psychiatrists/psychotherapists (for the mental), and clerics/religious (for the spiritual). Now, there is nothing wrong with being a specialist, so long as there is recognition that, first, the human being is multidimensional or compound and, second, there is a hierarchical ordering of those realms or elements from which the person is compounded, with each requiring its own mode of treatment. Advocates of holistic health who criticize conventional medical education and practice because it doesn't accomplish the things which psychology/ psychiatry and religion do make an irrelevant criticism. If your car needs repairs, you have a garage mechanic work on it; you don't go to a psychotherapist, shaman, or preacher. Conversely, you don't go to a mechanic for spiritual counseling or midlife-crisis guidance. By and large, conventional medical practice is not wrong; it is merely incomplete—a great difference. There's no need for holistic health advocates to throw out the baby with the bathwater.

The life of the twelfth-century Tibetan saint Milarepa offers an instructive example of the hierarchical nature of the compound individual and of the strengths inherent in each realm which are to be cultivated in the name of wholeness. Milarepa spent years meditating alone in a cave. He had forsaken all worldly contact and possessions. He lived as a naked yogi almost without any food except nettles, which he subsisted on for years. In fact, his skin had turned green from the unvarying diet. Yet he remained steadfast and determined to attain the jewel in the lotus: enlightenment. A song he composed to describe the situation says:

> Even though my bones have pierced my flesh on this cold stone floor,
> I have persevered.
> My body, inside and outside, has become like a nettle;
> It will never lose its greenness.
> In the solitary cave, in the wilderness,
> The recluse knows much loneliness.
> But my faithful heart never separates
> From the Lama-Buddha of the Three Ages.
>
> By the force of meditation arising from my efforts,
> Without doubt I will achieve self-realization.[1]

From whence comes such force of will? Not from even the most healthy diet and exercise program nor from scholarly study of philosophy and sacred texts. It comes from "awakening at the heart" to the possibility of enlightenment. Of course, Milarepa later learned moderation from such austerity, just as the Buddha had 1600 years earlier. After all, wholeness is wholeness—not just supreme cultivation of the spiritual realm alone. Proper care should be given to the requirements of body and mind also; the properties and limitations of each should be recognized and respected, without mistaking any of them (including the spiritual) as ultimate. Wholeness, *ultimate* wholeness, consists of the manifest and the unmanifest. As Ramana Maharshi put it paradoxically: "The world is illusion; Brahman alone is real; Brahman is the world." Thus, healing—as distinguished from cure—must properly diagnose the cause of an illness or disturbance and address it, as well as the symptoms.

The body is commonly said to be the temple of the spirit. True—but again, incomplete. *A Course in Miracles* (see Chapter 23) adds another dimension to the concept of temple by declaring that *relationships* are the temple of the spirit. That declaration brings balance and completeness to the body-as-temple concept, because all too often the body is wrongly worshiped by narcissists and spiritual materialists who leap aboard the latest food fad or health-product craze as the key to salvation. But neither spirulina nor snake-gall bladder, wheatgrass juice nor ayurvedic herbal compounds, flower essences nor crystals can restore health to bad relationships. As Swami Sivananda Radha of Canada puts it succinctly, pure food does not produce a pure mind. The body of relationships is the mystical body of Christ. Only open, honest, and loving relationships based on freedom and equality can bring health to that body.

The final obstacle to health is death, or so the materialist believes—whether genuine materialist or spiritual materialist. But this view is not necessarily true. In fact, it is totally challenged in various quarters ranging from ancient spiritual traditions to contemporary trends in health care, as I show in *A Practical Guide to Death and Dying*.

The fact that many medical practitioners have such a hard time dealing with is this: Death is inevitable. So much of the medical community's sense of purpose and identity is bound up in a struggle to *overcome* death. If one's self-image and self-esteem as a health practitioner are based on staving off death for patients or clients, it is a losing game because death cannot be cured. That is not to deny the value of biomedical research into life extension; I am strongly in favor of it and the immortalist movement. But, as a growing number of medical-care providers are coming to recognize, death need not be viewed as The Enemy. In fact, that view leads, ironically, to poorer medical care than a view which acknowledges death's place in the scheme of things and the need honestly and caringly to help terminal patients deal with their impending demise.

This is precisely the thrust of the hospice movement and certain lines of thantological work. Death may end a life, but it doesn't end a relationship. From a psychological point of view, that relationship continues among the living, for better or for worse. (Think of how many people still carry a deceased mommy or daddy around inside themselves as a heavy load of nagging guilt or scolding self-defeat.) From a parapsychological point of view, it continues between the living and the dead, for better or for worse. (Crisis apparitions are examples of it continuing for the better; emergency aid is extended to the living by the departed.)

Beyond the hospice movement's perspective is that offered by people such as Ram Dass and Steven Levine, who declare that dying is an opportunity for spiritual practice and that death can be a vehicle of awakening. (To be fair, it should be recognized that many hospice-staff members share this perspective and have worked extensively with it.)

The changes of consciousness the dying go through can lead to tremendous healing of relationships. Instances of deathbed reconciliation among fallen-out family members and friends are not infrequent and can lead to positively changed lives for those left behind. When such transformations of consciousness are deliberately cultivated during the dying process (by oneself or though trained practitioners), dying can indeed be a healing. Furthermore, it can have some degree of healing (through inspriation) on others who simply hear about such experiences.

The most inspiring examples of "dying the good death" come from the final moments of saints and holy people. Perhaps the ultimate healing-through-death was that offered compassionately by Jesus. As he died on the Cross, he said, "Father, forgive them, for they know not what they do"—and the world has never been the same. At that moment, the veil of the temple was rent in twain; symbolically speaking, the true nature of the human being and of relationships was revealed through the redemptive act of Jesus, which tore the "veil of maya" or delusion from our eyes to let Reality shine through.

Body, mind, and spirit: Any practice of healing must recognize that there are three great realms in creation and that ultimately the three are one—that is, manifestations of the One. Insofar as healing treats disease (dis-ease), it must be understood that there is no ease, no rest, until we rest in God. The leper who turned back to thank Jesus understood this. The lesson of that biblical passage, then, is this: *patients/clients must be dealt with in the context of ultimate wholeness and healing practitioners should seek to be whole themselves.* "Physician, heal thyself" applies to psychiatrists/psychotherapists and clerics/religious as well. In the context of ultimate wholeness, conventional healing is not always cure, nor does cure always involve conventional healing.

So long as there is embodied existence, there will be some degree of illness and malady, even for enlightened sages. But the awakened heart frees us of the egoic tendency to identify that illness or malady as problematic; it allows us to experience it as grace or the play of consciousness. When someone accidentally bumped into Ramana Maharshi, who was terminally ill with cancer, everyone near him saw a look of great agony flash across his face. His ravaged flesh was extremely sensitive; the pain from the contact was obviously enormous. Yet he made no comment until someone, thinking he was using yogic control, said to him, "Perhaps you don't feel the pain?" "There is pain," Maharshi replied, "but there is no suffering." His biological functioning was "doing its thing" by producing pain; so was his consciousness' transcendental perspective on existence, including his own fleshly life, by eliminating the egoic response to pain.

Paul Brunton puts it wisely in his *Notebooks* series (*Perspectives*, p. 131): "To pray for a bodily cure and nothing more is a limited and limiting procedure. Pray also to be enlightened as to *why* this sickness fell upon you. Ask also what *you* can do to remove its cause. And above all, ask for the Water of Life, as Jesus bade the woman at the well to ask."

10

The True Meaning of Yoga

To many Westerners the word *yoga* evokes an image of someone twisted like a pretzel or standing on his head. Another popularized image of yoga is the svelte-bodied female who lost thirty pounds and toned up through a yoga class at the local YWCA. While those images are not inaccurate, they are far from complete as a description of yoga. They are merely stereotypes, less-than-half-truths derived from photographs and sensationalized accounts in the media. Newspapers, magazines, books, lecture posters, films, advertisements—have all helped to dramatize and popularize these images.

The truth about yoga is something far greater. Yoga is a lot more than the stylized image of a skinny Indian yogi who has occult powers and bizarre behavior, wearing only a loincloth while sitting crosslegged on a mountaintop and chanting strange sounds. And yoga certainly is a lot more than a system of exercise, relaxation, and weight reduction. In fact, as one yogi put it, the whole of yoga can be reduced to learning just one basic posture which says it all: standing on your own two feet—being yourself authentically.

Yoga is one of the most ancient sacred traditions known to humanity. As Georg Feuerstein shows in his excellent *Yoga: The Technology of Ecstasy*, its roots go back at least 5000 years—far longer than any other major religion or spiritual path, except for shamanism and wicca. And of the three, yoga is the only one leading to enlightenment. Wicca—witchcraft or nature worship—is "earth religion." Shamanism leads to higher

106

realms and can be called "sky religion." Only yoga is founded in the Transcendental Domain, the *source* of earth and sky.

However, yoga is venerable not simply for its age. It is a time-honored tradition because it has inspected every facet of life, probed them to rock-bottom reality, discovered their secrets, and offered that knowledge openly to anyone who aspires to attain it.

Offered it openly—provided the aspirant recognizes that words alone are not sufficient. There must be practice; there must be direct experience, direct realization of truth.

And yoga offers that also. It has sage yet practical advice for people in all walks of life, of all personalities and professions, in all stages of health or illness, at all levels of education and intelligence. There is nothing unknown to the yogic tradition. I don't mean that every yogi is omniscient. None is, and even among the greatest there is a wide range in the degree of understanding and attainment. But if you inspect their entire tradition, everything you'll ever want is there, waiting for you to grow into it, to discover higher and higher levels of understanding and attainment, until the Secret of Life and the Universe itself—enlightenment—is made plain.

In short, yoga is a system for total human development: physically, mentally, and spiritually. The Sanskrit root *yug* from which the word *yoga* comes means "to yoke," "to join," "to unite." What is united is the individual and the cosmos. Through the methods of yoga, the individual (in yogi Rammurti Mishra's term) dehypnotizes himself, clears his mind of illusions and unconscious conditioning, so that total mastery of one's powers and potentialities is attained. Ultimately, the power and potentiality of our self is not other than that of the entire cosmos. Only the ego—the illusion of separate self—keeps us from realizing that we are truly divine, truly one with the universe, truly God in human form.

The practice of yoga, then, is both the means and the goal. Yoga has developed many branches or lines which differ from one another in emphasis or methodology, but theoretically all lead to the same condition, which is known as *moksha,* meaning "liberation" or "enlightenment." And what is liberation or enlightenment? As Mishra puts it in his *Fundamentals of Yoga,* "Moksha or *nirvanam* is the permanent abode of eternal consciousness. Knowledge, existence, blessings, happiness, and peace—Yoga is the infallible instrument to obtain *nirvanam.* Thus, the main goal of Yoga is freedom of the spirit from the fetters of material desires and permanent victory of consciousness over ignornace."[1]

That is what rightly should be said about yoga to those who casually approach it for a superficial degree of self-improvement or who snicker about "those funny postures" some branches of yoga include as part of their instruction. Yoga is a valuable resource for those seeking to discover their real self in the context of daily living.

Because self-discovery is the heart of the life-process, yoga can also be defined as "a science of consciousness." From the Latin *scire,* "to know," science has commonly been regarded, to quote Webster, as "accumulated knowledge systematized and formulated with reference to the discovery of general truths or the operational laws, especially when such knowledge relates to the physical world."

However, this dictionary definition is not complete. The essence of science is its *method,* not its data. Science is more a way of knowing than a body of knowledge. The accumulated information of science is obtained through trained observation and is empirically verifiable. Scientific method requires that research be presented for validation by the scientific community. A clear description of the techniques and materials used is necessary in the presentation. Then the procedures are carefully repeated by others. If the same results are obtained, the findings become accepted as scientific fact.

Understood that way, yoga is indeed a science by which others can verify the effects obtained by a previous researcher. That is why yoga emphasizes direct experience: it not only recognizes the need for personal realization but also provides the means for doing so. Unlike scientific experiment, yogic methods do not pertain primarily to the physical-material world but to the metaphysical-nonmaterial world. They deal primarily with the nature of self, that inescapable and fundamental element involved in all knowledge. (However, as I will show, yoga also has an extraordinary understanding of the human body and its capabilities. After all, it was yogis who first demonstrated for medical researchers that unconscious physiological processes such as heartbeat rate, brain waves, and blood pressure could be voluntarily controlled.)

Science has lately begun to recognize that a complete description of an event must include a description of the consciousness of the event's observer. The mind of the observer can not only bias the description, selecting data somewhat arbitrarily according to unconscious bias and philosophic assumptions, it can also (according to some parapsychological and quantum physics experiments) actually affect the outcome of the event itself. The mind can subtly engineer reality and can choose to experience the same event in a variety of ways. Thus there are no "pure" events unless there are pure minds—minds which are free from bias and prejudice and hidden desire and therefore do not affect the flow of events, but rather are one with reality.

Yoga excels in the purification of consciousness. This is where it demonstrates itself to be a true science. As with Western science, the steps to be followed (including postures, breath-control techniques, meditation practices, dietary regulation, rules for balanced living, and so on) are clearly delineated, and the "findings" (stages of enlightenment) have been attested to uniformly for millennia by people in every century who have carefully repeated these procedures.

In an article entitled "Yogic Methods of Knowing," yogi Christopher Hills of Boulder Creek, California, points out that both yoga and modern science are based on two distinct methods—induction and deduction. The inductive method is based on operations, with description, measurement, and analysis resulting in generalizations about things. The deductive method is based on logical postulates and rules for operating with them; it also results in knowledge about things.

"However," Hills writes, "yoga goes one step further in setting out for proof the hypothetical elements in a thesis in such a way which shows that knowledge *about* is not knowing directly. It is possible to know about horses without having ever seen one or ridden on one. . . . Such *knowing about* is judged in yogic terms as theoretical, and lacking in . . . other levels of consciousness."

The supreme work of yoga has been to guide people through those higher levels of consciousness so that knowledge about something is surpassed by direct knowledge. So long as there is some mental concept which splits or separates the knower from the known—so long as there is ego or the illusion of separateness—there will be only knowledge *about*. But when you pierce the veil of maya, when you see through the illusion of ego-isolated personality, the division between self and other is dissolved, healed. The knower and the known become one, the Self of all.

Knowledge of the Self is what modern science lacks and what makes it incomplete. But on the frontiers of research, science is coming to realize that, as Yale University physicist Henry Margenau puts it, "Consciousness . . . is the primary factor in all experience, hence it needs and merits the fullest attention any [scientist] can bestow on it."

Yoga aims at self-knowledge and self-mastery. Its goal is liberation or enlightenment—freedom from desire, compulsion, fear, limitation, and unhappiness. Ego is based on all which now masters us, dominates us, and causes suffering and confusion. Death appears to be the ultimate form of suffering and domination because it is inevitable, inescapable. Therefore death, from the ego's point of view, represents a threat to that which sustains the illusion of separate self. Awareness of death forces confrontation with the fiction on which we base our lives: ego. Liberation, enlightenment, self-mastery—this absolutely requires understanding of death and its role in our physical, mental, and spiritual existence.

Yoga can provide that. It has many methods and techniques which enable a person to overcome fear of death. Some of them deal with emotions, others with the intellect.

Beyond that, however, is the possibility of transcending death itself. Many stories exist about yogic masters living in the Himalayas who are hundreds, even thousands of years old. Enormous psychic and spiritual powers are attributed to these masters, but as incredible as the stories sound, they are more plausible than skeptics may believe. Consider the following data.

1. It is known that yoga techniques can be used to delay the aging process and, to some degree, actually reverse it for a time. A yogi I knew, Michael Volin of Nyack, New York, taught avatara yoga, which includes special exercises to retard degeneration and increase longevity. Known in India as Swami Karmananda, he was in his seventies when I met him nearly two decades ago. He demonstrated in his own person what avatara yoga can do. He had the youthful skin of a teenager and was in excellent physical condition.

2. In 1972, Dr. Daniel Goleman, who writes on psychology and human behavior for *The New York Times*, told the Biofeedback Society convention that when he was in India the previous year, he heard from credible sources of a yogi in Brindaban who was certified by the Indian government as being at least 212 years old. He also said that the yogis he met there were remarkable for their young-looking appearance. Although they were in their forties and fifties, he reported, they looked as if they were in their teens.

3. Ram Dass mentions in *Be Here Now* that his yoga teacher, Hari Dass, drank only two glasses of milk a day—nothing more. Ram Dass continues, "Even such a sparse diet as that is merely a step upon the path. At the conclusion, one is capable of living upon light alone."[2]

4. Sriman Tapasviji Marharaj, a yogi who died in 1955 at the well-attested age of 185, described to his devotees how he reversed the aging process three times to achieve such longevity. His rejuvenation was achieved through the ancient yogic practice of *kaya kalpa*, an aspect of ayurvedic medicine. The first time occurred in his eighties. According to his biography, *Maharaj*, all his teeth had fallen out, he was partially deaf, his eyesight was dim, his skin was wrinkled and hard, and his legs tottered when he walked. After the weeks-long process, "he got up from his bed with the ease of a man of twenty. He stood erect. His limbs and muscles were so supple that he could jump and skip. His vision was strong and his new teeth had grown to their normal size. His skin was bright and rosy and his hair was black. His voice, which had been feeble, was as strong as when he was twenty." Twice more he reversed the aging process before he finally succumbed to natural causes.

5. In *Death and Dying: The Tibetan Tradition*, Dr. Glenn Mullin describes "longevity yogas," practiced by Tibetan masters, which include nutrient pills used by yogis instead of food. According to Mullin, "The pills are made of a precise combination of mineral and herbal substances. I knew one yogi who had lived on them for two years, eating nothing but a half dozen of them a day. At first he lost a bit of weight, but after a few

months caught his second breath in the practice and gained the pill power, returning to his normal weight for the remainder of the time period."[3]

6. Paramhansa Yogananda, the renowned author of *Autobiography of a Yogi,* said in his book that yogis wear their hair long to facilitate intake of prana, the cosmic life-energy which is more fundamental than the four forces recognized by Western science.

7. Sri Aurobindo pointed to the final stage of yoga as one in which, after attaining union with the Supermind, the yogi begins a structural reorganization of his body on the molecular level. He alters his cellular construction and transmutes his physiological functioning.

8. In *Living with the Himalayan Masters,* Swami Rama of the Himalayan International Institute in Honesdale, Pennsylvania, tells incidents from his training in the Himalayas which showed him how yogis have completely mastered death. "Casting off the body" is done through various techniques, but always it is voluntary and achieved with full consciousness, so that the yogi continues to function in his nonphysical energy body, capable of interacting and communicating with living humans. Swami Rama reports these words of a sage who later demonstrated precisely what they say: "Death is a habit of the body. No one can live in this same body forever. It is subject to change, death and decay. You have to understand this. Very few people know the technique of gaining freedom from their clinging to life. That technique is called yoga. It is not the yoga that is popular in the modern world, but is the highest state of meditation. Once you know the right technique of meditation, you have command over other functions of your body, mind and soul. It is through *prana* and breath that a relationship is established between mind and body. When the breath ceases function, the link breaks and that separation is called death. But you still exist."[4]

If the foregoing are so, then consider this speculative probe. First, since a skin cell is not too differentiated from a plant leaf cell, perhaps physiological alteration might produce an ability to photosynthesize sunlight in the skin, thereby bypassing the usual energy conversion process from food. Note that a red-blood-cell molecule (hemoglobin) and a chlorophyll molecule are identical except for the central atom, which is iron in hemoglobin and magnesium in chlorophyll. In fact, a recent report in *Nature* indicates that plants probably have the genes needed to produce hemoglobin.[5] The report, by plant physiologists in Australia, France, and West Germany, suggests that hemoglobin has come down through evolution from a common ancestor of plants and animals.

Furthermore, the alchemical transmutation of elements by living organisms is now being recognized by science.[6]

Next, biofeedback research confirms that people can control bodily processes down to the single-cell level. That has only been observed with individual neurons so far, but if a person can consciously gain self-regulation of a single neuron, why not a single skin cell or a cell of an inner organ? Besides, control at the individual cell level may not be necessary in the matter of cellular reorganization and physiologic transmutation.

Also, Dr. Robert Becker of the Veterans Hospital in Syracuse, New York, has used electrical fields to induce organ regeneration in lower animals. A salamander can regrow a new tail, but no one ever saw a mouse grow a new leg until Dr. Becker showed that he could induce a stumplike regrowth through electrotechnology he developed. If it can be done in a mouse, why not a person? Moreover, anything we can do through technology we can probably also eventually accomplish through the direct application of consciousness and expanded mental powers.

Thus regeneration of limbs, organs—indeed, any and all parts of the human body—is now conceivable on scientific grounds. Couple that with the possibility of a person obtaining "food" directly from the sun through photosynthesis and from the atmosphere, and the "fanciful" stories of thousand-year-old yogis become plausible.

Thus, Yoga as a sacred tradition for higher human development has profound wisdom and experience to share with the questing individual. It is a means to "know thyself" and ultimate reality—to know it, master it, and live in accord with the meaning of the word: in conscious union with the divine dimension of all existence.

11

Kundalini: Sex, Evolution, and Enlightenment

It is dangerous to tell people of their bestial origins unless at the same time you tell them of their divine potential.

Blaise Pascal

Sexuality and spiritual experience have traditionally been linked in the literature of mysticism. Religious ecstasy seems strikingly similar to erotic excitement in the accounts of saints and holy people, who have spoken of enlightenment—knowing ultimate reality or, their usual term, God—in language which resorts to sexual imagery. Such images, they said, were the best they could find for describing an otherwise indescribable experience. Such terms as *rapture, passion, union,* and *ravish* occur frequently. Saint Theresa recorded that she felt stabbed through and through by Christ's spear. Madame Guyon wrote that "the soul . . . expires at last in the arms of love." Saint John of the Cross and others described themselves as "brides of Christ." Saint Francis de Sales spoke of sucking heavenly milk from the breast of God. Likewise, Sufi, Hindu, and Chinese mystics use highly erotic language. The Persian mystic Kabir spoke of himself as the "faithful wife" of Ram, one of the names for God. Hindu mythology tells of Krishna making love with many female cowherds.

113

Orthodox psychology tends smugly to dismiss such language as the product of aberrated minds whose main trouble was repressed sex, causing a regression to infantile behavior. But conventional psychological interpretations could be wrong. In an ironic turn of events, a physical linkage between sexual and spiritual experience is emerging which promises a major upheaval in Western psychology. From this emerging view, *sexuality is really unexpressed or unfulfilled religious experience.*

Notice that term: *religious experience.* The common element between it and sexual experience is consciousness. The states of consciousness experienced by lovers in union and mystics in God-intoxication are states in which the ususal sense of self as separate, isolated, lonely, and longing is dissolved. The individuals are no longer locked in the prison of ego, no longer in conflict with the world because of a socially conditioned image of who they are. Lovers sometimes attain this momentarily during orgasm and, afterward, universally regard it as one of their most cherished experiences. It has a sacred quality, as if they had contacted something greater than themselves, something at the wellspring of life itself, something which transcends the merely human and takes them into a higher state of existence.

Mystics, of course, experience this with greater frequency, intensity, and duration. Some of the greatest declared they were constantly in that state of mind, although to outward appearances they were simply performing their daily activities.

Try to imagine that: working, eating meals, driving the car, and doing everything else with the same sense of cosmic well-being you've felt at the peak of lovemaking. It's not just exquisite pleasure or intense passion. It's actually beyond emotion. It's tranquil, peaceful, serene; without any worries or cares; without attachments to status, fame, or wealth; without fear or failure or even death. None of our usual hang-ups and concerns. No anxiety. No past to regret, no future to worry about. Just pure being, pure consciousness, here and now. And all the while, everything necessary for living goes on. Nothing has changed, yet everything has changed because you no longer relate to reality in the same way. It is a new state of consciousness—not fleeting as in orgasm, but permanent. Erotic mysticism.

That would be foreign to our range of experience, even to our whole culture, and we lack the language to describe it well. But we have hints and glimpses of it given to us in the sacred writings of various religious traditions and revered spiritual teachers. Moreover, they tell us there are techniques and disciplines which can systematically be employed to alter consciousness toward that state. Meditation is an example of such a system. Yoga is another. So is tantra, which in some traditions uses *maithuna* (ritual sexual intercourse) for developing the psychosexual experience to religious heights.

In view of these facts, orthodox psychology ought to drop its illusion of knowing more than those poor, mixed-up mystics it labels as cases of infantile regression and recognize that there are realms of experience about which it is pathetically ignorant.

This, in fact, is happening. Because of rapidly increasing interest in consciousness research, psychology is being challenged in many directions. What transpersonal psychologist Abraham Maslow called "the farther ranges of human nature" is being considered more thoughtfully. Psychic phenomena, meditation, altered states of consciousness: The data from study of these are causing psychology to seriously examine ancient concepts and traditions from what Robert Ornstein, in *The Psychology of Consciousness,* calls "the esoteric psychologies."

The essence of the esoteric psychologies which so challenges conventional Western psychology is precisely what lovers and mystics have discovered to varying degrees for millennia: Humans have a potential for expanded awareness which can radically change their lives and transform them to the roots of their being. We may taste a small measure of that in moments of sexual ecstasy, but there is so much beyond the experience that in comparison orgasm is just a pale show.

So we find ourselves in the fascinating position of discovering new dimensions to the psyche, dimensions that could bring a tremendous evolutionary advance to humanity. If the nature of higher consciousness can be widely understood and experienced, a societal transformation around the globe would undoubtedly follow.

That is why research in this area is so important. That is also why I offer this essay summarizing the viewpoint of the Indian yogi-philosopher-scientist Gopi Krishna, who maintained that the language of sexual mysticism is to be understood literally and that it holds fundamental significance for psychology. There is, Gopi Krishna maintained, a direct physical linkage between sexual and spiritual experience. Ram Dass expressed the idea in the original title of *Be Here Now,* which was *From Bindu to Ojas.* As he explained it: "Bindu is sexual energy and [ojas] is spiritual energy, and it's the transformation of energy within the body through the conversion of a form of energy . . . it's called the raising of kundalini."

This ancient yogic concept, recorded in literature and oral tradition, is becoming widely known in the West as people such as Ram Dass and Shirley MacLaine speak and write about it. But the most important voice among them was Pandit Gopi Krishna, who died in 1984 at the age of eighty-one. He brought a marked degree of good sense and insight to the field of esoteric/New Age studies. I knew him personally, having interviewed him in Zurich for four days in 1976 and on several later occasions when he came to America from his home in Srinagar, Kashmir. I also read with deepest interest his dozen-plus books on the subject of kundalini, beginning shortly after his first (an autobiography entitled *Kundalini, the Evolutionary Energy in Man*) was published in the United States in 1970. I was deeply impressed by the man, not only for his obvious erudition and clear thinking about this profound human experience, but also by his character—his honesty, kindness, and humility. All that marked him in my judgment as a sage.

Pandit is an honorific meaning "learned man," so Gopi Krishna should not be thought of as a guru. He said clearly that he sought no followers, accepted no disciples, and made no demands for asceticism. Rather, his mission was to arouse interest in the nature of evolution and enlightenment, and to do that he wanted co-workers in scientific and scholarly research, not devotees. Most important, he said that the truth of his observations about a potent biological link between sex and higher consciousness (which he claimed is the motive force behind evolution and all spiritual and supernormal phenomena) should be tested, using the principles, methodology, and (insofar as possible) technology of science.

The essence of his claims is threefold: first, he had discovered that the reproductive system is also the mechanism by which evolution proceeds; second, religion is based on inherent evolutionary impulses in the psyche; and, third, there is a predetermined target for human evolution toward which the entire race is being irresistibly drawn. Whether humanity will arrive there or extinguish itself is another matter—which Gopi Krishna said was the fundamental motive behind his efforts to demonstrate our "divine destiny."

A New Species of Humanity

Kundalini is the key term in Gopi Krishna's theory of evolution. From ancient Sanskrit, it means "coiled up" like a snake or spring and implies the potential to expand or rise up, like the latent energy or potential power in a coiled snake or a wound spring. Gopi Krishna often translated it as "latest power-reservoir of energy" or "psychosomatic power center." Kundalini, he claimed, is the fundamental bioenergy of life, stored primarily in the sex organs but present throughout the entire body. This potent psychic radiation is normally associated with the genitals for simple continuance of the species by providing a sex drive. This is what Freud called libido (although the Freudian conception is strictly psychological and lacks the energy link to physics and biology which Gopi Krishna pointed out).

However, Gopi Krishna said, kundalini is also the basis for the attainment of a higher state of consciousness. The kundalini energy can be concentrated in the brain to produce enlightenment and genius—

higher mental perception. Its potency is our potential. Such a state, if widely attained, would mean a new species of humanity, a higher race. Thus, kundalini, the bridge between mind and matter, can be the evolutionary cause of creation as well as procreation. It is, Gopi Krishna said, the evolutionary energy and mechanism operating in the human race. He noted that in many ancient texts it is the key to attaining godlike stature and becoming "divinized."

Kundalini is traditionally symbolized in Hindu and Tantric texts as a sleeping serpent coiled around the base of the human spine to indicate its close relationship with the sex organs. The concept is not limited to Indian literature, however; it has been described in the ancient records of Tibet, Egypt, Sumer, China, Greece, and other cultures and traditions, including early Judaism and Christianity. The Pharaoh's headdress, the feathered serpent of Mexico and South America, the dragon of Oriental mythology, the serpent in the Garden of Eden—all are indicative of kundalini, Gopi Krishna maintained. So is the caduceus (the twin snakes coiled around a staff) symbolic of medical practitioners, which said to be derived from the god Hermes, founder of the hermetic tradition of higher knowledge.

In fact, nearly all the world's major religions, spiritual paths, and genuine occult traditions (which, unlike degenerate occultism, do not aim at psychic experiences or magical powers but at personal transformation and transcendence) see something akin to the kundalini experience as having significance in higher human development.

Nor is the concept limited to indicating the growth potential of an individual person. It embraces the entire race; it symbolically depicts the human species' evolutionary potential to grow and ascend over millennia from its "bestial origin" to a condition which is truly transhuman and godlike.

The kundalini concept, then, is a sort of map—a cartography of evolution and enlightenment, albeit in obscure language and veiled allusion—marking the transformational journey which must be undertaken individually but which, if sufficient numbers of individuals successfully complete it, can result in societal and planetary transformation and, eventually, a higher race.

The source of the "serpent power" is *prana*, a primal cosmic energy outside the electromagnetic spectrum and other forces known to official Western science. However, as I discussed in Chapter 7, many prescientific and unorthodox scientific traditions have identified a life force from which other energies and paranormal phenomena are derived. Apparently these are different labels for the same basic energy (or aspects of it) which permeates living organisms and is the source of all vital activity, including thought, feeling, perception, and movement. It especially focuses itself in the sexual organs, where the kundalini process begins.

Gene Kieffer, president of the Kundalini Research Foundation,[1] which is dedicated to Gopi Krishna's work, elaborated on the notion of prana as life energy: "The most powerful motivating force of life, as Freud has shown, is sex and the pleasure drawn from the sexual act. Similarly, the most powerful motivating force to draw humanity onto the evolutionary path, according to the traditional concept of kundalini, is *ananda,* a Sanskrit word meaning 'bliss.' This highly extended state of consciousness, permeated with an extreme form of rapture, is said to be possible only when the consumption of prana by the brain is greatly enhanced."

How can it be enhanced? As already mentioned, spiritual disciplines are the key. In a *New York Times* article Gopi Krishna pointed out that sublimation—raising up—of sex energy is the basic lever of all spiritual disciplines. But, he said, "the all-inclusive nature of sex energy has not yet been correctly understood by psychologists. In fact, the very term *reproductive,* or sex, *energy* is a misnomer. Reproduction is but one of the aspects of the life energy, of which the other theater of activity is the brain."

Surrounding and permeating the gross tissues of the body, Gopi Krishna wrote in *The Dawn of a New Science,* "a living electricity, acting intelligently and purposefully, controls the activity of every molecule of living matter. It carries the life principle from one place to the other, energizes, overhauls and purifies the neurons and maintains the lifegiving subtle area of the body much in the same way as the blood plasma maintains the grosser part."

That vital essence is extracted by the nervous system from surrounding tissue in the form of an extremely fine biochemical essence of a highly delicate and volatile nature. In humans this essence, existing at the molecular or submolecular level, especially focuses itself in the sexual organs, where the kundalini process begins.

From Sexuality to Spirituality

There is a subtle but direct connection between the brain and the organs of generation via the spine, Gopi Krishna maintained. The spinal cord and canal through which it runs serve as the avenue for transforming sexuality to spirituality. Through certain techniques known and practiced since ancient times, the kundalini energy can be aroused and guided up the center of the spinal cord (*sushumna,* in yogic terminology) to a dormant center called the Cave of Brahma *(Brahmarandhra)* in the brain's ventricular cavity, the site of the entryway to the seventh *chakra* (see below).

This "living electricity" or "superintelligent energy," as Gopi Krishna sometimes called it, is an ultrapotent, high-grade form of bioplasma: concentrated prana. But the techniques for controlling it are extremely dangerous, equivalent, figuratively speaking, to letting a child play with a nuclear reactor, and should be undertaken only under the guidance of a proven master of that tradition.

The nature of the chakras in yogic physiology is not clearly agreed upon by modern interpreters, so be careful of accepting dogmatic pronouncements by spiritual teachers and New Age commentators. For example, author Sam Keen and psychologist Robert Ornstein feel that the chakras are strictly metaphoric, lacking in any physical reality. Scholar Joseph Campbell likewise regarded them simply as psychological teaching devices, merely concepts. Others such as M. P. Pandit, an exponent of Sri Aurobindo, and William Tiller, professor of materials science at Stanford University, maintain that chakras exist in the "subtle body" of man, sometimes called the astral or etheric body, and influence the physical body through the endocrine system, with which they correlate at a nonphysical level of existence. Swami Agehananda Bharati, chairman of the anthropology department at Syracuse University, declares kundalini to be a lot of "claptrap" and "latter-day nonsense." Transpersonal psychologist Ken Wilber sees them as symbolic of levels of consciousness in the Great Chain of Being, having both physical and metaphysical reality in the evolutionary process of individual and racial consciousness unfoldment. Gopi Krishna, however, said that chakras are nerve plexes—major ganglia along the spine, observed directly in the body through clairvoyance by ancient yogis.

There are said to be six major chakras along the cerebrospinal column, but the location of the seventh chakra (termed *sahasrara*) is disputed. It has been identified by various authorities as the pineal gland, the pituitary gland, and the anterior fontanelle. Gopi Krishna, however, said it is the entire brain itself. In a letter to me, he wrote "The seventh centre in the brain is not actually designated as a 'chakra' but as 'sahasrara' in the Tantric books and 'Usha-Nisha-Kamala' in the Buddhist texts. It is often shown surrounding the head in the statues of the Buddha, more or less like a cap. In this sense, 'Sahasrara' refers to the cerebral cortex and, in fact, the whole of the brain. This is obvious from the fact that once Kundalini enters into the Brahma-randra . . . the whole of the cranium is illuminated and a new pattern of consciousness is born."

From its repository in the reproductive organs, a fine stream of living energy filters into the brain as fuel for the evolutionary process. As the energy moves upward it passes through various chakras along the central channel of the spinal cord into the topmost chakra, the brain. This does not happen in every case. In fact, it is quite rare for the kundalini process to be carried to completion. But the person to whom it happens experiences a golden-white light within his head. Apparently this is the same light which is seen by people as the aura or halo around saints and highly evolved sages.

The flow of kundalini into the brain has been described by mystics as "ambrosia" and "nectar," giving rise to exquisite sensations similar to those of orgasm but surpassing them by many orders of magnitude. The sensations are felt most intensely above the palate in the midbrain and in the hindbrain in a descending arc parallel to the curve of the palate. This is known in yoga physiology as the *sankini*, the curved duct through which the bioplasma passes into the brain.

Kundalini is at work all the time in everyone and is present from birth in mystics and seers, but in most people there is only a "dripping" rather than a "streaming." This upward streaming, which is a biological restatement of what Freud apparently meant by "sublimation of the libido," explains the source of an artist's or an intellectual's mental creativity. Beyond that are those rare people who Gopi Krishna called "finished specimens of the perfect man of the future," such as the Buddha, Jesus, and Vyasa. In them we see "an incredible combination of factors, both favorable heredity and cultural readiness, which produced those who, endowed with a superior type of consciousness and in possession of paranormal gifts, amazed their contemporaries with their extraordinary physical and intellectual talents which [ordinary people] ignorant of the Law [of evolution] ascribed to special prerogative from God."

Variations in the size of the energy stream determine the intellectual and aesthetic development of an individual, geniuses having a comparatively larger volume of bioplasma streaming into the brain. The wide variation in types of genius depends on the particular region of the brain which is irrigated and developed. Thus, through certain occult techniques and spiritual disciplines, an individual of normal intelligence can accelerate the evolutionary process to attain the stature of an intellectual prodigy and beyond, to genius. This concept directly challenges current notions that intelligence is basically determined at birth by one's genes.

The Secret Behind Yoga

Prana, the fine biological essence, is not in itself consciousness. It is only the means of nourishing our consciousness-receiving equipment, the nervous system—the body's link with universal consciousness. During the kundalini process, the entire nervous system, especially the brain, undergoes a microbiological change and is transformed. The results of a fully awakened and developed kundalini are both perceptible changes in the organism and a new state of consciousness, the cosmic consciousness of mystics and enlightened seers. This vital awareness of unity with God, Gopi Krishna said, is the core experience behind all the world's major religions and is the goal of all true spiritual and occult practices. Humanity has an innate hunger for this state of paranormal perception. Moreover, bountiful Nature has provided the means of achieving it: kundalini, the biological basis of religion and genius.

This is the "secret" behind yoga and all other spiritual disciplines, esoteric psychologies, hermetic philosophies, and genuine occult mysteries. It is also the key to genius, psychic power, artistic talents, scientific and intellectual creativity, and extreme longevity with good health. (An age of 120 with unimpaired mental faculties was commonly achieved among the ancient illuminati, Gopi Krishna said, and an age of 150 is quite probable in the kundalini-altered future.) But if improperly aroused, without right guidance and preparation, kundalini can be horribly painful and destructive, even fatal. Unsustained by a sensible, healthy manner of living—meaning regulated and balanced, not ascetic or orgiastic—kundalini can turn malignant and become the source of deteriorating health, terrible bodily heat and pain, many forms of mental illness, and even sudden death. In physiological terms, the pranic stream has gone astray into one of the two side channels of the spinal cord (the left side being called *ida* and the right side *pingala* in yogic physiology).

The pranic stream, Gopi Krishna said, is affected by "every shade of passion and emotion, by food and drink, by environment and mode of life." It is altered by desire and ambition, by conduct and behavior—and, in fact, by all the thousands of influences, from the most powerful to the slightest, which act on and shape life from birth to death. Thus the need for balanced, moral living is based on biological imperative.

There is another condition, too, even worse for humanity. Kundalini-gone-astray has been the cause of evil geniuses in history. However, in such cases the kundalini energy has been active since birth, as with all geniuses. Their lives are usually so filled with difficulties that the kundalini energy can become malignant if the finer qualities necessary for psychological stability have not been made a part of their upbringing. Lack of these finer traits constitutes a built-in safeguard of nature which bars the unstable individual from access to higher levels of consciousness. This moral dimension is what distinguishes seers and sages from psychics and gifted intellectuals who are otherwise quite ordinary.

Knowledge of kundalini, Gopi Krishna said, is the only real means of preventing future evil geniuses. It is also the best means of preventing history from ending in either the bang of nuclear holocaust or the whimpering slow death of an overpopulated, starving resourceless planet. "The only way to safety and survival lies in determining the evolutionary needs and in erecting our social and political systems in conformity with those needs," he maintained. His writings envisage a new structure of human society, a new social and political order to enable the entire race to devote itself to the development of the powers and possibilities latent within.

All reality is governed by one mighty law which is simultaneously biological and spiritual: *Thou shalt evolve to a higher state of consciousness via the kundalini process.* This law of evolution, he said, can be objectively demonstrated in people with unquestionable proof, using the techniques and technology of science: "The awakening of kundalini is the greatest enterprise and most wonderful achievement in front of man."

That is a vast claim, and most neurophysiologists and psychologists will probably regard it as simplistic, if not crackpot. After all, others from both East and West have talked and written about kundalini since early times. But Gopi Krishna, who made clear that he had only rediscovered an ancient tradition, was also a man of science. In that regard, he said something which had not been said before: Kundalini can be scientifically verified in the laboratory to prove the essential truth of religious tradition. We can get objective evidence which will show what has been the major claim of religious and spiritual teachers throughout history—that man was born to attain a higher state, a state of union with the divine. Until such proof is available, Gopi Krishna said, don't believe what I say, just do the research.

How did Gopi Krishna come to have such a radical message? What are the sources of knowledge for this man who flunked out of college, lived a simple life as husband and father, and worked most of his career as a minor civil servant in the Indian government? The answer is personal experience and scholarly research.

A White Serpent in Rapid Flight

In 1937, after seventeen years of steadfast meditation (he got up faithfully at 4:00 A.M. to meditate, even after his wedding night), the kundalini energy awakened in Gopi Krishna. In his autobiography he wrote: "There was a sound like a nerve thread snapping and instantaneously a silvery streak passed through the spinal cord, exactly like the sinuous movement of a white serpent in rapid flight, pouring an effulgent, cascading shower of brilliant vital energy into my brain, filling my head with a blissful luster."[2]

What began during meditation that Christmas morning was the development of a higher state of consciousness in Gopi Krishna. But the process was far from complete. What followed were years of hell, periods of severe ordeal when the changes being made in his nervous system caused enormous pain, prolonged sickness, near-death, bewilderment, and self-doubts about his sanity.

Slowly, carefully, he began to conduct experiments in the laboratory of his own body, observing the sometimes terrifying effects as he encountered the mysterious bioenergy: "I was destined to witness my own transformation . . . attended all along by great physical and mental suffering. But what I witnessed . . . is so contrary to many accepted notions of science . . . that when what I have experienced is proved empirically there must occur a far-reaching, revolutionary change in every sphere of human activity and conduct." The transformation included the spontaneous appearance of psychic, intellectual, and literary powers.

Local gurus and holy men were unable to give Gopi Krishna any relief or understanding, so he undertook a reading program through the literature of religion, psychology, and occultism. He found that kundalini was recognized at least 5000 years ago but was always a closely guarded secret recorded in veiled language and allusion which made little sense to someone who had no personal experience of it. Like acupuncture, which was also known that long ago, this knowledge had been lost to modern man. But, Gopi Krishna said, it can be recovered and grounded in scientific concepts and terminology through laboratory research and scholarly studies of the thousands of still-untranslated old texts dealing with kundalini. Thus, what has been recorded until now in occult terms will be demystified and explained in simple language.

How might the reality of kundalini be shown? First, a person in whom it is fully developed will clearly be a genius. *New* knowledge will come from him, knowledge such as Gopi Krishna himself offered which elegantly unites the entire psychic/occult/spiritual scene with evolutionary theory and the transpersonal psychology arising from Freud, Maslow, and Jung.

Next, as the kundalini process transforms a person, the nervous system and brain undergo changes which will be observable (although the necessary instruments for observing them may still be only on the drawing boards).

Third, the "food" the body uses to nourish the nervous system during transformation comes from the sex organs—the "essence" of seminal fluid in men and what Gopi Krishna called "the erotic fluids" in women. Thus, the reproductive organs increase their activity dramatically, producing many times more copiously than usual. This, incidentally, explains why ancient statuary and paintings show men, even a pharaoh and an Egyptian god, in meditation with an erect phallus. This is not meant by the artist to be erotic at all, Gopi Krishna said, but rather is a frank and literal depiction of a biological fact about kundalini.

This fluid sexual essence, existing probably at the molecular or even submolecular level, streams from the reproductive organs into the spinal canal and then upward into the brain. This can be verified by a spinal tap at the time the phenomenon is occurring.

The bloodstream also carries nerve food during this organic transformation. Hence, the composition of the blood changes due to the awakening of kundalini and ought to be examined in any research program. Heart activity (pulse rate) and other internal organs' functions undergo radical changes. Likewise, perception, digestion, and elimination change dramatically—still more clues to look for in the full spectrum of physical mental behavioral transmutations which necessarily must occur as nature prepares the organism through a total cellular reorganization for a higher state of being. These are matters which can be objectively determined by neurophysiologists and medical researchers.

In addition, the person will have high moral character and other traits typically associated with spiritual masters, such as psychic and literary talents. (Gopi Krishna said he was amazed to find himself at age fifty spontaneously writing poetry in nine languages, four of which were unknown to him. He had never taken any interest in poetry or attempted any literary performance, he claimed, yet long narrative powers in rhymed verse would impress themselves on his awareness so quickly that he could scarcely write them down.)

What About Celibacy?

What about celibacy? In growing to higher consciousness, is it necessary, as some claim, to abstain from sex and to "mortify the flesh"?

From Gopi Krishna's point of view, the answer is a firm no—with one exception. Since he himself was married and had three children, he strongly disagreed with those who regard sexual contact as detrimental to spiritual development. Moreover, he pointed out that during the Vedic Age thousands of years ago, when many of the great yogic scriptures were first written, several hundred inspired sages were recognized as enlightened men, and in almost every case they were married and had children.

Gopi Krishna felt that an enlightened person can enjoy an active sex life up to an age of a hundred—and even beyond! But he emphasizes the need, arising from the biological laws of spiritual evolution, of basing sexual activity on love and respect while avoiding immoderate or promiscuous behavior.

Generally speaking, he said, celibacy is contrary to nature, since enlightenment is an evolutionary process, with hereditary playing an important role by "stamping" the genes of the enlightened so that their biological gains through spiritual disciplines can be passed to their progeny. Suppression of sexuality out of contempt or hatred of our "lower nature" is an act of ignorance leading only to atrophy of the reproductive system. The biological fact that only the primates, especially humans, are perennially ready for sex is a clue to linkage between our animal origins and our higher destiny. But there is a critical period during the kundalini process lasting possibly as long as a year or two when celibacy is important. During that time, the fluid essence is needed for remolding the nervous system and brain. Otherwise, the kundalini awakening may be aborted through misuse. That is the only condition Gopi Krishna recognizes as demanding celibacy.

The "sage of Srinagar" broke new ground and (is it proper to say?) sowed seed. He wrote about his discovery of the mighty law linking biology, physics, and psychology in more than a dozen books and numerous articles. The scope and depth of Gopi Krishna's thought are awe-inspiring. In unraveling the kundalini experience, he apparently discovered the key to understanding practically every mystery and para-normal phenomenon which now puzzles science. The topics he raised relate to everyone on Planet Earth. They challenge the entire scientific community, a community which so far has been unable either to explain humanity or tame it. As Albert Einstein once observed, nuclear energy and the atomic bomb changed everything except our thinking. And as I pointed out in Chapter 1, the renowned neurosurgeon Wilder Penfield admitted in *The Mystery of the Mind* that all his experience in trying to understand mental experience—the mind—on the basis of brain studies came to almost nothing. "The mind is peculiar," he wrote. "It has energy. The form of that energy is different from that of neuronal potentials that travel the axone pathways."

Gopi Krishna felt that we can identify the mysterious mind energy which eluded Penfield. He also felt that it can do what Einstein hoped: change human thinking. That is because kundalini, as Gopi Krishna presents it, is the first testable field theory of psychophysical linkages among body, mind, and cosmos, covering the entire spectrum of psycho-logical, psychical, and spiritual phenomena. With it comes the possibility of objectively studying higher consciousness, thus answering questions presently beyond science and ending philosophical speculation about the condition.

That is a daring stance—daring, yet rationally and plausibly pre-sented. It is a sober and serious call for science to become involved in demonstrating the high spiritual destiny of the human race. Nothing since the 1925 Scopes "Monkey" trial so vigorously calls attention to the controversial cause of evolution. But whereas the Scopes trial inflamed antagonism between science and religion, Gopi Krishna made a breathtaking attempt to heal the split. And it is humorously ironic that

Western science and technology—often called the product of a godless, materialist approach to life—might be the means by which this is demonstrated to the world. Let Gopi Krishna, therefore, have the last word:

> The aim of the evolutionary impulse is to make man aware of himself. With this sublime awareness, he will regulate his life as a rational human being, free from egotism, violence, greed, ambition, and immoderate desire to lead to a state of unbroken peace and happiness on the earth. . . . Enlightenment, then, is a natural process ruled by biological laws as strict in their operation as the laws governing the continuance of the race. . . . This, I believe, is the purpose for which you and I are here—to realize ourselves . . . to bring the soul to a clear realization of its own divine nature . . .

12

Toward a Science
of Consciousness

Consciousness . . . is the primary factor in all experience, hence it needs and merits the fullest attention any science can bestow on it.
Henry Margenau, Introduction to Lawrence LeShan's *Toward a General Theory of the Paranormal*

Consciousness is the meeting ground for inner and outer reality. It is the common denominator of objective scientific knowledge and subjective religio-spiritual experience. But just what is consciousness? It is not the same as thinking because we can be aware of our thoughts, proving that they take place within consciousness and therefore are secondary to it. Likewise, we can be aware without having any thoughts, only perceptions. But again, they are secondary to the field of awareness in which they occur.

This simple demonstration shows that many things can be learned about the *contents of consciousness*—about thoughts, perceptions, feelings, ideas, values, beliefs, memories, sensations, related physiological processes, and so forth. The organization of these contents into a recognizable configuration is called psyche or mind (as in "I know his mind well"). And the nature of that organization and its relation to body—generally referred to as the mind-body problem—is gradually being clarified by the combined efforts of a host of disciplines from the neurosciences and linguistics to parapsychology and biofeedback. But *con-*

127

sciousness itself—not what we are aware of but the basic fact[1] of being aware that we are aware—remains the medium through which we know reality. Consciousness itself is primary and cannot be explained in terms of anything else. It can only be experienced. Apart from it, no observations or experiences are in any way possible. The word consciousness is, in fact, formed by the union of two Latin words—*con*, "with" and *scire*, "to know"—and literally means "that with which we know."

We can attempt to answer the question "What is consciousness?" by noting the principal senses in which the word is used. First, it means awareness, the capacity for perceiving and feeling. In this sense, animals display consciousness. But animals in their natural state do not display personal self-awareness, the conscious (as distinguished from the non-conscious/animal-like) aspect of mind reflecting a concept or image of oneself. Alan Watts says in *The Way of Zen* that "the power of thought enables us to construct symbols of things apart from the things themselves. This includes the ability to make a symbol, an idea, of ourselves apart from ourselves. Because the idea is so much more stable than the fact, we learn to identify ourselves with the idea of ourselves . . ."[2] This uniquely human trait, awareness of self and identification with some aspect of it, is the second sense in which we can answer the question "What is consciousness?"

The third sense takes us beyond the physical body. Since parapsychology has demonstrated that telepathy, clairvoyance, precognition, and psychokinesis are real phenomena, there must be some means through which the connection between physically separate objects and events can be made. That "connection" is also consciousness—in its most extended sense—as the universal field in which all experience and/or personal awareness occurs.

Although we can distinguish meanings, we cannot really define consciousness. To define is to delimit, to set boundaries. But who knows where consciousness begins or ends? Certainly animals are conscious (but not self-conscious). Arthur Koestler notes in *The Ghost in the Machine* that ethologists refuse to draw a lower limit for consciousness, while neurophysiologists talk of "spinal consciousness" in lower animals and biologists speak of the "protoplasmic consciousness" of protists, which are single-celled creatures without a nervous system. Exobiology suggests the probability (approaching absolute certainty) of other life forms in the universe. Since there are stellar systems significantly older than ours, it is likely that some life forms are more highly evolved than *Homo sapiens,* and thus possess higher consciousness. Contact with such intelligences seems likely, and some exobiologists who conduct radioscopic listening for signals believe it may occur soon. Some religious and philosophic traditions hold that all creation, even so-called inorganic matter, has a primal form of sentience or awareness. From their points of view, consciousness is everywhere and is the foundation of all existence—the organizing principle behind the physical universe. Call it the Logos, the Tao, God.

We cannot define consciousness, yet every day's living confirms its reality. We are conscious: this is the self-evident dimension of all knowing, all perception, all states of being. Whatever happens on the spectrum of our physical and mental life—waking, sleeping, dreaming, making love, feeling low, getting high, hungry or happy—is an alteration or disturbance of consciousness. And on the basis of psychic research, even death is an altered state of consciousness in a noncorporeal or discarnate condition.

The boundaries of personal awareness constantly shift like changing images on a movie screen, and with it, our perceptions, abilities, and understanding of reality. Further reflection leads to an awareness of awareness—an expansion of consciousness, if you will—and the possibility long maintained by many traditions of integrating the conscious and unconscious aspects of mind to develop a new and stable state of awareness, the ultraconscious. Other names for this state include cosmic consciousness, samadhi, satori, mystical union with the Ground of Being, the peace which passeth understanding.

The Consciousness (R)evolution

Recognition of the human potential for higher consciousness has led to a rising interest in the study of consciousness. This has been hastened by critical world conditions, which have led many social and political thinkers to see the imperative need for a transformation of consciousness in humanity if Planet Earth is to survive.

The signs of such a transformation are apparent: A consciousness revolution is occurring throughout human culture. We might ascribe its origin to the beginning of psychedelic drug research, when the "children of the Bomb" reached adolescence, but its roots go back much farther. In fact, traditions such as philosophy, religion, esoteric psychology, and the humanities have been concerned with the nature of consciousness for millennia. But not until recently has this interest flourished at the grass-roots level, and now the signs are everywhere. Some of the consciousness-raising developments prove faddish and ephemeral, of course, but even they help to lead people deeper into the search for expanded awareness.

What does the consciousness revolution mean? It is a revolution in the true sense of revolving, turning back. The consciousness revolution in its best aspect is both *radical,* in the etymological sense of *radix,* getting back to the root of the matter, and it is *conservative,* in the sense of returning to ancient traditions and recovering lost knowledge. It seeks to conserve the best of its root-traditions: the integrity of human life woven from the warp of the threatened ecosphere and the woof of sacred lifeways that have contributed to the liberation of mind, bodies, and the highest human potentials.

There is a profound wisdom in convention, but to truly appreciate it you first have to be unconventional. From that perspective, the consciousness revolution is also an evolution. It is not just a nostalgic retreat into the past. Rather, it is an upward spiraling, a quantum leap in awareness. Some who "turn back" do so in simpleminded fashion, as if it were possible to jettison all evolutionary mind-gains and just live in primitive fashion. Wiser "revolutionaries" understand the need to turn back in an upward spiral as *transcendence* rather than regression, so that you end up at the starting point but on a higher level. Regression merely negates; transcendence is progression because it includes what went before, but in a larger understanding which corrects errors, imbalances and incompleteness. In transcendence, both the past and the present are purified of destructive elements and fused in a lifestyle which humanizes technology as older ways of living close to the earth are revived with increased understanding of their value as conventions.

Science Meets Consciousness

What has this meant for science? Goaded by scholars and street people alike, who rightly criticize its image of objective, value-free neutrality, as well as its claim to be the ultimate arbiter of knowledge, science as a communal project is being transformed. And since science is really a method of knowing rather than a body of knowledge, it is only proper that science should start examining the means whereby it knows what it claims.

This examination is occurring in a variety of frontier areas as science looks ever deeper into the nature of man and the universe. From research on the perimeter of knowledge, a paradox has emerged: At the subtlest levels on which science can explore reality, objectivity becomes impossible. As "objective" sensitive instruments and sophisticated investigations probe the subatomic frontiers of the material world, the distinction between matter and energy dissolves. Further, the very act or means of observing those deep levels of reality requires a process of interaction which influences what was to have been observed. The observation cannot be separated from the observer. The consciousness of the experimenter is an essential part of the experiment. In a personal communication to me, Yale physicist Henry Margenau called it "epistemological feedback"—the interaction between the knower and the known which occurs wherever consciousness occurs. Its analogue, applicable to physical measurement by observation instruments, is better known as Heisenberg's uncertainty principle. For example, trying to measure the absolute temperature of a container of water proves impossible because the temperature of the thermometer or measuring instrument changes, to some degree, the temperature of the water.

Consciousness and Reality

To describe an event completely, you must include a description of the consciousness which is observing the event. But that cannot be done. Thus, absolute objectivity has been impossible from the start of science, and all human knowledge is finally subjective, a form of inner awareness. In a sense, the universe is a product of our minds. This is not to say that solipsism is ultimate reality or that we have created the universe. Rather, as the *Rg Veda* says (1:164:39), it means that knowledge is structured in consciousness, and our knowledge of absolute truth is directly proportional to the degree to which we can step outside ourselves and purify our consciousness.

In order to step out of our "self," we first have to know what self is. Only *Homo sapiens* has a sense of separate self, personhood, private individuality. This mentally held concept of identity begins to develop early in life (from about age two) because of various biological and social factors through which consciousness reflects back upon itself. The result, as Alan Watts noted, is a self-image we carry within our minds which we normally consider to be our true self but which is none other than ego, the I-concept. Thus, uncovering the true source of cognitive awareness as distinguished from an illusory image of self is tricky business. Our brains and sensory organs have perceptual filters built in. Enculturation processes such as language and religion likewise erect conceptual screens. Our picture of the universe (our "reality construct") is thus built from limited information shared ("validated") by society as "common sense." As the Talmud says, we do not see things as they are—we see things as we are. *A Course in Miracles* likewise points out that perception is a choice; perception selects and makes the world we see. Hence, in the language of consciousness—explorers such as Joseph Chilton Pearce *(The Crack in the Cosmic Egg)* and John Lilly *(The Center of the Cyclone)*—a reality construct is built by consensual validation. (This is one of the primary lessons which Don Juan imparted to his student, Carlos Castenada.)

But if "reality" varies from culture to culture and is a function of mind-state, how can I truly know—and how can I know that I truly know?

Again in our quest for ultimate truth, we are faced with the problem of consciousness, the source and ground of all experience. The variety of approaches to the question "What is consciousness?" is wide, but a convergence of many disciplines in the scientific, religio-spiritual, and humanistic domains is becoming apparent. The thrust of them all fundamentally contradicts the mechanistic-materialistic view which reduces consciousness to a byproduct ("epiphenomenon," as the Skinnerian-behaviorist psychologists would say) of the brain's electrochemical processes. Psychologist David McKay states the opposing view: "My own consciousness is a primary datum, which it would be nonsense to doubt because it is the platform on which my doubting is built."[3]

Consciousness is something more than the brain and egoic self-concept. Various religious and philsophic traditions concluded that long ago; some, such as yoga, concluded so on grounds which include neurophysiology! For example, the founder of Transcendental Meditation, Maharishi Mahesh Yogi, restates vedic philosophy by explaining that brain/body and mind are, respectively, the gross and subtle manifestations of consciousness, states which are lower than the causal and—the ultimate state—the transcendental. When your state of consciousness changes or ascends to higher levels, brain/body and mental functioning change also.

This is the fundamental premise on which TM and all other meditative traditions are based. Through their various techniques and practices for refining awareness, the meditator can expand his consciousness and directly experience the larger dimensions of the psyche until, finally, there is no distinction between personal mind and universal consciousness. This is what Buddhism calls "original mind" and Jesus called "the kingdom of Heaven." In those dimensions, the supersensible becomes perceptible and metaphysics comes down to Earth in ways which utterly confound physics, such as psychic phenomena.

Consciousness Public and Private

An examination of the etymological relation of "science," "conscience," and "consciousness" shows an interesting aspect of the situation we are examining here. John Dewey pointed out in *Education and Democracy* that consciousness was viewed by the classical Greeks as a shared, communal sense of knowing rather than the private, individual mode generally assumed for it today. (His observation can be more generally applied to tribal peoples.) And conscience meant "knowing together."

Knowing what? Plato defined science as "the clear intellectual perception of fundamental moral truth." That was what was known together: an understanding of ultimate reality, the deep structure of the cosmos, based on direct insight. The facts of science pertaining to the physical world were understood as reflections of the same metaphysical world from which the customs and laws of the wisely governed society arose. To transgress the rules of human behavior was to act in disharmony with the functioning of the universe. Thus, in the early Western view of the nature of consciousness, facts, values, and principles of societal organization were all grounded and unified in the nature of existence.

But as the fully formed egoic state of consciousness became the dominant mode of awareness in humanity, there arose a bifurcation of mind which T. S. Eliot termed "a dissociation of sensibilities." Psychologists today refer to it as hemispheric dominance or the bicameral mind. This "split-mindedness" has given rise to the controversies recorded in history as science versus religion and faith versus knowledge. One side emphasizes the objective/rational/analytical/experimental mode of knowing; it can be called the Aristotelian mode. The other elevates the subjective/intuitive/synthetic/experiential mode; it can be called the Platonic mode. Each leads to a way of "seeing" the world and interacting with it, a way which is valid but incomplete.

The inherent strengths and weaknesses of both are now apparent. The need at this point in history is for a balanced, integrated mode of mentation.

And this search for wholeness is precisely the best aspect of the New Age movement. Although it is still in a nascent stage, a process of unification is occurring in the body of human knowledge which is leading to a renewed harmony between both our split-minded modes of cognition and our senses of personal and public reality. Work in the physical, psychological, and behavioral sciences—inner space and outer space research—is coming together and overlapping to reveal an underlying unity. The need for a holistic approach to problem-solving is apparent, and the traditional compartmentalization of scientific disciplines is being supplemented by interdisciplinary studies.

All Knowledge Is One

Given the fundamental connectedness of all experience and existence, this is not unexpected. Fragmentation is giving way to integration and the fundamental connectedness of all things is coming into sharper focus with each new insight. Ken Wilber, whose brilliant theoretical work in transpersonal psychology qualifies him as the Einstein of consciousness research, points out:

Eastern and Western approaches to consciousness (and reality) can be meaningfully correlated and unified if we regard consciousness as a spectrum composed of various levels or modalities, much as the electromagnetic spectrum consists of numerous vibratory bands. Just as Herschel and Curie attended to different bands of the electromagnetic spectrum (IR and gamma, respectively), without realizing that they both were working with the same spectrum of radiation, so now many investigators are attending to different "bands" within the spectrum of consciousness without realizing that they are working with the same reality approached from different levels.

Taken together, then, these Eastern and Western approaches offer a fundamental complementarity, for—generally speaking—the levels that the West has heretofore ignored have been thoroughly investigated by the East, while the converse is also true. The East has extensively explored those paths leading to the Absolute Noumenon, while the West has restricted itself to scientific investigations of phenomenal psychology. Man, considered as absolute subjectivity, is the Godhead—this is the concern of the East; man, considered as an object of knowledge, is the phenomenal ego—this is the concern of the West. Taken together they span the entire spectrum of consciousness.[4]

This trend toward unification of knowledge and awareness of ever-larger wholes is leading from physics through paraphysics to metaphysics, from orthodox psychology to transpersonal psychology, from biology to theology and philosophy. These disciplines have been concerned in their own way with knowledge, especially self-knowledge. Their ultimate concern can be formulated in the ancient question: Who am I?

This same question is now emerging as the problematic focus for science, as well as for the humanities, arts, and religion. That recognition is leading us toward a science of consciousness—a knowing about ourselves and the universe based on public observation and verification of data obtained in the private "laboratories" of our inner awareness.

Noetics, the Science of Consciousness

A science of consciousness is emerging. It has been termed "noetics" by Dr. Charles Musès, editor of the no-longer-published *Journal for the Study of Consciousness* and a mathematical investigator who enunciated a theory of consciousness in terms of new mathematical parameters which he calls hypernumbers. Musès, who first used the term in 1967, defined noetics in his 1972 book *Consciousness and Reality* as "the science of the study of consciousness and its alterations." Apollo 14 astronaut Edgar D. Mitchell has popularized the term by establishing a research organization called the Institute of Noetic Sciences[5] to investigate the nature of consciousness, mind-body interaction, and human potential.

Noetic as an adjective, from the Greek root *nous* meaning "mind," has a history of usage in English going back to the seventeenth-century, although Plato apparently coined the term. As he used it in his *Republic*, noetic meant "discriminating" or "thinking"—a stage on the way to pure knowledge, gnosis. When the word passed into the English language, it first meant purely intellectual or rational knowledge. In the last century, Harvard psychologist William James gave it the additional meaning of directly knowing eternal truths (see his *Varieties of Religious Experience*), an apprehension of knowledge surpassing the usual processes of logical reasoning by the intellect. Today it means the nonrational or transrational (but not irrational) direct cognition or "knowingness" which comes through creative intuition, psychic perception, spiritual apprehension, and religious transcendental experience.

Knowledge of this sort seems to bypass most of the filters and screens which nature and nurture impose on us. It is less-mediated cognition and hence "purer." Nevertheless, those filters and screens (Henri Bergson called the brain a "reducing valve") often serve useful biological purposes. Some unmediated perceptions may distract an organism from survival tasks. In such a situation, the filter or screen helps to focus attention on what is necessary to maintain physical well-being or survival. Also, some perceptions are delusional (based on false belief) or hallucinatory (based on false sensory data), as in the case of paranoid schizophrenia. So it seems that intuition alone is not entirely trustworthy because there can be an admixture of fantasy and irrational material along with the rational. However, with practice, intuition can be cultivated, just as reason and logical thinking can be enhanced. Balance and integration are necessary for the clear perception of reality.

Informed Intuition: Knowledge Plus Experience

Noetics recognizes the need for this balance. It doesn't take an anti-intellectual or anti-science stance in favor of mysticism or transcendental knowledge. On the contrary, it makes full use of the scientific method. But it is aware that technological science has its inherent limitations. Noetics also makes a valid distinction between the scientific method and scientism, which is the attempt by some dogmatic scientists to turn their personal philosophy—a reductionistic, atheistic materialism—into a binding world view for all scientists and, beyond them, the public.

Noetics takes the position of Albert Einstein when he said, "Science without religion is lame; religion without science is blind." Noetics seeks to understand the operations of consciousness and mind-body interaction through *informed intuition*. To paraphrase Einstein, "Knowledge without experience is lame; experience without knowledge is blind." By bringing the rational and nonrational/transrational together in a multidisciplinary, holistic fashion—what the physicist C. F. von Weizsäcker in *The History of Nature* calls "a fusion of insight and instinct"—one achieves, in science historian Theodore Roszack's term, gnosis. As with Plato, this is "a kind of knowledge older than scientific knowledge that is augmentive rather than reductive, that honors and invites the aesthetic, sensuous, compassionate, and visionary possibilities of experience as well as the rational and technical. The term is not meant to exclude scientific knowledge, but to embrace it within the program Abraham Maslow called 'hierarchical integration'."[6] Thus, our complete faculties are brought to bear for an increased understanding of the human being and the universe.

The phrase "complete faculties" includes those being demonstrated by parapsychology. Evidence shows that people have abilities which are outside the sensory and motor systems as described by mainstream science. The implications are clear: If human consciousness can operate external to the body at remote distances, then perhaps it can operate without a fleshly body at all. Indeed, evidence from psychical research supports this conclusion, and, as a result, raises a host of profound questions about human nature and cosmology. It also suggests that our knowledge of ultimate reality is *not* limited by an inability to "step outside ourselves." The problem, rather, is why we first conceived ourselves in a fragmented way as private egos. Again, the question of self-knowledge arises, and the mystics' perennial answer (from the topmost band on the spectrum of consciousness) to the question "Who am I?" now seems understandable when they reply "I am the universe." They have no bifurcation of consciousness into "self" and "other" with which they identify. They have broken through the illusion of ego and freed themselves from *maya*. Their "center" of existence is not the body or even the mind. It is pure, undifferentiated, nondual, nontemporal consciousness.

What Is Science?

In order to develop a science of consciousness, we must ask "What is science?" as well as "What is consciousness?" Coming from *scire,* "to know," science has been defined as "accumulated knowledge systematized and formulated with reference to the discovery of general truths or the operational laws, especially when such knowledge relates to the physical world." This is not a complete definition, however. The essence of science is its method, not its data. The accumulated knowledge of science is obtained through trained observation and is empirically verifiable. Scientific method requires that research be presented for validation by the scientific community. A clear description of the techniques and materials used is necessary in the presentation. Then the procedures are carefully repeated by others. If the same results are obtained, the findings become scientific "fact."

Ths definition follows Aristotle's division of all knowledge into science and metaphysics (which deals with those aspects of reality "beyond" the physical). And it is just this view which noetics is challenging. Noetics recognizes consciousness as the meeting ground for inner and outer reality—the common denominator of objective scientific knowledge and subjective religio-spiritual experience. This recognition allows it to extend the domain of both in a socially useful, humane manner. It recognizes the authenticity of the experiences and phenomena which various nonscientific traditions have long valued, and brings an end to those perennial controversies, science versus religion and faith versus knowledge. This is so because the world's major religious and spiritual traditions have an aspect which is indeed scientific.

That aspect is entirely empirical and centers around consciousness-altering disciplines, techniques, and procedures aimed at giving the practitioner direct religio-spiritual experience of the sort which occurred to the tradition's founder. Unfortunately, religious and spiritual traditions are generally identified as formalized ceremony, doctrines, prescriptions, and prohibitions, rather than recognizing the deeper basis in psychotechnology. As an example, consider yoga as a science for the study of consciousness. For more than four millennia, the validation of knowledge has been its prime discipline. I pointed out in "The True Meaning of Yoga" that the steps to be followed for enlightenment are clearly delineated and the "findings" have been attested to by people who have carefully repeated the procedures described by their predecessors. Again, as with psychic research, we have a demonstration that human knowledge of ultimate reality is not limited to data obtained through the physical senses, but rather that we have access to metaphysical reality.

The same can be said about other sacred traditions, genuine occult systems, and higher psychotechnologies such as Sufism, meditative Buddhism, the cabalistic tradition of Judaism, and certain esoteric traditions in Christianity such as Hesychastic prayer or the spiritual exercises of Saint Ignatius Loyola. Modern systems of occult thought such as Theosophy, Rosicrucianism, and Anthrosophy display an intriguing ability to integrate scientific and religio-spiritual experience in order to objectively demonstrate the supersensible aspect of the universe which has been described and mapped by centuries of spiritual explorers. Interestingly, there is emerging a paraphysical technology by which lower levels of this "other" reality can be objectively demonstrated, measured, and harnessed in the manner by which conventional technology has extended human perception through the recognized senses.

Thus, noetics is an expansion of science which rises above science's traditional shortcomings in a way which can substantially contribute to the advancement of other human endeavors, particularly those called "spiritual" or "religious." From the perspective of noetics, a new image of humanity is emerging—an image in which the spirit of science is leading to a true science of the spirit.

Toward a Science of Consciousness

But while there is progress, there are also problems. Noetics is just beginning to organize and articulate itself. Because it is still in its infancy, it has perhaps a lower ratio of information to noise than other fields of science. The spectrum of psychic, paranormal, and mystical experiences being investigated is bewildering to the general public, and consciousness researchers themselves sometimes show the same confusion. The unfamiliar terrain is being mapped in ways which are not always congruent. And many "authorities," becoming aware of higher levels in the spectrum of consciousness, have been humbled by the depth of experience systematized in spiritual traditions. Ignorance, inexperience, and bias frequently enter into definitions of what constitutes "higher" consciousness.

What standards exist by which we can measure and judge states of consciousness? In his *States of Consciousness*, psychologist Charles Tart has offered a useful foundation with his state-specific sciences, which he defines as sciences particular to various discrete altered states of consciousness whose overall pattern of functioning is radically different from one another. Another of his books, *Transpersonal Psychologies*, also contributes toward developing noetics into a sophisticated science. Other explorations in consciousness are available from various writers and researchers such as Robert Ornstein's *The Nature of Human Consciousness*, Charles Hampden-Turner's *Maps of the Mind*, my own *Frontiers of Consciousness* and *What Is Enlightenment?* and Gopi Krishna's books on kundalini, notably *The Secret of Yoga* and *Higher Consciousness*. The most important, in my judgment, are Ken Wilber's matched pair of books, *The Atman Project*, which examines the noetic development of the individual from birth to enlightenment, and *Up from Eden*, which offers a transpersonal view of the development of the human race.

Perhaps the primary problem in noetics is simply lack of experience on the part of those interested in research. It would be presumptuous, if not arrogant, for an "outsider" to judge the value and/or validity of knowledge claimed by a spiritual tradition or sacred lifeway. Just as anthropologists have to go into the field or live within a culture, so, too, must would-be noeticists bring back firsthand reports by sincerely and diligently practicing one or more psychotechnologies. Reading, conversation, and speculation are not enough. There must be depth of personal experience.

If these problems can be adequately resolved, useful strides may then be taken at all levels of society toward building "a better world" because facts arising from the domain of amoral science will become linked with time-honored values arising from religio-spiritual, humanistic, and philosophic experience. The split in human consciousness could be transcended in a unified state which enjoys advantages of both "lower" states while overcoming their inherent limitations.

The knowledge already gained by noetic explorers shows many intriguing avenues deserving further investigation. Of course, points of contention are being raised, and this is to be expected. Nevertheless, the laws and techniques of noetics are slowly being clarified, concurrent with a highly creative technology which brings us considerably closer to the externalization of the internal conditions and processes of our own consciousness. That is how it works as we move through the revolution of awareness toward a science of consciousness.

13

Consciousness and Substance: The Primal Forms of God

There is a widespread notion among New Age–oriented people and spiritual seekers that consciousness is energy and that working with energy will per se change one's consciousness and bring enlightenment. This is a fallacy, and a spiritually dangerous one. States of consciousness can be *correlated* with states of energy, but they cannot be *equated*.

Consciousness is wholly outside the realm of matter and energy, although at the same time it is coextensive with the whole of it. As Da Love-Ananda puts it in *The Hymn of the Master*, "I AM smaller than the atom. I AM larger than the universe" (verse 97). Consciousness is omnipresent throughout manifest creation as a universal "field," yet it is not inherently a property of any part of that creation. As is classically (and paradoxically) said about enlightenment, consciousness is that which is totally involved with, yet totally unattached to, the realm of nature and phenomena. In other words, consciousness is uncreated. It wholly transcends the cosmos, including energy in all its forms, from the most solid matter to the most subtle radiations and etheric/celestial vibrations. Consciousness permeates or bathes all creation. In Da Love-Ananda's terms, everything resides or inheres in consciousness. But consciousness was present before creation itself and, in that far-distant future when the cosmos is annihilated and withdrawn into the unmanifest state of God, consciousness will remain.

140

That is not to say God is consciousness alone. God includes consciousness (God includes *everything*) but God cannot be *defined* as anything, even consciousness. To define is to delimit, but God is unlimited, infinite, and infinitely beyond definition or description. God is ultimately mysterious, beyond all human attempts to encompass in words and thoughts and intellectual formulae. God cannot be comprehended, only apprehended.

Yet in our apprehension of the Ultimate Mystery, we can nevertheless say that the two primal aspects of God are consciousness and substance (or matter/energy). In the terminology of Da Love-Ananda, God or the Transcendental Domain, which enfolds all creation, issues forth into creation as the Radiant Transcendental Consciousness and the Radiant Life-Current. All objects, entities, and organisms in the cosmos, all planes of being and forms of experience result from combinations and premutations of these aspects of God. They are the poles of existence from which humanity begins (although it begins in the sleep of ignorance-nescience) and to which humanity is called to awaken in knowledge-conscience and realization of reality. They are the poles to which evolving humanity must align and yield itself in radical understanding, transcending all sense of separateness and independence.

Consciousness and substance are the two primal aspects of Being, and we must release our attention and open our body-minds to them in profound conductivity if we are to fulfill our destiny and become enlightened. To identify only with one or the other is to assume an incomplete, unfulfilled, and therefore unhappy stance in the world. The person whose sense of self is thus posited is forever seeking yet perpetually self-defeated by the implicitly drawn boundary in his or her consciousness which divides existence into self and non-self, inner and outer, subject and object. Duality and universal opposites characterize such a person's perception of reality. It is a most bleak, absurd, and sour (*dukkha*, as the Buddha put it) existence.

Spinoza remarked that matter is God as extension. That is true, but it would be more accurate to say that substance (both matter and energy) is God as extension. However, even the totality of the universe does not define God; that is simply pantheism. To complete the picture of manifest creation, we must say that if substance is God as *ex*tension, consciousness is God as *in*tention. Will, volition, purpose, meaning, motivation—these are aspects of ourselves which can never be explained in electrochemical terms, astrophysical terms, or anything whatsoever which is some form of matter/energy from the realm of nature. Thus, substance and consciousness are the objective and subjective aspects of God. They are, in theological terms, the traditional aspects of God described as omnipresent and immanent. Although this does not define

God either (for there is the transcendent/unmanifest aspect of God which is entirely beyond the universe) it is more accurate and comprehensive than Spinoza's remark and has been called panentheism by Whitehead. To use the phrasing of Da Love-Ananda, God or the Transcendental Being is the Identity or Subject of all selves or subjects and the Condition or Objective source of all not-selves or objects.

We see this situation reflected in miniature in ourselves. We are both object and subject. We are creatures but we are also aware of ourselves as creatures. We can say, "I have a body, but I am not my body; I have a mind, but I am not my mind." We are not merely a body-mind, however complex and subtle it appears. Our true identity transcends the entire body-mind complex. So we can also say that consciousness is self-created, but that the creative self is not our egoic body-mind self. Rather, it is the Self of all—which is a traditional term for God, the Supreme Identity, the Radiant Transcendental Being who is the One-in-all.

Consciousness and substance coexist and intereact universally on all levels of manifest reality, from the most subtle and rarefied to the gross/physical, and thus consciousness is present in the most rudimentary forms of energy and matter, even subatomic particles. Nevertheless, for theoretical purposes of understanding, it is necessary to distinguish consciousness from energy/matter. Otherwise we run the risk of thinking that generating energetic effects in our bodies or in the environment is the same as changing consciousness.

Some spiritual seekers, failing to understand this distinction, become "energy junkies." They learn with fine detail how to manipulate energy inside themselves or attract energy to themselves from outside. They may generate effects in the body-mind which are often very dramatic, even overwhelming. They may, for example, experience great bursts of internal light, ecstatic mind-states, loss of body-awareness, blissful celestial sounds, skyrides of unearthly colors, and so forth. Yet when the experience is over, their consciousness has not changed a whit. They don't understand what occurred, nor do they seem to care to *radically* understand. After the internal pyrotechnics have subsided, it is consciousness alone which can bring understanding to the person. Without that reflection upon experience, without self-awareness of what it is which can observe experience or energy at all, they are not mystical, merely mystified. Their ego is still the dominant focus of awareness and the only effect of the experience is to sharpen their desire for still more experience (through drugs, sex, or other energy-arousing situations, including certain meditative practices which are not true or real meditation) rather than getting rid of the experiencer—the egocentric state of consciousness which seeks experience for personal gain rather than resting freely in God, the Source of all experience, the Condition of all conditions.

Ask yourself: What is "reflection upon experience"? It is essentially *transcendence* of experience. It is disengagement and disidentification from the experience in all its subjectivity so that understanding is gained through objectivity. Psychologically speaking, for liberation to occur, the entire universe must ultimately become an object of consciousness. Only when the cosmos—the entire realm of nature and phenomena—is transcended in consciousness can there be enlightenment. Yet in that moment of objective clarity and transcendence of all creation is the paradoxical discovery that one's true being includes all which is transcended. Transcendence is not mere negation. That, to repeat, is why enlightenment is described as that condition of consciousness which is totally involved in the universe yet also totally detached from the universe. And thus arises the yogic ideal of nonattachment, nonaversion: perfect equanimity, the unity of opposites.

Energetic effects may accompany changes in consciousness, and often do, but they are not at all necessary. Energy junkies don't understand that it is their own consciousness which first of all directs them toward an experience, prior to all manifestations of energy, and then imposes itself upon energy to create the experience sought. They don't understand that it is only because we are first of all *conscious* of our energies that we can work intelligently with and through our energies.

Furthermore, energy junkies compound their basic mistake of thinking that energy equals consciousness by then saying there are two forms of energy—positive and negative or masculine and feminine—with which to work. This is nonsense. There is no such thing as positive and negative or masculine and feminine energy; there is only energy—period.[1] The perceived duality of energy is a reflection of the mind perceiving the energy, not the energy itself. As Saint Paul put it: To the pure in heart all things are pure. There are positive and negative *effects,* but those effects are a function of how the energy is applied or experienced, and it is always consciousness which applies or directs or experiences energy in all its forms. The mind interprets things as positive or negative, according to its understanding (which is to say, according to its level of consciousness), but the energy itself remains undivided, as seamless as the universe itself.

Even healing, one of the best possible uses of energy, does not necessarily change consciousness in the healee. Remember the story of Jesus cleansing the ten lepers. Only one of them responded spiritually to Jesus' use of energy, because that one alone reflected in consciousness upon his experience. The other nine went their way without the least thought of expressing thanks to Jesus. Their awareness was not changed by the healing energy; they remained egoic, self-centered, bound.

The eye does not see itself and energy does not direct itself. It is always subject to direction and control by a senior influence. That influence is consciousness. Nothing—absolutely nothing—can be done with energy in and of itself to change consciousness. Enlightenment is not possible in any way whatsoever through the manipulation of energy, no matter how subtle or ethereal the energy, no matter how celestially vast the field of energy. All that does is produce phenomena, whereas enlightenment is transcendence of all phenomena. All that does is produce illusion and hallucination, whereas enlightenment is the clear perception of Reality through release of attention from all partial states and from all identification with phenomena. Transcendence does not deny or reject partial states, nor does it reject or deny phenomena. Transcendence simply sees them in perspective—as less than infinite and ultimate—so that attention rests freely in its source-condition, which is unbound consciousness, consciousness which does not recoil from infinity. That infinite consciousness is your primal identity, beyond all partial circumstances and conditional phenomena. And it is none other than God.

An incredible amount of energy-oriented nonsense occurs today in the name of higher consciousness. It leads people to become energy junkies, all because of the mistaken notion that consciousness and energy are the same thing. But they are not. The frenzied search energy junkies make for this or that "energy high" is (I have to say it) pathetic. It is sadly ironic that their glamorous, alluring notions about energy as the key to spiritual growth are *precisely* what prevents their own enlightenment. Some people urge you to wear crystals or gemstones to "cleanse and balance your aura" for spiritual growth. Others solemnly declare that you must meditate at rare "power points" of the planet or else sit inside a pyramid or other geometric form so you can "receive the positive energies." Still others say you cannot gain higher consciousness unless you receive an initiation from a guru who'll transfer vital force to you so that your chakras are opened and your kundalini energy is awakened. (So how do they explain Gopi Krishna's enlightenment—or the Buddha's?) But it is all—*all*—the work of Narcissus—ego—and it leads nowhere except to addiction, compulsion, seeking, and suffering: dukkha.

So long as something (other than the universe itself) is seen or conceived or experienced as an object of consciousness—as a *content of consciousness*—it is still only partial, less than the infinite, ultimate wholeness which is *consciousness itself*. The yogic "sword of discrimination" recognized long ago that consciousness or *chitshakti* must be distinguished from energy or *pranashakti*. The latter is the content of consciousness or that which is perceived. Chitshakti is consciousness itself or that which perceives. It is essentially the same distinction as the paired Sanskrit terms *Purusha* (spirit, Self) and *Prakriti* (matter, Nature). Enlightenment is the condition which understands their difference in the manifest universe and their ultimate unity at the Source of both, the perfect poise of Being-amid-becoming. Enlightenment is the condition of being aware of the universe *as* the universe—being cosmically conscious. It is the realization of the union of opposites—of Shiva/consciousness and Shakti/energy, of nirvana and samsara—and the transcendence of all separateness and all boundaries in the extraordinary, yet perfectly ordinary, experience of the cosmos being conscious of itself through an individual. And *that* is our condition, our matrix, our identity prior to all separation, division, and differentiation. As I have said before and will say again: There is only God.

PART **II**

SPIRIT—THE DESCENT OF THE DIVINE

Commentary

Human history is a process of ascent to godhead. That process is best described, individually and collectively, as evolution. Humanity is proceeding from a prepersonal state of simple animal consciousness through the personalized state of self-reflective, egoic consciousness to the transpersonal state of self-transcendence or consciousness beyond ego.

However, as mystics, myths, and mystery schools point out, ascent would not be possible unless there first was descent. We cannot spiritually lift ourselves by our own bootstraps. We cannot create higher consciousness from electrochemical reactions. Consciousness is immaterial; it cannot be squeezed from test tubes or neurons. It operates *through* them but cannot be reduced *to* them. As a plant grows toward the light, so does humanity yearn for God and greater awareness because, like a plant's inherent capacity to perceive and respond to light, there is a teleological design at work in us from the start. As Evelyn Underhill, author of the classic *Mysticism,* put it, "We recognize the growth of conscious mind from the humblest animal origins as consistent with the divine creative will . . ." (But, she added, "we have not seen the extent of this will.") Underhill echoed what Shakespeare said through Hamlet: "There's a divinity that shapes our ends, rough-hew them how we will."

That divinity is not simply external, transcendent, apart from the world. It is also, as I show throughout this book but especially in "What Is Spirituality?", internal and immanent (and also omnipresent). We are concerned with God because God is first of all involved with us. Discovery of "God within" and the human capacity for cultivating that immanence is the principle theme of the New Age movement. Underhill,

149

quoting Saint Augustine, observed, "He created us for Himself to continue His line of creation beyond nature to *more*."

I use the word "involve" in its metaphysical sense: the act of enfolding. Involution has two aspects: origination and preservation. The universe originated—exists—at all only because it is a form of God. God enfolds the universe; it inheres in God. The involutionary process by which God manifested it billions of years ago continues even now, this very instant, from moment to moment, sustaining and preserving that which was originally wrought. Without involution, without God's presence as what Teilhard de Chardin called the "withinness" of things, the cosmos would be instantly annihilated. With it the cosmos is unfolding and evolving, stellar sequence by stellar sequence.

Within that larger context, we humans have also been brought forth as a form of God. But we are not a static form. Like the cosmos, we are evolving. We have a purpose, a direction, a meaning: growth to godhood. Evolution is the natural fruition of God's plan for humanity.

As we're evolved, our idea of God has likewise evolved. Throughout history, in step with the expansion of human consciousness, there has been a deepening apprehension of the nature of God and an ever-finer expression of it. Of course, the atheist or rationalist maintains that the idea of God is merely an invention of the human mind, and that any evolution of the idea simply reflects humanity's increased capacity for conceptual thought imaginatively projected onto the heavens.

That is not the case, of course. Rather, the case is that God is Ultimate Reality and our understanding of the nature of God is a function of our state of consciousness. The atheist and rationalist simply have not seen through the limitations of their position, which is not so much wrong as incomplete because it is simply an intermediate stage of understanding. As we evolve in consciousness, we apprehend reality ever more clearly. In the enlightened state Ultimate Reality is apprehended directly, immediately, beyond all concepts, intellectual constructs, and social conditioning. One aspect of that apprehension is the *presence* of God—here, now, everywhere, always. God descended into the world by the act of creating it; God remains in the world by the act of sustaining it: involution.

That realization has been intuited by humanity since it first acquired human status, although the form of the realization was pale and distorted. But with each evolutionary advance came clearer, more illuminated perception.

The animism of paleolithic Man was apparently the earliest form of the human apprehension of God. Nature was thought to be animated by spiritual powers which took individuality—but not personality—as trees, rivers, mountains, lightning, clouds, the sun, and so forth, and humans could interact with those powers via ceremony and sacrifice. *Homo sapiens* at that time was still without a well-formed sense of egoic identity; the self was still sensed as collective, tribal, immersed in nature. The cave paintings of Altamira Font de Gaume and Lascaux depict this.

As human consciousness enlarged and the sense of self-operating in the race became more solidified, the religion of the Great Mother or Earth Mother arose. Matriarchy dominated human culture. This is the time, as Merlin Stone entitled his book, when God was a woman.

The next major change in the human understanding of God was polytheism. The transcendent realm was conceived as populated with divine forms, some human-like, some animal-like, but all with personality and distinctly human qualities, including gender. The emergence of polytheism in neolithic times was coincident with the emergence of a well-formed sense of ego in the most advanced members of humanity and a clear sense of being disengaged from nature, though still attuned to it. The "gods" emerged to human understanding about 5000 B.C., and with it a male-oriented urge to dominate nature. The feminine qualities present in culture were subdued by masculine aggression and quest for power—hallmarks of ego.

As the pace of human evolution accelerated, producing individuals who were capable of sustaining self-identity via a state of consciousness beyond ego, their enhanced awareness and perception showed still more clearly the nature of God. And thus emerged the next major phase of humanity's religio-spiritual understanding: monotheism. The "gods" were now understood as lesser beings—the divinities of the mid-heavens—who were subservient to the transcendent God-above-all-gods. Monotheism arose with the pharaoh Akhnaton in Egypt about 2000 B.C. The One God, although depicted as male, was actually understood to be genderless—neither male nor female but beyond or above or prior to the division into the sexes.

Akhnaton was clearly, for his time, an evolved member of the race. In fact, as I explain more fully in "The Sparkle of Spirit," the pharaonic rulers were themselves perceived as semidivine. They were regarded as clearly and qualitatively above the mass of humanity. Likewise, around the world, leaders and rulers of the tribe or community were seen as god-men and god-women, having both human and divine qualities.

That view still holds forth in the consciousness of many people today, indicating their own level of development to be short of even self-actualization or fully-functioning ego. Think of various recent world events in which charismatic leaders have commanded millions to do their bidding, no matter how absurd or brutal the command might be. Think of the childish adulation given by the masses to glamourous film stars and singers. The adoring followers of such people have not yet developed a sense of self strong enough to support personal autonomy and to see the superficiality of their world view. Their identity still resides largely outside themselves, in the collectivity and its leader. It is the leader—the chieftain, king, or emperor—who thinks for them and provides in his or her person an external symbol of higher consciousness and a conduit to the god-realm or, if a celebrity in a secular society, who gives a vicarious and false sense of transcendence of the human condition.

But as Ken Wilber points out in *Up from Eden,* his brilliant study of human evolution, by the sixth century B.C., a few members of the human race had attained to the ultimate state of consciousness: enlightenment. Buddha, Lao Tzu, Rama, and, shortly after, Socrates, Plato, Zoroaster, Pythagoras, Jesus, and others demonstrated self-transcendence to the point where they could say, as Jesus did, that "I and the Father are one," meaning their sense of self-identity was totally divested of ego and totally invested in the Divine Domain, the transcendental realm from which all creation arises.

Such evolutionarily advanced people were so far beyond the understanding of the masses that they were perceived as incarnations of God. The term most commonly used to describe that condition is *avatar,* a Sanskrit word meaning literally "he descends" (*avator* in Hindi). An avatar is said to be a deity who voluntarily assumes a physical body to participate in creation. An avatar is the divine in human form—God walking the Earth among men and women. More specifically, according to Hindu tradition, an avatar is an incarnation of Vishnu, and there have been nine such incarnations, with a tenth still to come. The avatar concept itself originated about the sixth century B.C., according to Daniel Bassuk in his 1987 *Incarnation in Hinduism and Christianity.*

Avatars, Bassuk tells us, are traditionally regarded as perfect beings, not perfected beings. Ichor flows through their veins, not blood. They are believed to have been born in a supernatural way, to have no karma to expiate, to remember all their previous lives, and to be conscious of their mission from birth. Avatars, from the traditional point of view, originate in heaven, not on Earth. They are qualitatively different from the spiritually liberated human who gradually becomes divinized, enlightened, freed from the wheel of death-and-rebirth. Ancient thought holds that while it is humanly possible to become a man-god, it is impossible for a human to become a god-man, for, as Bassuk points out, "when matter is spiritualized it is through the will and actions of man, but when spirit materializes as in the case of the Avatar, it is by the will of God alone" (p. 6).

That is the traditional view. A new age, however, would end certain views and traditions. That is precisely the case here. The traditional understanding of avatars must be revised as the ongoing evolution of consciousness makes clear to us that the received view originated in the minds of people who were to one degree or another still in the prepersonal, pre-egoic condition. If knowledge is structured in consciousness, then the portrait of avatars which emerged from such consciousness clearly can be improved upon by those who have ascended above the masses in their perception of reality. The concept of avatar is no longer tenable in its traditional sense. If Jesus was a god-man, how can we explain the fact that blood, not ichor, flowed from him on the cross? Likewise, if Buddha was a god-man, how can we explain the fact that he died of food poisoning? Moreover, we have the testimony of avatars themselves—notably Jesus and Buddha—that their condition of consciousness is attainable by others.

In short, the traditional understanding of avatars is a distorted understanding which needs to be demythologized and divested of its superstition, romance, and ignorance. Human evolution has reached a state where avatarhood is becoming comprehensible and frequent. (Unfortunately for undiscerning spiritual seekers, it is also being claimed by some people who have a degree of transpersonal understanding but are still egoically enough driven to seek self-aggrandizement through assertions of avatarhood. As the enlightened spiritual teacher Da Love-Ananda remarked a few years ago, we've got avatars all over the front yard.)

It is time to see Spirit through the light of science. Not *by* the light of science, of course, because that would be reductionism. But science has given us a powerful understanding of the evolutionary process. With that understanding, the workings of Spirit become ever more illuminated. Our understanding of the avatar concept—the descent of the divine—is deepened by humanity's collective effort to ascend into higher realms of reality via science.

With that meeting of science and Spirit, it becomes clear that the *jivanmukta,* the liberated mortal who ascends in consciousness to the Divine Domain, is not qualitatively different from those beings who are presumed to descend from the eternal to the temporal, from the unconditional to the conditioned, from the infinite to the finite. For deity is not simply incarnate in Man—it is incarnate in all life. If humanity is the flowering of life, then avatars are the flowering of humanity. That has now become obvious; it has also become obvious as a possibility for the human race on a species-wide basis. That is what any movement toward a New Age must be all about. The Great Ones, Masters, Mahatmas, Adepts, and Avatars of history are, in simplest terms, the elder brothers of the human race. They are men, not spirits, G. de Purucker tells us in *Masters of the Occult Path:*

> They are men who have evolved through self-devised efforts in individual evolution, always advancing forwards and upwards until they attained the lofty supremacy that now they hold. They were not so created by any extra-cosmic

Deity, but they are men who have become what they are by means of inward
spiritual striving, by spiritual and intellectual yearning, by aspiration to be
greater and better, nobler and higher. They are not what they are by any
favoritism either of a god or of Fate, but have merely run ahead of the great
multitude of men (pp. 5–6).

They point the way for us to become deified. They show that, from a
evolutionary perspective, we are humans having a spiritual experience,
but that from an involutionary perspective, we are Spirit having a human
experience. In Chapter 21 I show in detail what this means about the life
and teaching of Jesus. Sri Aurobindo (see "Karma, Reincarnation, and
Evolution"), himself an enlightened being who was sometimes described
by naïve devotees as an avatar, explicitly denied that such was the case. He
declared that anyone who thought he was just another avatar come to
start another religion or to enlarge the number of gods by one had sadly
misunderstood him. Avatar-worship and sectarianism had no place in his
teaching, except to be recognized as holdovers of an earlier time which
need to be discarded in the name of consciousness expansion and higher
evolution. The descent of the Supermind is intended for all humanity.
"The full emergence of supermind may be accomplished by a sovereign
manifestation, a descent into earth-consciousness and a rapid assumption of its powers and disclosing of its forms and the creation of a
supramental race and a supramental life: this must be the full result of its
action in Nature," he wrote in *The Mind of Light* (pp. 108–109).

The divine has indeed descended and has been, without question,
beautifully represented in certain noble specimens of humanity who were
forerunners of a higher race. But the descent is not sporadic and momentary; it is ongoing in a lawful manner. In the realm of physics, it
operates as the forces which sustain the cosmos. In the biological realm,
it operates, as Gopi Krishna put it in his elucidation of the kundalini
experience, as a biological process applying to all of the human family.

In fact, this can be discerned in the very myth of the avatar. Tradition
maintains there have been nine incarnations of Vishnu, who, according
to Manly Palmer Hall in his 1932 *Man—The Grand Symbol of the
Mysteries*, "in his most abstract form, signifies the Divine Spirit either of
the universe or of man" moving from form to form and is "the true
explanation of the transitions constantly taking place in Nature" (p. 107).
Vishnu is the second god of the Hindu trinity, being regarded as the
supreme god, the preserver and sustainer, encompassing Brahma the
creator and Shiva the destroyer. The first incarnation of Vishnu was
Matsya the Fish, divinity of the primal age. The second was Kurma the
Tortoise. Next came Varaha the Boar, followed by Narasimha the Lion-
Man. Fifth was Vamana the Dwarf. Parashu Rama, "the man with the
axe," was the sixth incarnation of Vishnu. Ramachandra, hero of the

great Indian epic, the *Ramayana,* was the seventh. Krishna (and, in some versions, Balarama the Plowman) was the eighth avatar, Buddha the ninth. (Although this is the same god-man revered by Buddhists, they do not attribute avatar status to the Enlightened One.) The tenth avatar of Vishnu is Kalki, who, it is believed, has yet to appear on Earth, but will do so when it is time for a righteous age to begin.

These strange-sounding and unlikely appearing divinities, taken literally, are simply another form of religious superstition and have no significance for evolving humanity's present condition. But taken mythologically—that is, as what Bassuk calls "a rich, meaningful and significant interpretation of reality"—the avatar concept becomes an insightful parable of evolution.

The history of evolution is presented this way. Eons ago, the first forms of life emerged on Earth; the fish avatar symbolizes that. Then amphibians gained ascendence; Kurma the tortoise represents that stage of Earth's life. The next avatar is a boar—a mammal which figuratively indicates the succession of higher life forms. Then comes Narasimha, half man and half lion, suggestive of the stage when humanity began to develop. Although it was hominid, no longer anthropoid, it was still far from being the genus *Homo*—perhaps *Australopithecus*. Vamana the Dwarf is better understood as Vamana the short man or not-yet-complete-man. Parashu Rama, or the man with the axe, can be thought of as the beginnings of true humanity, when the Neanderthal people's stone and bone technology distinguished them from their non-toolmaking or, at best, extremely crude toolmaking predecessors. The next avatar, Rama, was a hunter who used a bow and arrow—an invention of the Cro-Magnon people. Balarama the Plowman is emblematic of the emergence of agricultural society as human evolution surpassed the hunter-gatherer stage. Krishna, whose flute delights all who hear it, is the artist, the deepening esthetic and spiritual dimension of human consciousness. Buddha's significance as the most recent avatar should be obvious: He represents the full expression of the human potential in the individual. Kalki, then, symbolizes the full appearance of that potential throughout the race as a higher humanity.

Madame Helena P. Blavatsky, founder of Theosophy, pointed out the evolutionary aspect of the avatar myth at the end of the last century. In *Isis Unveiled,* she observed that in the myth:

> we see traced the gradual evolution and transformation of all species out of the ante-Silurian mud of Darwin . . . Beginning with the Azoic time, corresponding to the *ilus* in which Brahma implants the creative germ, we pass through the Paleozoic and Mesozoic times, covered by the first and second incarnations as the fish and tortoise; and the Cenozoic, which is embraced by the incarnations in the animal and semi-human forms of the boar and man-lion; and we come to the

fifth and crowning geological period, designated as the 'era of mind, or age of man,' whose symbol in the Hindu mythology is the dwarf—the first attempt of nature at the creature of men . . . and then . . . Parasu Rama physically, a perfect, spiritually, an undeveloped entity, until [we see] mankind personified by one god-like man, to the apex of physical and spiritual perfection—a god on earth.

Manly Palmer Hall pointed to an additional aspect of the evolution-ary import of avatars: ". . .the analogies between the origin of life upon the planet and the development of the embryo in the womb are appar-ent." He finds similarities between the nine avatars and the characteristics of the prenatal human's nine months of intrauterine growth. "The tenth avatara of Vishnu has no correspondence in the prenatal state of man, but rather corresponds to his whole life after birth . . . Vishnu, 'he who pervades,' comes forth for the last time not as a man but rather through man. He is the invisible god who rules in the chariot of the human heart. The world awaits the coming of its Redeemer—the perfect man. To the philosopher, this perfect man is rather the perfection in man. The immortality that lay asleep in the germ from which man sprang awakens and, in the course of countless ages, releases itself, tincturing all bodies and lifting all men into the perfection of its own state" (p. 119).

The essays in this section expand on that theme. I discuss the mean-ing of "divine descent" and how it operates in us, as individuals and as a race. In an Afterword, I expand on the concept of *Homo noeticus* as the citizens of a new age.

A passage in *Messages of Sri Aurobindo and the Mother* eloquently summarizes the perspective I offer here—a perspective which sees involu-tion and evolution working in complementary fashion as aspects of Ultimate Wholeness, and matter and Spirit as complementary ex-pressions of the One Reality.

> The process of evolution has been the development from and in inconscient Matter of a subconscient and then a conscious Life, a conscious mind first in animal life and then fully in conscious and thinking man, the highest preset achievement of evolutionary Nature. The achievement of mental being is at present her highest and tends to be regarded as her final work; but it is possible to conceive a still further step of the evolution: Nature may have in view beyond the imperfect mind of man a consciousness that passes out of the mind's igno-rance and possesses truth as its inherent right and nature. There is truth-consciousness as it is called in the Veda, a supermind, as I have termed it, possessing Knowledge, not having to seek after it and constantly miss it. In one of the Upanishads a being of knowledge is stated to be the next step above the mental being; into that the soul has to rise and through it to attain the perfect bliss of spiritual existence. If that could be achieved as the next evolutionary step of Nature here, then she would be fulfilled and we could conceive of the perfec-tion of life even here, its attainment of a full spiritual living even in this body or it may be in a perfected body. We could even speak of a divine life on earth; our human dream of perfectibility would be accomplished and at the same time the

aspiration to a heaven on earth common to several religions and spiritual seers and thinkers.

The ascent of the human soul to the supreme Spirit is that soul's highest aim and necessity, for that is the supreme reality; but there can be too the descent of the Spirit and its powers into the world and that would justify the existence of the material world also, give a meaning, a divine purpose to the creation and solve its riddle. East and West could be reconciled in the pursuit of the highest and largest ideal, Spirit embrace Matter and Matter find its own truly reality and the hidden Reality in all things in the Spirit.

14

The Sparkle of Spirit

Have you ever wondered why people value gold and jewels? What makes them precious? You can't eat them or live in them or keep your body warm with them. They have no utilitarian value, so what makes them desirable?

The answer, I think, is that they are primarily visible reminders of divinity. Think about that the next time you hear someone say "Oh, what a divine necklace" or "What a heavenly ring" or "It's simply out of this world!" There is greater wisdom in those words than the speaker is probably aware of.

The simple truth is that gold and jewels are precious because originally, early in human history, they were considered tangible symbols of a higher state of being, a state characterized by radiance and permanence. Because they were so durable, one might say eternal, and because they seemed to come from a world of timelessness and light, they were reminders of paradise. They still have that quality and we still experience them that way, although for most people the experience is subconscious. Nevertheless, gold (more broadly, precious metals) and gems are fundamentally sparkles of the Spirit, symbols of the Ultimate Reality from which creation springs.

Let's think about that a bit more. Think, for example, about why royalty wear crowns. Why do they place gold and jewels upon their heads? The answer: It creates an effect emblematic of the greater reality originally to be found embodied in rulers and leaders which has been lost through the ages.

What was that quality? It's the same thing we see implied by the halo depicted around angels' and saints' heads. A crown represents a halo, which is the sign of divinity or beings from an order of creation beyond the human.

But even a halo is only a symbol of something else—something the artist could not represent directly and realistically. What is that something?

Both crowns and halos, when we penetrate to their true meaning, are symbolic forms of what clairvoyants call the aura, the envelope of light surrounding the human body. The word *aura* itself is derived from the Latin *aurum*, "gold." The color, intensity, and shape of the aura are said to be indicators of a person's physical, mental, and spiritual condition. A highly spiritual person—one who is deeply attuned to God or to Brahman, to Allah, to the Tao, to the Cosmic Intelligence, the Divine Wisdom, the Transcendental Source—can be identified by his or her aura, it is said, because it has an unmistakable golden-white color. It flashes and scintillates like sunlight and has its greatest dimension and intensity around the person's head, where it is called the corona, like the ring of light seen around the sun during an eclipse.

That is what crowns and halos represent, and they are associated by tradition only with royalty, with holy people, and with supernatural beings such as angels because when human society arose leaders and heads of state were quite literally considered god-kings or agents of divinity. There was no difference between a spiritual leader and a political leader. Those who led the people in either sphere of activity were one and the same. (This condition, theocracy, continues today. The Dalai Lama of Tibet, the now-deceased Ayatollah Khomeini, and, until World War II, the Emperor of Japan are examples of spiritual leaders as heads of state. But there the similarity ends; the Dalai Lama is personally much more enlightened than either of the others.) The god-kings had charisma, they had extraordinary powers, they were literally power-full. And there was no question in the minds of the people ruled because, at least according to esoteric teachings such as those of the mystic scientist Rudolf Steiner, people in general had the faculty of clairvoyance and other psychic abilities such as telepathy.

These psychic faculties were widespread in the population. Thus, if you were clairvoyant and could see auras as readily as you see your clothing or food, you would have no doubt about the aura of the king or queen or chieftain you followed. Everyone would know it and agree on it. It would quite literally be common sense, a commonly shared perception, to do so. The aura would be a directly perceived indicator of the special qualities embodied in that person and would be without question or doubt the mark of his or her right to govern, to rule, to direct the lives of people in a manner best suited to their happiness and well-being.

What seems to have happened over the ages, however, is that, first, as the power of intellect emerged, people lost their psychic abilities—their channels of supersensory perception—and, second, at the same time rulers and leaders lost their ability to govern wisely because they lost their contact with higher wisdom, the divine source of our being. In short, the sparkle of spirit has apparently dimmed since humanity's primeval existence.

I say "apparently" because I am stating the case as it is commonly believed among many New Age people and spiritual seekers. From my perspective, there is something else going on in history: something which is regenerative, not degenerative, something which is evolutionary rather than devolutionary. To anticipate for a moment, I'll simply say that the sparkle of spirit has in no way dimmed. It has only appeared to do so because its purpose has been better served that way.

The true situation, I think, was just the opposite of what is widely believed and is best described in Ken Wilber's *Up from Eden,* a study of humanity's origin and divine destiny. What actually was lost to humanity with the emergence of intellectual-rational thought is a rudimentary state of consciousness characterized by a simple sense of self. That primitive mode of awareness invested self-identity in the group and its ruler, much as a herd of animals is led by a dominant one. Individuality is essentially impossibile for this simple self-sense; only the chieftain, only the king or queen or emperor has a strong enough sense of separate selfhood (in other words, enough ego-strength) to stand out alone, on his own, and it is precisely that individuality which brings him to a position of leadership. For others, existence will be a life of fellowship. For them, separation from the tribe or clan will be akin to depersonalization and loss of identity.

To put the matter briefly, what was lost was only a simple form of psychic perception and primary-process knowing. These are actually pre-egoic faculties, seen in young children and primitive peoples still in tribal consciousness. And the sense of contact with the divine was only a rudimentary awareness of a transhuman condition—a sense which, from the egoic point of view, creates the illusion of greater harmony with Earth and heaven when there was actually no greater harmony, only less self-distinction between Man and nature.

That is not to say there is no harmony to be attained. There is, and we can attain it, but only by going *beyond ego* to a higher level of consciousness, a higher self-knowing. Regression to an earlier, simple mode of consciousness is impossible for contemporary humanity, although many people in the New Age movement mistakenly think so. Their attempts to adopt a more "natural" lifestyle are really movements toward a more primitive mindstyle. That is not the simplicity and higher innocence of mystic union with God; it is the simplistic, naïve reduction of one's mental potential. The evolutionary thrust of human affairs says: There's no turning back. There can only be *progression*.

If so, then, how can we begin to enter into direct and conscious contact with the Spirit? How can we move from simply observing light— the glitter of jewels and the shine of gold—to being light, to being enlightened? How can we make the experience of divinity or awareness of God our constant, living condition? How can we become as elevated and wise and skillful and helpful and as worthy of reverence as a true god-king?

The Indian holy man Sathya Sai Baba put it very simply: First you seek the light, next you're in the light, then you are the light. But you don't have to search out a holy man in India for that experience, because God's love and light are omnipresent. They can be found everywhere, and sometimes in the most surprising way. Listen to what Canadian psychiatrist Richard Maurice Bucke said at the end of his 1901 classic *Cosmic Consciousness*, in which he wrote about himself in the third person. Here's what happened to Bucke:

> He and two friends had spent the evening reading Wordsworth, Shelley, Keats, Browning, and especially Whitman. They parted at midnight, and he had a long drive in a hansom. His mind, deeply under the influence of the ideas, images and emotions called up by the reading and talk of the evening, was calm and peaceful. He was in a state of quiet, almost passive enjoyment.
>
> All at once, without warning of any kind, he found himself wrapped around, as it were, by a flame-colored cloud. For an instant he thought of fire—some sudden conflagration in the great city. The next [instant] he knew that the light was within himself.
>
> Directly after there came upon him a sense of exultation, of immense joyousness, accompanied or immediately followed by an intellectual illumination quite impossible to describe. Into his brain streamed one momentary lightning-flash of the Brahmic splendor which ever since lightened his life. Upon his heart fell one drop of the Brahmic Bliss, leaving thenceforward for always an aftertaste of Heaven. Among other things, he did not come to believe, he saw and knew that the Cosmos is not dead matter but a living Presence, that the soul of man is immortal, that the universe is so built and ordered that without any peradventure all things work together for the good of each and all, that the foundation principle of the world is what we call love and that the happiness of every one is in the long run absolutely certain. He claims that he learned more within the few seconds during which the illumination lasted than in previous months or even years of study, and that he learned much that no study could ever have taught.[1]

Bucke's experience fundamentally transformed his life, and he began a study of those great people in history whom the world has regarded as illuminated, enlightened, in higher consciousness. What he concluded was this: Evolution has not stopped. The human race is slowly moving toward a transhuman, godlike state. It is slowly evolving to a condition as far beyond us as we are presently beyond the animals and as animals are beyond the vegetal level of life. The great geniuses, the spiritual teachers, the mystics, sages, and saviors of history are best understood as indicators of the coming race. They are evolutionary forerunners of the new breed which is to inherit the Earth. The fundamental difference between them and us is not an exterior change of appearance but an interior one, a change of consciousness. And so the higher humanity will be one in which there is a new receptivity to the light of creation, a fuller manifestation of the sparkle of Spirit.

Five decades after Bucke wrote his book, the French Jesuit anthropologist Pierre Teilhard de Chardin spoke of noogenesis—the birth of higher consciousness—in his magnificent *The Phenomenon of Man*. Like Bucke, he saw a potential in the human race which is still to be realized. "Man," he wrote, "is not yet zoologically mature. Psychologically he has not spoken his last word. In one form or another something ultra-human is being born which, through the direct or indirect effect of socialization, cannot fail to make its appearance in the near future: a future which is not simply unfolding of Time, but which is being constructed in advance of us."[2] About the same time, the Indian mystic-philosopher Sri Aurobindo described "the mind of light" which would be displayed in us as the human journey toward perfection continued. *The Mind of Light* testifies to the descent of the Supermind.

Since Bucke wrote his book we've had two terrible world wars and many lesser ones. We've seen economic depressions, political chaos, and social upheavals. And, in more recent years, we've added the threat of nuclear annihilation, environmental destruction, and biological/chemical warfare. This sort of makes Bucke, Aurobindo, and Teilhard de Chardin look like foolish dreamers, doesn't it?

Perhaps, but only if evidence which supports and advances their view is lacking. Is there nothing but darkness in this world—nothing but blind selfish instincts, nothing but greed and aggression which seek to reduce life to the lowest level of brutality, masked only by a thin veneer of "civilized" behavior? Is existence what novelist Joseph Conrad described in *Heart of Darkness* (and, following him, filmmaker Francis Ford Coppola in *Apocalypse Now*) as "the horror, the horror"?

I say there is something else. And I'm not alone. In 1977, for example, a Gallup Poll found a ground swell in religion, with tens of millions of Americans being energized by this spiritual renewal movement. Gallup remarked that the United States appeared to be in an early stage of a profound religious revival.

Another Gallup Poll in the early 1980s found that an estimated eight million Americans had undergone a near-death experience (NDE), which is significant in light of the effects an NDE has on people. Researchers have learned that NDEers undergo a remarkable transformation as a result of having died and revived. Their lives are reoriented in terms of values and behavior. It can be said, in a highly simplified way, that they awaken to love and selfless service. Their values shift from materialism to spirituality, from careless disregard for others to caring concern, from insensitivity to the environment to a respect for nature, from egotistic pursuits to community-minded activities.

These are just two indicators of a widespread search today for release of the human potential and a conscious reconnection with the infinite. There are many others. Look at the sales of books such as *Jonathan Livingston Seagull, The Aquarian Conspiracy,* the Don Juan series by Carlos Castaneda, and various New Age titles. Look at the proliferation of personal-growth centers and development organizations which are consulting even for mainstream industries and Fortune 500 corporations. Look at the integration of meditation and yoga techniques into medicine for stress management and holistic health care. And recall the many other indications I noted in the Introduction.

Call it a great awakening, a rebirth of the Spirit, a consciousness revolution, the coming of the Aquarian Age, or the New Age. Whatever the name, a new and growing phenomenon is making itself felt today throughout society as a significant part of the population seeks a higher state of being. People want to grow—physical, mentally, and spiritually. They want to actualize their inner resources. They want to rise above the old forms and institutions which limited freedom and understanding and self-expression. They want to rise above the conventional values and ways of life which brought about the suffering and oppression we see in the world. They want to experience the transcendent dimensions of their existence and bring that experience back to Earth and anchor it here in society. They want to fix it in the world. They want to transform the groaning Earth and lighten its heavy load.

This is a tremendously exciting situation because no longer is society a place where an occasional illumined teacher or mystic appears among us. Now there are larger and larger numbers of spiritually motivated men and women emerging from the masses of humanity and directing people's consciousness to the light of Spirit. It's becoming almost commonplace.

Of course, there is a lot of faddishness, nonsense, and ripoff happening in the name of higher consciousness. All that glitters is not gold. You've got to be alert for it because in the spiritual supermarket there are, frankly, a lot of hustlers passing counterfeit coins and jewelery. Pretty soon you'll probably be able to join a Guru-of-the-Month Club. And you'll probably see books such as *Yoga for Self-Promotion, Win His*

Heart through Zen Cooking, Meditate Your Way to Better Grades, and *Let God Boost Your Profits.* That's not what spiritual growth is all about, of course.

So we have to be careful not to fall into the many traps and dead ends which clearly exist on the path of self-unfoldment. Substituting cult for culture isn't enough. In the search for transcendence of the human condition, in the search for mystical experience, people sometimes mistakenly accept substitutes for God. These substitutes can be dangerous and can even degenerate to the tragic level of Jonestown, Guyana, where in the 1970s a charismatic but psychotic and deadly leader convinced his naïve followers that he alone was God and triggered the mass suicide-execution of more than 900 people.

No, the situation is one which requires you to build for yourself what I call a spiritual crap detector, an inherent ability like the aura-reading of our ancestors. Then you run claims through the crap detector to see how the needle reads. For there will be more Jim Joneses, I think, who'll emerge, get notice, and gather a following. We must be alert to these people: They run the needle into the red danger area.

Now, with that cautionary advice, consider what might happen if a large number of genuinely enlightened people should appear in society at the same time. Think about it—enlightened leaders in government and industry; in education, science, religion, business. The result could well be transformative of society itself. In fact, the result could lead to an evolutionary change, an advancement of the entire human race to a higher state of being.

That, I suggest, is precisely what is happening today. Many of the events in the news today are, from my perspective, signs that a higher form of humanity is emerging. Amid all the dissatisfied groping and frantic seeking, what is coming to pass today is not a communications gap, not a generation gap but rather a species gap. The chaos and confusion and societal unrest around us are signs of what I call "moral evolution." Think about the movements toward political reform, educational reform, ecological reform, nutritional reform, medical reform, judicial reform—social reformation in general. And think about the greatly accelerated interest and exploration in psychotechnologies, in spiritual disciplines and sacred traditions. To me, these are signs that a higher humanity is coming onto the planet and asserting its right to life.

A new species, *Homo noeticus,* is making its way onto the surface of the globe, and the result is a big sorting-out process among people. They're trying to find out what species they belong to. They sense something is wrong, something isn't working right in society, but they're not quite sure what it is.

Now, this can be terribly painful and anxiety-provoking—to stand

AMEN

with one foot in the old world and one foot in the new, sensing that a great gulf or gap is directly beneath you. But the marvelous and hopeful thing is that Nature, in its wisdom, has given us the wherewithal to take conscious, voluntary control of our own evolution. We can systematically work on ourselves in a safe, reliable manner which brings down the light, which draws the sparkle of spirit to us and helps us make a quantum leap over the species gap. How? That's what meditation and other spiritual disciplines are all about. The test of their value is whether they are in tune with the biological imperative to evolve, to advance the entire fabric of life in refinement and intensity of consciousness.

I daresay that you, by virtue of reading this, feel kinship with this emerging, evolving race. You sense you belong to it because it is in tune with the evolutionary purpose of life, with our human potential, which is to grow into higher and higher states of consciousness and ultimately return to the godhead which evoked us in the first place.

Through their experience of higher consciousness, our mystics, saints, sages, and spiritual geniuses were able to foresee across the centuries the vast sweep of human destiny—a climb from darkness to illumination, from savagery to a godlike condition, from blindness to "the light which lighteth the world." They were able to see the human race poised midway between the apes and the angels, ready to become fully the gods-in-hiding we are now.

This vision has been preserved for us and handed down through the ages until now, because so many people are personally experiencing for themselves a vision of the future of human evolution, we are in a condition where sweeping planetwide transformation can occur. This is the start of the long-sought Kingdom, the utopian dream becoming reality.

But it is not inevitable. The choice to actualize it is ours. We have the means to accomplish it within us. And we have the necessary operating instructions and technical manuals to do it in the form of sacred scriptures and spiritual teachings of holy men and women throughout history who have discovered the sparkle of Spirit within themselves, this evolutionary potential, and recognized it as a gift from the Creator. They have offered their lives to us as examples, as models, as guides to higher consciousness and world transformation.

That alone, however, won't do it. We must apply the teachings. We must install in our lives the instructions preserved by sacred traditions and spiritual paths. We must understand that the day of the god-king is past and will not come again except as we ourselves become god-kings and god-queens. We must actualize what is latent within us. We must realize it—make it real by letting our light shine forth. For too long now, humanity has looked upon its god-kings and saviors as something completely beyond what humans might themselves become. Thus, people have worshiped rather than revered them. People have made personality cults out of what should be understood as transpersonal events. And this immature understanding is exactly what has led to religious wars and the Guyana jungle tragedy.

The genuine spiritual teachers of history did not call upon people to worship them, but to honor them by following their examples and their teachings, by practicing them and putting them into action in their own lives. Those teachings and those examples have at their center the development of a new and higher state of consciousness—God-consciousness, the peace which passeth understanding, the direct experience of divinity dwelling in us, now and forever, creating us, preserving us, urging us to ever higher states of being.

The real significance of our god-kings and saviors is not that they were human like us but that we are gods like them—or at least have the potential to be. The Cosmic Intelligence has provided it, implanted it, and instructed us in it. That is the sparkle of Spirit.

But it's not going to be activated magically by a touch of the hand or some romantic event out of a fairy tale. The choice to unfold your human potential is no one's but your own. No amount of gold or jewels will do it for you, but if you once experience the sparkle of Spirit, you'll never be the same. And then no amount of gems and precious metals will satisfy the craving you'll have for more of the true spiritual light. It's addictive but, unlike drugs, the sparkle of Spirit is regenerative, not degenerative. God-intoxication is the point of human existence. Any others ultimately prove unsatisfying and self-defeating.

There will never be a better world until there are better people in it. In order for that to occur, we must all start with ourselves. And in doing so, we become, in a sense, co-creators with God—co-creators of a renewed world on its way to paradise, as it was in the beginning. And therefore, as it was in our mythic beginning, we should all say to ourselves "Let there be light, and let it begin with me."

15

The Spirit of Creativity and the Creative Spirit

The path of all . . . leads from being a creation of God to becoming co-creator with Him.

Ernst Lehrs, *Man or Matter*

The greatest art results from a process in which the artist transcends his usual sense of individuality, egotism, separation from existence. Creativity is a process of self-transcendence which brings the creator deeply, intimately in touch with the Creator or Ultimate Reality—the Source of all knowledge, beauty, goodness. Rightly considered, creativity is a process of God-discovery—the God beyond God, as Paul Tillich put it, directing our attention past anthropomorphic concepts of divinity to the living reality which can never be adequately conceptualized, but only realized.

Time after time, the world's greatest artists, musicians, sculptors, inventors, scientists, writers, dancers, and so forth have testified to the transcendent dimension of the creative process: "It wasn't me doing it." "It was something higher working through me." "I seemed to see myself from a great distance while the work was going on, as if I were simply a channel for it from a higher source."

The act of creation, then, is one in which the individual attunes himself deeply to the very foundation of the universe, the primal dimension which, astrophysically speaking, is constantly creating the cosmos anew from moment to moment by awesome forces which can be described as Love or that which unifies. If those forces were to cease

168

operating, the universe would instantly be annihilated. Thus, Love sustains the universe. That attunement to Love, that alignment to the transcendent source, that opening of our little, everyday self to the foundations of the cosmos brings experience which has traditionally defied description but belongs to the realm of mysticism.

The mystic creator discovers his true identity to be one with all creation, precisely as God is One. Then, having realized his divinity, the mystic creator brings his experience "down level" by translating the formless into form, the speechless into speech, the ineffable into the conceptual.

But always there remains in the completed work a sense of the numinous, the profound source from which it was drawn. Its creative energies work on the consciousness of the viewer, the listener, the audience. It sends little tendrils of godness and goodness through the cracks in our ego-armor, tickling our stony sensibilities . . . teasing our suppressed senses . . . offering joy, peace, and love . . . awakening us to our potential for fuller, richer living.

It was exactly that understanding which led James Joyce to have Stephan Dedalus say in *A Portrait of the Artist as a Young Man,* "The artist [is] like the God of creation. . . ." At the novel's end, Dedalus declares his intent "to forge in the smithy of my soul the uncreated conscience of my race."

The artist, Joyce implies, aims at nothing less than effecting a profound change of consciousness in humanity—a change which would eliminate the egoic state of mind which acts without conscience against fellow humans, creating only suffering, mistrust, hatred, confusion, despair.

Conscience is a "knowing with" or "knowing together"—the capacity for sensing or experiencing life as if we were someone else and thus able to know how our acts will feel or seem to that person. Conscience is that empathy which allows us to "walk a mile in another's shoes." We act in good conscience because we know feelingly that to do otherwise will break what novelist John Fowles calls the eleventh commandment: Thou shalt not commit pain.

This brings us to destruction, the other side of the creation coin. World mythologies recognize the aspect of God which destroys, consumes, devours: Kali, the Great Flood, Armageddon, The Great Cleansing. But God's destruction is conscious and part of the mysterious process by which existence is sustained and evolution proceeds.

Most human destruction is simply creativity unaware of itself. Our inherent drive for self-transcendence, our godward urge gets pathetically suppressed and distorted, and may become pathological. When that happens, we turn on ourselves in anger, hatred, blind aggression, and naked fury. The sad story which follows is man's perennial inhumanity to man: wars, slavery, crusades and jihads, gulags, "scorched earth," genocide, and, lately, the looming threat of nuclear annihilation and global ecocide.

What's going on here, and why? As I said, human destruction is only creativity unaware of itself. All aggression, all suffering can be traced to the human ego. Ego is that self-centered attempt to play God instead of surrendering oneself to the bliss, the ecstasy of recognition that prior to ego, prior to the sense of separate self which fears that otherness will smother it and make it give up its individuality, its false identity—*all* is God. To protect itself from seeing through the illusion of separate self, ego seeks to refashion the universe as if the ego were ultimate. Humanity-unaware strives for immortality, permanence, freedom from all which threatens its illusory sense of security. It strives for it by trying to impress its identity onto all creation. That is the pride of Lucifer, the sin of Satan: I shall bend all reality to my will; I shall create heaven and Earth in my image.

So the drive and energy behind creativity are not sufficient in themselves to produce great art or great anything. Without wisdom, without self-awareness, without attunement to Truth, the result is at best flawed, at worst deadly. "He was an artist, not an angel," a musician said of a deceased rock group member known for the riotous ways which led to a very mixed-up life and, ultimately, his death. High intelligence or special talent is no substitute for the character refinement and value-realization which lead to love-wisdom. Given all these, however, the result is sublime: Beethoven's ninth symphony, Michelangelo's Sistine Chapel frescoes, Joyce's *Ulysses,* Hokusai's "Breaking Wave."

A creative person can't get enough time and materials for all he wants to do. He is brimming with energy and ideas. He is enthusiastic about his work. Enthusiasm: from the Greek *en theos,* literally "God within" or "inspired" but better understood as "filled with God," "overflowing with a sense of divinity," or "one who experiences the presence of God." Not the conceptual God, not the anthropomorphic God, but the Living Presence beyond all categories of thought and intellect which is the source of all wisdom, all learning, all science, all art in precisely the sense Einstein meant when he remarked that the highest form of insight is mysticism.

But for all his enthusiasm, the creator is also disciplined and aims at mastery of the discipline. The truth is, you've got to learn the rules before you can creatively break them. Short of that, the result is usually cliché, mediocrity, hackwork.

Discipline involves character development, "working on yourself," which in turn leads to self-mastery. But then, *surprise:* The artist, while fashioning his creation, has ultimately been working on himself, creating a higher humanity, beginning at home.

Of course, God is at the root of all urge for self-expression, self-mastery. Thus, if creativity is essentially the process of ascending in consciousness to realization and demonstration of God as love-wisdom, the ultimate art medium becomes the human body-mind and the ultimate artform becomes human relations. The body-mind becomes a holy temple for the Master Builder; individuals become members in the mystical body of God, which builds a spiritual earth. As we grow in love and wisdom, we naturally express it in our daily lives. Everyone we come in contact with is material for the art of "divinizing" humanity. From our most transcendent moments to the mundane, from our most intimate relations to the routine and ordinary, God is the content of our lives, seeking expression in everything and everyone.

The ultimate artist, then, is the one who creates as the Creator creates, by fashioning little bits of individual consciousness known as people into vehicles for grace and God-realization. Such an artist may be widely known and revered by millions as a savior, guru, enlightened teacher; he may also work quietly behind scenes, devoting his effort to a relatively small "batch of material" on which he lavishes the most loving care and attention to detail: shaping, sculpting, drawing out impurities, releasing the light, the music, the glory and imprisoned splendor he sees in the material. Each artist-creator chooses the appropriate forum for his creativity and then patiently, skillfully applies his talent to the Great Work of creating heaven on Earth—that condition in which creature, creation, and Creator are realized as One.

16

Channeling and Higher Human Development

Higher human development—evolution—has been accelerating in the last few centuries. The pace of change is now unprecedented for our species and what is to come is, I believe, a *new* species. We are witnessing the final phase of Homo sapiens and the simultaneous emergence, still quite tentative because of the nuclear and environmental threats to life, of what I have named *Homo noeticus,* a more advanced form of humanity.

It will take several centuries more to thoroughly demark the new age and the new humanity from the present one, and the transition will not be easy. Evolution never is. But as we pass from the Age of Ego to the Age of God, civilization will be transformed from top to bottom. A new, global society will be created, a civilization founded on love and the perennial wisdom of sacred traditions.

The change of consciousness underlying this passage involves transcendence of ego and the recognition of the unity of life in all its kingdoms—mineral, plant, animal, human, and spirit. However, information is necessary for transformation; there is no ascent into higher states of being without an attendant change in the content of consciousness. How does the human race get such information?

The expanding perimeter of human knowledge depends, first of all, on those courageous pioneers, those noetic heroes who push into new territories of mind and new realms of reality. Through a combination of their own steadfast, selfless effort and divine grace from above, new understanding is gained, new information is revealed. Their experiences, their discoveries, their visions are then communicated to others through conventional means: speaking, writing, and teaching. Slowly the word goes forth, drawing more and more people into sympathy and synchrony with the new understanding.

A second source of information for transformation is revelation. This is communication from nonphysical intelligences through people with special talent for receiving such transmissions. The modern term for such people is *channel,* but traditionally they have been called oracles, mediums, trance communicators, shamans, and other less precise terms such as visionary or seer (although the latter terms properly belong to those who achieved their insight primarily through spiritual practice rather than through the aid of nonphysical entities).

Channeled communications have a long and honorable history in human affairs. Of course, like anything else noble and elevated, they have their sleazy imitators and questionable claimants. Metaphysical bookstores are filled with books alleged to be from wise discarnates who, upon examination, don't speak two clear sentences in a row and who, if they were in physical form, probably couldn't walk and chew gum at the same time. These "revealed" works, however well intended, are generally a mixture of delusional fantasy and subconsciously recycled material from other sources which may or may not be genuine. In some instances there is deliberate intent to plagiarize, invent, or commit fraud. For every book of Revelation (John of Patmos said he received it from Jesus in His celestial form) there are dozens of revealed books not worth the paper they're printed on. The channels for such works are so bad in "audio" which we can be thankful they're not available in "video." Higher consciousness it's not. As one perceptive commentator noted, both drinking water and sewage flow in channels.

Spiritual counterfeits aside, the human race has been uplifted by words of wisdom originating, it seems, from levels of existence beyond the human which are inhabited by more highly evolved beings who are compassionately concerned for us and whose existence is, the communications say, inextricably entwined with our own. There is said to be a great variety of these superhuman and nonhuman forms of life: angels, archangels, devas, ascended masters and mahatmas, spirit guides, exusiai, cherubim, seraphim, extraterrestrials, metaterrestrials, ultraphysicals, Space Brothers, and so on. These entities and their native realms interpenetrate our own three-dimensional framework, creating a spiritual hierarchy, a great chain of being leading up to the source of creation, Godhead.

Whatever their name or form, the existence of these more highly evolved intelligences is on a scale enormously beyond the human, and from their level of reality they influence human affairs in a noncompulsory manner. From their point of view, the future of the human race already exists to some unspecified degree because they can see with overarching vision the possibilities ahead for us and can gently guide us toward desirable ends. Through a sort of mutual induction process, higher consciousness reaches down to humanity while, in turn, humanity—through its soul travelers, sages, saints, and seers—reaches up to higher consciousness. Thus evolution proceeds.

Think of some examples:

- Moses heard a voice from a burning bush.
- Socrates had his daimon, a voice he perceived inwardly from childhood on, which counseled him and offered prognostications.
- Saul, while journeying to Damascus to persecute Christians, heard the voice of Jesus and thereafter became Paul.
- Muhammad was given the Koran by dictation from the archangel Gabriel.
- Nostradamus, in trance, received precognitive information from what he described as divine revelation, inspiration, and good angels.
- Theosophy owes its existence to the discourses received by H. P. Blavatsky and several of her colleagues from discarnate mahatmas named Kuthumi and Djwal Kul.
- Another ascended master, The Tibetan, produced numerous works through Alice A. Bailey.
- Edgar Cayce's readings were never clearly identified as to source, but a number of indications suggest they originated at the transhuman level of existence called Overmind by Sri Aurobindo.
- Aurobindo himself began his spiritual development by trying his hand at automatic writing; his book, *Yogic Sadhana,* was written under the inspiration of Ram Mohan Roy, a deceased yogi who brought yoga to Great Britain in 1830. (Also, on two occasions in his early unfoldment, Aurobindo heard a voice from above commanding him to go to certain locations which were absolutely necessary for his safety, since he was being pursued by British authorities for his part in the Indian independence movement. He acted immediately, barely evading capture.)
- *The Urantia Book* is a collection of "papers" channeled during sleep by a Chicago physician in the 1930s; it is a gigantic work with many anticipatory insights into modern astrophysics and psychology.
- Krishnamurti, writing in his early teens under the pen name Alcyone, transcribed *At the Feet of the Master,* claiming he merely re-

corded what was said to him by an ascended master while he, Krishnamurti, visited him at night through astral projection.

• Through the mediumship of Elizabeth ("Betty") White, a number of high-level discourses were received from discarnate intelligences she and her husband, Stewart Edward White, termed simply "The Invisibles"; her *Betty Book* and his *The Unobstructed Universe,* received from Betty through another medium after she died, are regarded as classics of mediumistic literature.

The phenomenon continues today and increases at ever faster pace, so widespread as to be a fad. Fads are usually superficial; however, there are many serious and notable examples of channeling which has helped give rise to the current public interest.

• While imprisoned in solitary confinement in 1973, Timothy Leary received a "Starseed communication" from what he termed Higher Intelligence; the communicator's point of origin seemed to be extraterrestrial and was reminiscent of the earlier communications occultist Aleister Crowley claimed to have received from Aiwass, a native of the Sirius star system.

• Paul Solomon, a trance psychic in Virginia Beach, Virginia, gives medical information about people in the fashion Edgar Cayce did; he speaks aloud without conscious recall what is told to him by the Source.

• Aron Abrahamsen of Everett, Washington, also enters trance in a Caycelike manner to produce health readings for people and even to locate objects and minerals in remote places.

• In the 1970s Eileen Caddy and David Spangler of the Findhorn Community in Scotland channeled discourses from various nonphysical entities—devas, angels, and archangels—such as John and Limitless Light and Love.

• From the early 1970s a multidimensional being, Seth, spoke through the now-deceased channel Jane Roberts, producing a stream of books which included the well-known *The Seth Material.*

• *Jonathan Livingston Seagull* was written by Richard Bach after he heard a disembodied voice tell him the story; Bach says the voice, not he, is the real author.

• In 1981 a Westport, Connecticut, housewife named Meredith Young sensed a vibrational presence during meditation, followed by an urge to write. Three years later her channeled book, *Agartha,* presented the teachings of a group of nonphysical beings who refer to themselves simply as Mentor (teacher).

• Perhaps the most spiritually pure and practical of all channeled communications in modern times are the text, student workbook, and teacher's manual known collectively as *A Course in Miracles,* whose unnamed author is believed by many to be Jesus. (I do not subscribe to that view of its origin, as I explain in Chapter 23, but its beneficial influence on the lives of thousands of people is testimony to its divinely inspired source.)

Determining the Source

But what *is* the source of channeled communications? Is it genuinely external to the psyche of the channel or is it an aspect of the channel's own mind?

The answer is ambiguous. It may be either; both are possible. You have to examine each case individually and even then "it" may not be perfectly clear. One of the greatest channels, parapsychologist Eileen Garrett, channeled several distinct personalities, but after decades of experience and rigorous scientific investigation into paranormal phenomena, she was still not entirely certain of the source of her communications.

Benevolent discarnate entities of great wisdom are undoubtedly contacting humanity. Age-old tradition and contemporary experience attest this. Likewise, the human potential for growth to godhood includes the capacity for people to utter inspired discourses from what esoteric psychology calls the High Self—the aspect of us beyond ego and individualism which is in touch with the transcendent dimension of reality. As discussed earlier, many great artists have attested the fact that their music, art, mathematical insights, and so forth seem to come from a higher source. Even technological breakthroughs have originated in dreams and visions.

But the proliferation of channeled discourses today seems to have discarnate entity population working overtime. I estimate that perhaps nine out of ten channels are "bringing through" nothing more than a fabricated subpersonality of their own creation. Most of the material I see from channels is banal or trivial, stylistically awkward, and often factually erroneous (like the case I cite in *Pole Shift*, where an "ascended master" incorrectly stated that Arcturus is the pole star and that Earth has several magnetic axes). In a small portion of these instances there may be elevated speech, ennobling thoughts, and sound psychological guidance, but it is nevertheless, as I evaluate it, simply a production of the individual's own unrecognized talent for subtle information-gathering and theatrical dramatization, dressed up in the guise of some noble personality. This legitimizes the experience to the channel, who otherwise is not ready to accept it as an aspect of himself and to acknowledge the enormous creativity in the depths of his own psyche.

Now, there is nothing wrong with this capacity in and of itself. In fact, its development should be considered a positive step *if* the channel recognizes it as a manifestation of his or her own capacity to access the High Self. That Self transcends not only our own individualtiy but also that of discarnate entities, ascended masters, Space Brothers, and the like. It is the Ultimate Source of us all.

However, channeled information for personal growth—no matter how wise the information and regardless of the source—is useless for the channel until applied to his or her own life. Trance channels rarely are aware of what they channel. For example, until late in life Edgar Cayce had no idea of what came through while he gave readings. (To his credit, Cayce did try to live in accordance with the principles enunciated in them.) I know channels who can give stunning information but have to play back a tape recording of what they say in order to know what it is. Simply vacating your body while an entity speaks through you is *not* spiritual practice. The emptying of self which sacred traditions talk about results in mind*ful*ness, not mind*less*ness. For this reason, Theosophy frowns upon mediumship, even though it was part of Madame Blavatsky's own experience. Likewise, Rudolf Steiner, the founder of Anthroposophy, declared that knowledge of the higher worlds should be obtained in the full light of waking consciousness.

A channel must recognize the indisputable fact that his or her own mind has a tremendous capacity for fantasizing, plausibly fabricating, and spontaneously dramatizing something based on the slimmest data and subtlest cues. Why might a channel unconsciously fabricate? Escapism into fantasy, wish fulfillment, increased self-esteem, a subtle power trip—there are many reasons. The channel must beware and *be aware*. Reality testing is absolutely necessary. Without it lies the possibility of the channel succumbing to delusions of grandeur, depersonalization, multiple personality disorder, and even possession.

With it, ideally speaking, channeling can help a person to grow *beyond* channeling to the stature of a sage whose every word, however casually uttered, is full of wisdom and grace. There is no need for such a person to go through trance-induction procedures into an altered state of consciousness, assume a different personality, and after a period of effortful theatrics resume an ordinary, colorless existence. Instead, the Source has infused the individual so fully that he or she can say, as Jesus did about his Father, that they are one. In *How to Be a Channel*, J. Donald Walters (formerly Swami Kriyananda) writes about his teacher, the renowned yogi Paramhansa Yogananda: "There was nothing ritualistic about his channeling, nothing portentous, nothing to make us feel that we had the rare blessing of being given ringside seats at some special and extraordinary event. He was so natural in everything he said, so unaffected, so seemingly casual, that, not infrequently, his most amazing statements almost passed unnoticed—only to be remembered later on with awe."[1] I recommend Walters' sensible commentary and instructions on channeling.

Practical Advice for Channeling

It is not infrequent for people who are consciously on a spiritual path, following a tradition and practicing a discipline, to begin experiencing themselves as channels. It likewise can occur spontaneously for people not involved in such pursuits. What should you do if that happens?

The first thing is to remain calm. Don't panic; you're not losing your sanity.[2] Initial channeling experiences are analogous to visiting a foreign country with a very different climate and culture. You need time to get used to it. While the experience can be disorienting at first, remember that you are simply gaining access to other levels of consciousness, other realms of reality, and learning to function in them.

Most spiritual traditions urge you to ignore or avoid developing such abilities, declaring them to be a trap or a dead end. The path to God doesn't depend upon such experiences, these traditions maintain. Enlightenment is direct God-realization—beyond all mediated knowledge from discarnate sources who, however advanced they may be, are not ultimate. Krishnamurti came to understand this; later in life he abandoned the practice which led to *At the Feet of the Master,* saying there was no need to seek enlightenment through an occult hierarchy. "Truth is a pathless land," he declared. A wise friend, experienced in occultism and channeling, put the same thing to me differently when, pointing heavenward, he said: "Straight up with no tangents."

If you decide to use channeling as a spiritual tool (and it can be a useful one) you must exercise discernment, discrimination, and caution, at least as much as you would for more earthly forms of human activity. There are distinct dangers.

One of the great soul-travelers with profound knowledge of inner space, the eighteenth-century Swedish mystic-philosopher Emmanuel Swedenborg, said: "When spirits [meaning low, not angelic, ones] begin to speak with a man, he must beware that he believe nothing that they say. For nearly everything they say is fabricated by them, and they lie—for if they are permitted to narrate anything, as what heaven is and how things in the heavens are to be understood, they would tell so many lies that a man would be astonished. This they would do with solemn affirmation. . . . Wherefore men must beware and not believe them."

Spiritual traditions warn us to "try the spirits" and test our visions to see whether they are truly from God. Jesus put it simply: By their fruits ye shall know them. It is easy to be deceived by ego-created fantasies, hallucinations, and delusions. Likewise, the unwary can fall prey to deceptive messages and messengers. Low-level entities lurk in metaphysical realms, ready to rush in where fools tread. Sensible use of channeling requires a high degree of character development and a balanced, well-integrated personality. Without that, the channel can run into difficulties such as spirit obsession or even possession.

Several recent books offer valuable guidance in the matter. I've already mentioned Walters'. Jon Klimo's *Channeling: Investigations on Receiving Information from Paranormal Sources* is the most scholarly and comprehensive, covering the history and theories of channeling; it also offers instructions on how to channel and how to do so safely.[3] William Kautz and Melanie Branon's *Channeling: The Intuitive Connection* is less theoretical and more how-to, but no less sound in its advice and spiritual perspective. Finally, I recommend Corinne McLaughlin's "How to Evaluate Psychic Guidance and Channeling" (a brief pamphlet available from the School of Spiritual Science, Sirius Community, Baker Road, Shutesbury, MA 01072).

To put my cautionary advice in a few sentences, here are what I see as the primary questions to consider in testing the nature, orientation, and spiritual quality of channeled communications.

• **Are the communications compatible with the body of scientific knowledge?** If not, why not? Even genuinely new knowledge will at least be compatible, however revolutionary or advanced it may otherwise be. For example, some UFO contactees claim to have been given predictions of world-shaking events and are urged by the aliens or extraterrestrials to make them widely known. Many contactees have done so. Almost invariably, the predicted events don't occur, leaving the contactees looking foolish for having made their public statements. This is a pretty good indication that the entities are either figments of imagination or astral tricksters—or worse.

Beyond that, you must understand that any finite being is not omniscient, no matter how far up the spiritual hierarchy it may be. Even the most highly evolved spiritual figures, incarnate or otherwise, can overreach themselves and make mistakes. Sometimes this may be a statement which is demonstrably false or is at least open to debate and differing interpretation by others who, although not equally evolved in consciousness, are nevertheless qualified with regard to the particular topic or issue.

• **Are the communications compatible with the teachings of the world's major religions and spiritual traditions?** Again, if not, why not? Is recognized spiritual authority and the collective experience of thousands of years to be lightly ignored? Remember that such wisdom and authority come from people who, like you, were searching for spiritual truth.

All sacred traditions have made explicit warnings about psychic phenomena (including channeling) and have formulated doctrinal statements and instructional statements to guide practitioners safely along the path to enlightenment or God-realization. Remember: Psychic development is not the same as spiritual growth.

• **Does the communicator recognize a higher power?** Anything which claims in personal terms to be ultimate, isn't. If you are a Christian, ask whether the communicator recognizes the spiritual authority of Jesus. If you belong to another tradition, ask about the highest authority of that tradition.

• **Is there patient regard by the communicator for your own sense of truth and you need to test the veracity of the communications?** Meredith Young was told by Mentor, "You must trust us based on your reaction to our teachings." This concern for the channel's sense of truth is an important indication of the benign nature and trustworthiness of the communicator. The other sort may begin speaking sweetly, but soon the tone changes and becomes demanding, frantic, and hostile.

• **Does the communicator ask permission to continue communication?** Seeking permission is a sign of respect. If the communicator does not ask permission, if it shows no regard for the integrity of the communication channel, beware. I know people who have experienced communicators breaking in on them without warning, day or night, whether the person is prepared or not, alone or in a group. This sort of entity will disrupt activities, creating havoc in daily affairs and frightening anyone around, alienating them from the channel, who appears to be (and, in fact, is) out of control.

• **Do the communications encourage your own growth to independence of the communicator and other external authorities?**

Kyros, an entity channeled by Sandra Radhoff of Albuquerque, New Mexico recently stated: "A good channel is one who attempts to guide others into the awareness of their own abilities to connect with their own higher guidance. But many [people] move from channel to channel (from Ramtha to Lazaris to Mafu) like that which are termed 'groupies' following rock stars. . . . Some entities depend on channels to tell them what to do in their lives or to tell them what will happen in the future." It should be clear that such dependence is only a step away from addiction, and spiritual addiction to anything other than God is as detrimental to higher human development as physical addictions are. A meditation junkie, a bliss ninny, a spook chaser is still an addict. That is not the same as God-intoxication.

If your channeling doesn't pass all these tests, I suggest you close down that line of communication altogether. Simply give it no more attention, and refuse any requests from the entity for further contact.

Your mental health could be at stake. (There may, of course, be other entities you've learned to trust and can safely continue to bring through.)

Channeling, done properly, can be a valid means of spiritual growth, and the spiritually aspiring person should welcome whatever assistance he gets along the way, whether from ordinary or extraordinary means. For some seekers, it is not the channeled communications that are important but rather the experience of opening themselves in love and trust to a higher reality; for others, however, the important thing is the harsh experience of having the glamour removed from their illusions about spirituality and higher consciousness when they find their much-valued channeling capability has led them into foolishness or worse.

Whatever the case, it is important to recognize that psychic communications are merely signposts pointing the way for the spiritual traveler; they are not the ultimate destination. The destination is the Kingdom of God, the Transcendental Domain.

You see, the very act of communication presumes some kind of separation—a split or division between sender and receiver—and assumes some kind of knowledge to be transmitted from one to another. Communication of any sort is at best a bridge, and a bridge presupposes some degree of separation between the parts being connected.

The Kingdom, however, is union with God—the transcendence of all sense of separation or gulf between God, humanity, and the cosmos. Spiritual traditions tell us that our true identity is the One, the Whole, which manifests with infinite variety but which is never anything less than the all-in-One-and-One-in-all. It is profoundly mysterious, and although people can name it and talk about it, its reality is beyond all knowledge which can be verbalized. It can never be adequately communicated; it can only be experienced.

Therefore, the best channels contacting the highest source are those which produce not words but deeds. Channeled information is useful and valuable only if it leads to human transformation; otherwise it remains merely a philosophy or a curiosity. As Karl Marx said (and we can appreciate it without being Marxist): Philosophers have sought to explain the world; the thing to do, however, is change it. Authentic channeling, whether from discarnate entities or from a person's own High Self, involves a dimension of reality which seeks to go beyond communication to communion. It seeks to transform people and, indeed, human society itself. Is that not, in its ultimate sense, precisely what the coming of the Kingdom is all about?

We are all, therefore, called by Universal Mind to be channelers in the service of higher human development. We are called to transform ourselves and to assist others in that process. Words can be important in that regard, but deeds are more so. Channeled words abound; there is, in fact, a surfeit. But the channeling we are truly called to do—the channeling most needed today by a groaning planet—was described elegantly in a simple prayer, the Prayer of Saint Francis:

> Lord, make me a channel of your peace.
> Where there is hatred, let me sow love,
> Where there is injury, pardon,
> Where there is doubt, faith,
> Where there is despair, hope,
> Where there is darkness, light,
> And where there is sadness, joy.
>
> Lord, grant that I may seek to comfort rather than be comforted,
> To understand than be understood,
> To love than be loved.
>
> For it is in giving that we receive,
> It is in pardoning that we are pardoned,
> And in dying that we are born to eternal life.

17

Gurus, Devotees, and Politics

When Swami Muktananda first came to the United States in 1974, one of his devotees urged me to meet him. I was glad to because I'd heard so many stories about him. Ram Dass had publicly extoled him and his miracle-working powers, or *siddhis*. Moreover, I was associated with an organization, the Institute of Noetic Sciences, which was vigorously engaged in psychic research. So, though the devotee, I had *darshan* (audience) with Muktananda at his ashram near the San Francisco Bay. It was a pleasant educational experience. I didn't witness any miracles or paranormal phenomena, but he did tell me (since I was working with Apollo 14 astronaut Edgar Mitchell, founder of the Institut) that he had also been to the moon. However, he said through his interpreter, he had not gone in a spacecraft; he had gone through out-of-body experience in his astral form.

A few days later the ashram staff asked me to help plan a reception for Muktananda at the home of a devotee who lived near me. Many Bay Area luminaries were to attend. Again, I was pleased to have the opportunity to experience the presence of Muktananda.

The reception took place in May 1974 on the day after India exploded its first atomic bomb. Now, my four years in the Navy during the 1960s had included duty as a nuclear weapons officer. That had deeply affected me and led me to conclude that the only sane thing to do with nuclear weapons was abolish them. I was, and still am, deeply concerned about the proliferation of nuclear weapons, which I see as the foremost threat to the well-being of Planet Earth, bar none. And if you've ever had your finger on the button which could unleash kilotons of fiery death

183

(see the next chapter for more details) as I have, while your deepest sense of human community tells you that what you're doing is sheer madness, you'll understand why I was so concerned about India's entry into the nuclear club.

Since the Indian atomic test was headlining the news on the day of the reception, I asked Muktananda what he thought about it. He replied that, first, he had not known about it until I informed him and, second, it probably was a good thing since India's neighbors already had nuclear weapons. India, he said, had to develop the bomb.

I was stunned. His reply struck me as insensitive and uncomprehending. I felt he was uttering nothing more than the superficial rhetoric and platitudes I'd heard from a thousand politicians and military strategists. I could understand that such nonsense would come from them. But from a spiritual teacher, a guru? I couldn't believe my ears!

However, I wasn't about to get into a political argument with Muktananda on an occasion in his honor, so I dropped the topic and spoke of other matters, and the reception continued. But the magnitude of the threat presented by India's action continued to loom large for me. It was not inconceivable to me that India, then on the verge of economic collapse, might in desperation sell atomic weapons to some petrodollar-rich Arab nation, thus priming the Middle East for atomic Armageddon. I felt conscience-bound to do what little I could to influence Indian policy on the matter, so I wrote to several Indian acquaintances, urging them to make their voices heard in protest against nuclear arms for India. One of my correspondents was Swami Chinmayananda, whom I'd met a few years earlier in New York. He is a delightful person—warm, witty, insightful, learned—and a contributor to my anthology *What Is Meditation?* I felt confident he'd agree with my aims.

You can imagine my shock when he wrote back in terms which agreed completely with Muktananda (whose views I had not mentioned) and in terms which said plainly but lovingly that I was being foolish. With Russia and China aiming nuclear weapons across India's borders, he said, India did what it *had* to do. "Think, think, think!" he ended his letter.

The score was 2–0. I had received a hard blow to my views and values. "Am I naïve?" I asked myself. Is it foolish to urge the abolition of nuclear arms? Is it unrealistic to believe there can be a safe and peaceful world? Is it simply stereotyped thinking on my part to expect spiritual teachers such as Muktananda and Chinmayananda to speak out vigorously for nuclear disarmament? Was I missing part of their message?

I was wrestling with my basic image of what a spiritual teacher or guru is all about, and I wasn't getting any revelations. Knocked for a spiritual loop of sorts, I felt I ought to re-examine my values and beliefs to see if perhaps there was a perspective I'd failed to discover. My values and beliefs had arisen from deep personal experience, but I was well aware of the adage "Man convinced against his will/Is of the same opinion still." Therefore I tried to be very honest in examining myself on the subject, and also very open to change. I began a process which was no urgent formal investigation, just a quiet, ongoing contemplation from the Witness consciousness point of view which lasted several months.

When I felt all the data were in, I pressed the "compute" button, so to speak. The answer came out loud and clear: No more nuclear weapons, despite what Muktananda and Chinmayananda said. I had thought, thought, thought—and I could not accept their words as wisdom on this particular issue. They ran the needle on my spiritual crap detector into the red danger area (no pun intended). With undiminished love for them and respect for their missions, I mentally bade them goodbye on the question of India's nuclear arming.

Shortly afterward, I had a chance to raise the subject with another spiritual teacher, Munishri Chitrabhanu. Muni was at that time acknowledged as leader by nearly six million Jains. He was born in India and lived there most of his life, thirty of those years in a monastery.

Without mentioning my views or those of Muktananda and Chinmayananda, I asked Muni what he thought of India exploding the bomb. I was gratified to hear him say unequivocally that it was morally indefensible. However, he added, it was politically understandable. He could see why many felt it was a good thing. But those people, he said, simply didn't see things clearly.

The score was 2–1.

I describe all this for two reasons. First, I'm still convinced that nuclear weapons are the Devil's work. It would be my position, even if I hadn't heard confirmation from Muni. Second, and more important: Spiritual teachers are quite properly revered for their expertise—the skillful unfolding of the inner life—but their opinions in areas outside that expertise ought not to be automatically accepted as truth. Saints and mystics don't have omniscience.

Is it trite and obvious to point out that opinion is opinion, no matter what the source? There can be expert opinion, informed opinion, and ignorant opinion among professionals of all kinds, including spiritual teachers. Just as you respect a doctor for his medical training but can take or leave his views on solving the problem of, say, welfare cheating, so too you ought to recognize that the label *guru* doesn't carry Ph.D. status in politics. Muktananda and Chinmayanda, it seems to me, were nationalistic rather than planetary in their approach to the issue of nuclear arms. It was shocking to run into that in men I'd expected to be beyond it. But the experience cut away an illusion and provided a useful lesson. It showed in still another way what I'd already seen in other areas: gurus are, after all, only human. They have their blind spots and prejudices in varying degrees, and their education, as well as their devotees', is still going on—or *should* be.

(In fairness to Muktananda and Chinmayananda, I'll also say that the intervening years have led me to modify my own view somewhat. I still stand for the abolition of nuclear weapons, but not for unilateral disarmament. A negotiated, multilateral, verifiable disarmament: yes. Unilateral: no. So I perhaps had my own blind spot—not recognizing that good will can be resisted and that unverifiable treaties could bring about the very suffering I hoped to prevent. I trust that both Muktananda and Chinmayananda would agree with that.)

Devotees must recognize that spiritual mastery does not confer omniscience, and that spiritual wisdom is not the same as socioeconomic expertise, business acumen, medical proficiency, geopolitical authority, public relations competence, or any other form of worldly accomplishment. To become spiritually mature, devotees must think for themselves and take responsibility for their actions in all fields of life-experience, from workplace to worship, recognizing that there are many areas where resort to their teacher or the teaching will be insufficient or impossible. They must be prepared to "go it alone" at times, remaining open for "situation guidance" in lieu of authoritative pronouncements from the teacher and possibly even in divergence from the teacher/teaching.

I'm reminded of a delightful lesson Swami Kriyananda (a different one than J. Donald Walters) gave to his audience at Swami Rama's first annual International Conference on Meditation and Yoga in 1976. Kriyananda, sitting in half lotus, told the assemblage that he was going to demonstrate the single most difficult *asana* in all of yoga—the position which is the essence of the entire tradition. The audience hushed. Kriyananda rose slowly to his feet, planted them squarely on the stage, placed his hands on his hips, and silently looked on the audience with strength and love.

"Standing on your own two feet," he said. "That's what it's all about."

His demonstration humorously epitomized the theme of this essay: The guru's truth is not your truth until you've discovered it through firsthand experience. The guru's role is to help you discover truth for yourself, not hand it to you as a party line. The wise student/devotee knows that and—to put it bluntly—uses his guru skillfully rather than swallowing whole and untested everything he or she may say. The "sword of discrimination" ought to be employed so that the student/devotee recognizes where the guru's expertise ends and where his or her ordinariness begins, with all its ignorance and provincialism. In spiritual life, as much as in politics, the goal is liberation, but before there can be liberation there must be deliberation.

18

The Paranormal
in Judeo-Christian
Tradition

The Bible is a rich storehouse of psychic lore and tales of supernatural events. The paranormal is integral to the Judeo-Christian tradition, but its ultimate significance is not that it provides evidence of unseen realms in the cosmos or of untapped powers in the human race. Those are real, but phenomena in and of themselves are not ultimate, whether they are called psychic, paranormal, supernatural, transphysical, or miraculous. Spiritually naïve people may become fascinated with such phenomena (it may be awe from simple ignorance or power-lust from egotism) but for the mature person whose life reflects the presence of what is traditionally referred to as the Holy Spirit, paranormal phenomena always point beyond themselves to their source, God.

The god of the Bible is, of course, the Living God and thus the Holy Spirit, as an aspect of God, is a living being. That does not mean, however, that the Holy Spirit is a person or a ghost (even a holy one) or—as some religious art depicts—a dove. Those familiar conceptions are intended symbolically, but when taken literally they become misconceptions or misunderstanding of God: spiritual truth seen "through a glass darkly." The Holy Spirit does not have any form which human thought can conceive.

For the modern mind, nurtured in a scientific culture, the Holy Spirit can best be understood as the universal power through which God performs miraculous or supernatural events. It is one of the modes the Divine uses to operate in the universe. As such, it is the matrix or field from which all psychic or paranormal phenomena are generated. Properly understood, then, paranormal phenomena are instances of a general condition: the Power of the Living God, the Force Field of the Life Source. Those phrases are closer to the terminology of science, but they are only contemporary expressions for the more traditional term *Holy Spirit*.

Ideally, then, the psychic and the paranormal realms draw us toward a deeper understanding of the nature of reality. When Jesus performed miracles, he always pointed beyond himself to the source of his power, God. So did the Hebrew prophets.

Jesus and the Hebrew prophets taught people that God is the source of creation and that our personal power, our life—indeed, our very being, including our postmortem existence—is a miracle freely granted through God's unconditional love. Their teachings sought to counter the materialistic views and values which ignored or denied the presence of Holy Spirit, and their paranormal demonstrations served to reinforce that realization in people. The teachings and demonstrations asked: What have we done—what *can* we do—to deserve the gift of life, the abundance and happiness which is ours when we yield ourselves wholly to God? The answer is: Absolutely nothing. Life itself, they implicitly said, is the ultimate paranormal event and the Love, the Creative Power, the Life Force which brings it forth is wondrous. Recognize that and give thanks to God for the amazing grace which sustains us and the entire universe moment to moment, eternally. It is a miracle beyond comprehension.

That is the significance of the paranormal in the Judeo-Christian tradition. It has perhaps been said most elegantly and succinctly in the poetic prose of *A Course in Miracles:* "Miracles occur naturally as expressions of love. The real miracle is the love that inspires them. In this sense everything that comes from love is a miracle."

19

Empty Self, No Sword: Enlightenment and the Martial Arts

Whenever you cross swords with an enemy, you must not think of cutting him either strongly or weakly; just think of cutting and killing him. Be intent solely upon killing the enemy.

> Miyamoto Musashi,
> a 17th-century samurai,
> *A Book of Five Rings*[1]

To subdue the enemy without fighting is the highest skill.

> Gichin Funakoshi,
> father of modern karate,
> *Karate-do: My Way of Life*[2]

What is the source of hostility and aggression in human affairs? Must an attack be met with violence, or can it be neutralized by nonviolence? Is there a gentle way to resolve conflict between people and nations?

These questions have concerned me for decades. As part of my continuing inquiry into the human condition, I recently went to the Zen Mountain Monastery in Mount Tremper, New York, to attend a seminar on Zen and the Martial Arts. The weekend took its name from Joe Hyams' 1979 book of the same title[3] and was spent exploring the

189

"warrior spirit" through talks and demonstrations by martial artists, through practice sessions, and through meditation.

In his discourse the first night, the monastery's abbot, Sensei John Daido Loori, pointed out that there is common ground between Zen and the martial arts which is profoundly spiritual. He spoke about overcoming anger, developing single-pointedness of mind, breaking through fear, and realizing the self.

Although my interest in the martial arts is fairly recent, my interest in Zen began in 1962, when I discovered Alan Watts' books during an agonized search for inner peace. As I previously mentioned, I was a nuclear weapons officer in the Navy, and although I'd gone into military service voluntarily, filled with adolescent dreams of gallantry and glory, I soon found that the reality of being a professional killer, however much sanctioned by government, was deeply opposed to my humanitarian instincts and values. The honor of combat in defense of my country was overshadowed by the realization that I literally had my hand on a button which could release kilotons of blazing death for people I'd never met. The code of combat, with its emphasis on chivalry and valor, had no consolation for me at the thought of how idiotic it was for people to fight over political ideologies instead of reasoning together in good will, and how I might have to die for that idiocy, never to see my wife and young children again.

My soul was in turmoil. When my ship went to Vietnam in 1964 to set up a forward base from which to load atomic depth bombs onto seaplanes in response to the Gulf of Tonkin events, I performed my duties, but my heart wasn't in them. (A lovely card and note I got from Watts at that time in response to a letter, and a visit to a zendo in Tokyo while on liberty, were two of the few moments when I felt connected to anything real beyond the insanity of militarism.)

My experience in the Pacific, both in and out of the war zone, clarified existence deeply for me. It confirmed the age-old insight of spiritual psychology: the ego is the source of all human aggression. My country might have been at war, but I was not. I attained what novelist John Knowles calls a separate peace. (At the end of this chapter I offer a poem which I wrote then on the theme.) The Pacific led me to pacifism. When my ship returned to the States, I went to my executive officer, declared myself a pacifist in international relations (I smile now to think I may be the first pacifist nuclear weapons officer in history), and firmly resolved that, when my service was completed, I would leave the war machine to become part of a peace machine—as an educator. The Latin *educere* means "to draw out." An educator, therefore, is one who draws out of students or actualizes the potential within them. As an educator, I would help people see Ultimate Reality and thus discover their true self beyond ego. I'd awakened to this possibility several years earlier through my suffering-searching and had realized it more deeply the year before through a spontaneous mystical experience. I saw the wisdom of the anonymous sixth-century B.C. Chinese poet who wrote:

> If you are thinking a year ahead, sow a seed.
> If you are thinking ten years ahead, plant a tree.
> If you are thinking one hundred years ahead, educate the people.
>
> By sowing seed, you will harvest once.
> By planting a tree, you will harvest tenfold.
> By educating the people, you will harvest one hundredfold.

Educating people into fulfilling their human potential for enlightenment would be slow, difficult, and uncertain work, I saw, but awakening compassion and opening the wisdom-eye was the only way to world safety and sanity. Inner peace would become outer peace by eliminating human aggression where it arises. The simple wish of a young father to enjoy his children growing up led me to the heart of existence.

With such a background, it may seem strange that I am now involved in the martial arts, which have an image of violence and bloodthirst. But that is an incomplete image of them. Yet, the violence and bloodthirst are there in the tradition, but so is something else—something deeper. My involvement is simply a natural progression as I continue my explorations in consciousness research and higher human development. My abiding interest throughout has been the nature of enlightenment and its potential for world peace; the martial arts speak directly to that.

The conflict I saw so vividly on the Cuban Blockade, in Vietnam, and soon afterward here in America when I became active in the antiwar movement were outward expressions of divisiveness in the human psyche. It became clear to me, as I said in my Introduction to *The Highest State of Consciousness,* that "political action, social work, this *ism,* that *ology,* are all incomplete, futile actions unless accompanied by a new and elevated mode of awareness."[4] Reforms intended to tame the violence in people will not succeed unless they accomplish a change of consciousness in people because consciousness is primary. Legislation may control behavior (that is the legitimate function of law) but it can't control minds and thus won't eliminate the cause of bad behavior. Only understanding, only the removal of ignorance, can do that. Since Zen and other sacred traditions claim to have the means for changing a person's consciousness by removing ignorance of the true self, I have immersed myself in study of the psychotechnologies they offer for that goal.

Now, although I'd read widely in Zen literature, visited zendos, and interacted with Zen people for twenty-plus years, I never knew until recently that the martial arts have an organic connection to Zen and a deeper significance than chop-socky movies portray. Somehow it escaped my attention, partly because it seems to be notably absent from books about Zen but also because, considering myself a man of peace, I had little interest in what appeared to be the epitome of violence on a personal level. Like most other Westerners, I had a stereotypic view of the martial arts: Bruce Lee and Chuck Norris bashing heads or elite military forces kicking ass. I'd been involved in consciousness research and sacred traditions for decades, yet Bodhidharma, whom I knew as the first patriarch of Zen, remained unknown to me as a member of the warrior caste who migrated from India to China in the sixth century, where he trained monks at the Shaolin Temple (the same one David Carradine recreated in his *Kung Fu* television program) in combat skills to strengthen themselves for more arduous meditative practice and to defend themselves from brigands seeking their treasures. According to Jay Gluck, around A.D. 528 Bodhidharma emerged from solitary meditation in a cave and announced:

> war and killing are wrong, but so also is it wrong not to be prepared to defend oneself. We may not have knives, so make every finger like unto a dagger; our maces are confiscated, so make every fist like unto a mace. Without spears every arm must be like unto a spear and every open hand a sword.[5]

Gluck comments that Bodhidharma's system required that the fighter first divorce himself from any emotion toward his opponent and the weapon, so that "right action" was performed with "right attitude." In other words, Bodhidharma would, as Gluck puts it, "arm the man of peace; pacify the man of arms." From that event most Oriental forms of weaponless combat are derived.

Thus the common ground Sensei Daido talked about is both historical and psychological, and I was delighted to learn this several years ago when a friend who is studying a Korean martial art and I began to discuss the philosophical dimension of fighting. He recommended *Zen and the Martial Arts* and loaned me his copy. It blew me away. A veil was removed from my mind; a wholly new dimension of the martial arts emerged to my view and converged intimately with my longtime interest in self-transcendence and global peace. I'd been reading and discussing the martial arts sporadically for several years, but Hyams' book crystallized things for me: There is a "warrior path to enlightenment" not incompatible with a desire for a peaceful world. I began to read voraciously about the martial arts and to practice an Okinawan form of karate, Shorin-ryu—the oldest style, from which all others are derived.

As the saying goes, when the student is ready, the teacher appears. I was ready; teachers appeared everywhere. Besides my own sensei and his staff, there were books, magazines, videotapes, students of other martial arts, visits to their schools and to martial art supply houses, and one street situation where I faced a berserk man seemingly ready to kill me. (Fortunately, I was able to leave the confrontation quietly with neither of us getting hurt. It provided an occasion for deep reflection.)

To put in simplest terms what I consider most important about the martial arts, I'll quote a friend: "The martial arts don't train you to fight; they train you *not* to fight."

To elaborate, I'll point out first that the traditional name for a martial art school or practice hall, *dojo,* means "place of enlightenment" or, more precisely, "a place *(jo)* to practice the Way *(do)* to enlightenment." Enlightenment, of course, is what Zen and all sacred traditions are about, and although most practitioners of the martial arts are not enlightened or, for that matter, even aware of the possibility of enlightenment, the highest wisdom of the martial arts declares that the ultimate enemy is one's own ego. As Eugen Herrigel writes in *Zen and the Art of Archery,* quoting his master: ". . . this is what the art of archery means: a profound and far-reaching contest of the archer with himself."[6] Karate master Richard Kim puts it similarly in *The Weaponless Warriors:* "He who conquers himself is the greatest warrior."[7] Writing about morality in karate, Kim says:

> This raises the question, "If we are fully aware of the violence inherent in man's nature, are we not turning out killers? Are we not teaching an art that enables man to destroy man?"
>
> The answer must be, as the great Okinawan masters have always answered, "Yes, we are fully aware of the violence inherent in man, and that the art of karate embraces within itself techniques to kill with the empty hand. But there is a morality involved, woven in the fabric of karate, that controls the violence and the use of the art except under one condition—absolute necessity and dire peril."[8]

That is why it is said in karate that, when confronted, a karate person does not make the first move. Karate is never for offense, only for defense. That is also why tenth degree black belt Eizo Shimabukuro, grandmaster of Shobayashi Shorin-ryu Karate, says the first thing a teacher should do with a student is "fix the heart." Yes, there are martial artists who abuse their skills and position, such as the dojo owner in *The Karate Kid.* But it is Mr. Miyagi, the Karate Kid's sensei, who demonstrates the truth of karate.

More than technical proficiency, self-mastery or ego-transcendence is the ideal of the martial arts. The peacefulness, loving compassion, and reverence for life which flow from that state are characteristically shown by great martial artists. They have a sense of harmony with the universe which allows them to go through life without the chronic anxiety the ego experiences because of its apparent separateness from creation. This openness to infinity, this "empty self" means freedom from the ego's habitual mental guardedness and its behavioral expression—belligerence, defensiveness, self-aggrandizement, power lust, and all the other versions of man's inhumanity to man arising from the illusion of separate self. Not that all martial art masters, who may have their quirks and shortcomings as well, exhibit this completely, but to one degree or another it is there, quietly drawing people who hunger for freedom from insecurity and from the unhappiness of disharmony. The quotations at the beginning of this essay were identified by Terrence Webster-Doyle in his excellent exploration of the roots of conflict and violence, *Karate: The Art of Empty Self*,[9] to illustrate the difference between technical skill and true mastery in the martial arts. As Webster-Doyle states, "It is impossible to attack emptiness or to attack from nothingness."[10]

This is beautifully exemplified in the life of Yamaoka Tesshu, a nineteenth-century Zen Buddhist who engaged in thousands upon thousands of contests with the best swordsmen in Japan, yet never took another's life. According to his biographer John Stevens, Tesshu "never resorted to the ruthless cut-the-enemy-down-by-any-means tactics of Musashi, disarming his opponents instead with the power of 'no-sword' [*muto ryo*]."[11] The "sword of no-sword," Tesshu wrote, is a state of awareness of "the heart of things where one can directly confront life and death." Students of Tesshu's system of swordsmanship were told, "The purpose of Muto Ryo swordsmanship is not to fight to defeat others in contests; training in my dojo is to foster enlightenment."[12] Despite his sometimes fierce manner, Tesshu, who achieved enlightenment at age forty-five, was noted for his generosity and kindness to people and animals.

Compare that with Miyamoto Musashi, who is far better known than Tesshu and is popularly regarded in Japan as the master swordsman of all time. Cunning and seemingly invincible, he killed more than sixty people before he was thirty. Yet for all his martial prowess, he was personally unhappy and spiritually confused. Hounded by enemies created through his arrogance, he knew no peace until the last few years of life, when he retired to a cave to contemplate the mystery of existence. That is when he wrote *A Book of Five Rings* and, according to a poster I saw in a dojo, said, "In looking back over the events of my life, I can see now that I began to understand the way of the warrior when first I began to feel compassion."

This view of the martial arts was expressed by Joe Hyams in an interview I had with him recently. I said to Hyams, "My sensei teaches that the word *karate* means 'empty hand.' He says that, ideally, the empty hand is extended in friendship openly to show there is no hostility toward anyone in the world, the idea being that the true martial artist is a person of peace."

Hyams replied: "There is no question about that. Some people come to the martial arts because they're interested in glamour and power. But if they stay with it awhile, they'll find there is a deeper aspect to the martial arts. There is more than just chop-socky, flailing the arms and hands. And that deeper aspect is cultivation of the self, development of character, mindfulness, and one's human potential. That's where true peace is found."

Taisen Deshimaru, a Zen master who led a session on Zen and the martial arts at Zinal, Switzerland, in 1975, pointed out that Zen became known in medieval Japan as "the religion of the samurai"[13] because, as author–aikido master George Leonard put it in his introduction to Deshimaru's *The Zen Way to the Martial Arts,* zazen training could "still the restless mind, perceive the ultimate harmony beneath seeming discord, and achieve the oneness of intuition and action so necessary for kenjutsu (swordfighting)."[14] Leonard, summarizing Deshimaru's teaching about the stages common to Zen and the martial arts, comments "Throughout this lifelong process [of training in the martial arts], there is an inexorable shift in emphasis . . . from technique and strength of body in the beginning to exquisite intuition and a realization of spirit in the end."[15]

Leonard adds: "Master Morihei Uyeshiba, the founder of modern aikido, realized the true potential of his art only after he turned seventy, when he could no longer count on the power of his body. Most of the films which show his seemingly miraculous feats were made in the 1960s, when he was between eighty and eight-four years old."[16] His name, Morihei Uyeshiba, means "abundant peace." Uyeshiba, John Stevens tells us, was "undoubtedly the greatest martial artist who ever lived" and aikido is "a path of harmony and love, unifying body and mind, self and others, man and the universe."[17] That state was what C. W. Nicol's karate sensei meant when he told Nicol, who was practicing *kata* in a Tokyo dojo, "If you practice you will develop a mind that is as calm as still water. Karate is moving Zen, and it is the Zen state that you must strive for."[18]

The Zen state, the enlightened state, is characterized principally by serenity . . . tranquility . . . equanimity amid all circumstances, even life-threatening ones such as mortal combat. It is an ideal condition in which "empty self, no sword" epitomizes the Tibetan Buddhist adage "Insightful wisdom requires skillful means to produce effective action."

But, some may wonder, what about the admonition of Jesus to "resist not evil"? Or Gandhi and Martin Luther King's advocacy of non-violence? Were they all wimps?

I don't think so; their courage is admirable and beyond question. But it is a sad fact of human life that good will can be resisted and innocence slaughtered—witness the Holocaust, the 6000 razed temples and monasteries of Tibet, the massacre at Tiananmen Square. Sometimes turning the other cheek will only get you slapped a second time, even fatally so.

How can resistance to good will be overcome effectively so that antagonisms are resolved instead of perpetuated? There is no sure and simple way. Education to enlightenment is slow, difficult, and uncertain, often requiring tremendous sacrifices in the name of love. The way of Gandhi and King is for some; I have no argument with it—only deep respect. However, as philosopher Paul Brunton notes, the person who invokes the doctrine of pacifism for universal practice misapplies an ethical rule meant only for monks and ascetics who have renounced the world and misconceives a mystical doctrine meant only for inward realization. Pacifism, Brunton says, is admirable in a mystic but out of place in a person of the world. In fact, he points out that for people who have not retired from the world, "there is a bounden duty to protect human life, because of its superior value, when it is endangered by wild beasts—even if we have to kill those beasts. . . . Circumstances arise when it is right and proper to arm oneself in defence of one's country and slay aggressive invaders, or when it is ethically correct to destroy a murderous assailant."[19] He immediately adds, however, that the infliction of unnecessary pain must always be avoided.

The way of martial artistry offers people of peace who are still "of the world" an avenue for understanding more deeply the nature of human conflict and how to deal with it skillfully—meaning compassionately and wisely. In the words of Okinawan karate master Morio Higaonna, "Karate is a pacifist philosophy."[20]

How can that be? First of all, martial arts training builds self-confidence, and with that comes a lessening of the urge to fight. Few people enter the martial arts for spiritual reasons. Most simply want to learn self-defense because they're afraid of being attacked. Like any other ego-driven human, the novice martial arts practitioner has a mental attitude of fear and to some extent is living with a constant expectation of conflict. Martial arts training can instill a degree of assuredness that the person can deal with attack. This, in turn, leads to greater mental calmness and capacity for seeking nonviolent means to end a confrontation. It also leads the person to project a certain aura or bearing which subtly signals to potential aggressors they will not find him an easy mark, thereby further deterring the possibility of attack. The martial arts are thus a reasonable, conscious alternative to the fight-or-flight reflex which otherwise governs (unless a person's fear is so overwhelming as to "freeze" him). Psychiatrist Stuart Twemlow, who has a dojo in Topeka, Kansas, told me:

At a recent gathering or experienced black belts from many traditional styles, very few [indicated they] had been in any sort of fight since shodan [first degree black belt rank]. How interesting. The answer, I think, is in the altered state of consciousness the practice produces; it is peaceful and powerful, and once this balance of opposites is achieved, there is no enemy.[21]

Research data support that clinical observation. Carl Becker points out in "Philosophical Perspectives on the Martial Arts in America":

Recent studies by Rothpearl at Fordham documented that suspicion and aggression levels may be slightly increased for martial artists in their intermediate ranks, but that this quality changed to one of nonviolence in the more advanced students. Rothpearl suggested that it is their specific training to restrain themselves from violence which may be responsible for this shift. In any case, the evidence is fairly clear that these Eastern "combat sports" do *not* have the negative effects feared by [some], but on the contrary tend to reduce violent tendencies and curb them.[22]

Second, martial arts training clarifies the nature of violence and aggression. It provides a structured, intense but safe and supportive context for self-examination. It shows that violence and aggression are mental in nature—a mentality present in everyone until faced, inspected, understood, and transcended. With that understanding, there is "no enemy." Misguided opponents, yes—enemies, no. For with understanding comes the awakening of compassion. One realizes that "there but for the grace of God go I."

Now, I do not mean to present martial artistry as a panacea. A front snap kick won't stop a hail of bullets from an assault gun, and a drug-crazed thief needing money for a fix isn't likely to be deterred from robbery by a friendly invitation to talk about his problem. As Aldous Huxley pointed out about international politics, the work of the pacifist needs to be done *before* hostilities break out. Once those jackboots march across your border or that intruder enters your home, it's a question of another's life or yours and your loved ones'. And while it is true that "greater love hath no man than to lay down his life for [another]," wisdom, it seems to me, declares that invasion or break-in are not situations where such great love is warranted. The self-sacrifice of Jesus, Gandhi, and King was the act of men supremely aware of their destiny in the world's affairs. But yielding your life needlessly to a criminal or a brute serves no higher purpose. Everyone has the right to life, liberty, and the pursuit of happiness, but the next person's right stops at your chin and vice versa. To quote Brunton again:

The sage . . . does not wish to confirm the wrong-doer in wrong-doing, and does not wish either to smooth the latter's path and thus encourage evil, or to practise partiality towards him. A meek submission to an aggressor's will makes the aggressor believe that his methods pay, whereas a determined resistance checks his downward course, arouses doubts and even provides instruction should he suffer punishment.[23]

Speaking for myself, as the tide of crime and violence rises in society, I intend to be prepared for situations where predatory people might regard me as prey. So, unless situation wisdom immediately bids me otherwise, in such an event, as some law enforcement officers and NRA members put it, I'd rather be tried by twelve men than carried by six. Becoming an unwilling victim of a bully or savage is neither wise nor compassionate—it's foolish and futile. Morihei Uyeshiba's comment makes good sense: "Your Golden Rule says turn the other cheek when someone would strike you. This is aiki[do] except that we would turn it before being struck. Thus the attacked is saved hurt and the attacker is saved from committing sin."[24]

The pace of evolution is accelerating and humanity is poised for a quantum leap forward into a New Age of peace and love. However, that will not happen overnight—it will take several centuries at least—and in the interim, holdovers from an older age will be around, robbing, raping, mugging, and mayheming. Aggression and violence have been with us for a long time and will continue to be. Those ancient bandits who tried to pillage the Shaolin Temple treasures are still around, some holding positions of great power and influence in world affairs, ranging from politicians and financiers to military dictators and druglords. As sentient beings, they should be dealt with compassionately. As drags on evolution, however, they need to be dealt with skillfully, with the wisdom-eye as well as the heart—as I elaborate on in Appendix 3. So consider them jack-asses. To deal with a jackass, you first have to get its attention, and the way to do that, folk wisdom says, is to hit it between the eyes with a two-by-four. Otherwise it will ignore you or continue stubbornly in its inappropriate behavior. Translated into human terms, that means some-times the most compassionate and wise thing you can do for a person is to figuratively punch him in the mouth—and perhaps even literally, if circumstances require it. This right action should be given with the right attitude, of course—that of a loving parent who sees his misbehaving, thoughtless child needing correction or that of a Zen master who strikes his disciple with a *teisho* stick. The Zen master is practicing "skillful means," which has been known to induce *kensho,* spiritual awakening. The blow is intended to educate, not eradicate. It is *forceful* but not *violent.* Of course, it takes insightful wisdom to know whether that blow will induce kensho, but it takes only ordinary self-respect to know that thieves, thugs, and terrorists must not be allowed to control your life. In either case, the punch is justified.

When Bodhidharma found the Shaolin Temple in need of security and the monks in need of personal protection from harm and greater physical endurance for spiritual practice, he took direct action which was profound in its simplicity: he gave martial arts training. That is still "skillful means." So, as our planet heads into a New Age I look for warrior-sages, for (pardon me) "Rambodhisattvas" to demonstrate a new level of attainment in the human potential for self-directed growth in body, mind, and spirit aimed at the liberation of all sentient beings.

> The real value of martial arts study . . . has nothing to do with physical feats such as brick-breaking; in fact, it is not even primarily concerned with fighting. In our modern technologized society, it would be easier to buy a gun, or carry a can of mace. Their real value lies in what the martial arts can tell us about ourselves: that we can be much more than we are now; that we have no need of fear; that our capacities for energy, awareness, courage, and compassion are far greater than we have been led to believe. They tell us that all our personal limits—and by extension, our destructive social and historical patterns—can be transcended.[25]

I *gassho* (revently bow) to the wisdom of Bodhidharma.

. . . the really final truth [is] that, when carried to the extreme, opposites meet.
—Carl Jung

PACIFIC DAWN
(FOR ALAN WATTS)

Pacific dawn
With golden fingers
Establishes reign of the sky.
Gray clouds mask the horizon
Merging mountains on distant islands with sea and air.
The kingdom of light slowly spreads its hand
And captures the sky in mute celestial battle
That is not hostility at all.
The brilliant rays reach out from unseen sun.
Violet night fades rose, flamingo, buff.
Watching this daily miracle—
Pacific war of night and day—
One feels the wisdom which led the Japanese
To choose the dawn as symbol for their flag.

Sunset is a tenable philosophy
And perhaps characterizes the direction of our times:
The approach of night.
And yet the Western world has much to learn
Of good and evil, of life and death.
Yin-yang, the Chinese called it:
The eternal principles of light and dark
Which, though opposed to one another,
Cannot exist without the other—
Implying a deeper unity.

Therefore I see a possibility for salvation
Before annihilation.
As I stand here watching the sun rise
In kind antagonism to darkness' realm
I feel the calm peace of some ancient sage
And envision a meeting of East and West
As natural as this dawn.

The Sea of Japan, 1964

Headnote
This poem spontaneously arose in me during a bridge watch on my ship, while watching sunrise in the Sea of Japan, after leaving the Vietnam war zone in August 1964.

20

Enlightenment and the Spiritual Journey

What is enlightenment? The question has been asked throughout history by people looking for the meaning of existence. So precious has understanding seemed, so important for their happiness has it seemed that men and women in all ages have devoted themselves exclusively to finding an answer, despite hardship, privation, and even, at times, social ostracism. Their search has been motivated by a hunger for self-knowledge: Who am I? Why am I here? Where am I going? What is life all about? These are all aspects of that fundamental question: What is enlightenment?

Today an increasing number of spiritual seekers are following in the steps of their predecessors. Public opinion polls indicate a revival of religio-spiritual searching in the West. There is restlessness and dissatisfaction with the status quo, which has provided neither answers nor happiness. In addition, the age-old question is now being asked by consciousness researchers in science and by the merely curious who hear vague but alluring stories about something called enlightenment which makes living blissful and worthwhile. In fact, so widespread is the urge to know about enlightenment that, for the first time in history, people and organizations claiming to understand it have developed into a thriving field of commerce. The enlightenment industry is big business. Everywhere ads proclaim that no longer is the search relegated to years of arduous discipline in remote sanctuaries. Today, enlightenment is for everyone.

201

Ego and the Enlightenment Industry

Now, it is true in the ultimate sense that enlightenment *is* for everyone. That, thank God, is precisely the point toward which all creation drives. But one of the unfortunate aspects of all the commercialism has been devaluation of the term *enlightenment.* A surge of books, articles, tapes, lectures, and seminars on enlightenment offer conflicting opinions, claims, and counterclaims about it. There has also been a veritable explosion of psychotechnologies and consciousness-altering devices claiming to induce mystical, transformative, and "enlightened" states. Hypnotic tape recordings, past-life recall sessions, alpha and theta brain-wave training, out-of-body astral sounds, various meditation systems, sensory isolation flotation tanks, enlightenment crystals—these are typical of the wares being offered today in spiritual supermarkets. However, the spiritual "consumer" should ask: Do any have real value? If so, how much? What are they useful for?

All these products and services and systems have value of a limited sort: value for the novice, value for the person just beginning to become aware of the higher ranges of being which are culturally denied and educationally excluded in Western society. They are capable of delivering experiences which open our window on reality a bit wider than normal. They can show the limitations of everyday consciousness and the possibility of something beyond it. But the critical point to be understood is this: The value of mystical and transformative states is not in producing some new experience but in *getting rid of the experiencer.* Getting rid, that is, of the egocentric consciousness which experiences life from a contracted, self-centered point of view rather than the free, unbound perspective of a sage who knows he or she is infinity operating through a finite form.

What Enlightenment Is Not

Now, if that last statement sounds too vague, perhaps it would help to be specific about what enlightenment is not. It is not an altered state of consciousness, whether induced through meditation, drugs, sex, or any other mind-altering psychotechnology. It is not a dazzling display of psychic phenomena or paranormal powers. It is not a vision which transports one momentarily to some celestial realm. It is not sitting immobile in trance while experiencing an inner world of fascinating colors and sound or, alternatively, a complete blankness of mind. Enlightenment can include all that but it also infinitely transcends all that. *Anything* less than ultimate is not the answer, and all phenomena are passing, nonultimate. And *caveat emptor,* that applies to nearly everything offered by the enlightenment industry.

So as all the excitement about quick fixes, bliss machines, effortless systems, and instant ego cures winds down without noticeable results, as the froth of commercialism subsides and people begin to see deeper into the nature of self-transformation and spiritual quest, they are left confused and dissatisfied. And again the question arises: What is enlightenment?

The Perennial Wisdom

If that has been the perennial question, the answer has been called the perennial wisdom. This is the goal of the spiritual journey: radical understanding which gets to the heart of human experience, illuminating every facet, removing all doubt about the meaning of existence and the nature of reality. It is not so much a matter of factual knowledge as feeling-wisdom, not omniscience but certitude. (However, there is a vast body of literature on enlightenment and my *What Is Enlightenment?* draws from it to offer a comprehensive collection. Its introduction, expanded here, is intended to offer an intellectually sound understanding which is, in effect, a map of reality.)

The perennial wisdom is unchanging; truth is one. That is agreed upon by the sages of all major religions and sacred tradition, all hermetic philosophies, genuine mystery schools, and higher occult paths. Enlightenment is the core truth of them all. Even more broadly, it is the essence of life—the goal of all growth, development, evolution. It is the discovery of what we ultimately are, the answer to the questions Who am I? Why am I here? Where am I going? What is life all about?

The Paradox of Being and Becoming

Paradoxically, the answer we seek is none other than what we *already are* in essence: Being, the ultimate wholeness which is the source and ground of all Becoming. *Enlightenment is realization of the truth of Being.* Our native condition, our true self is Being, traditionally called God, the Cosmic Person, the Supreme Being, the One-in-all. (Some enlightened teachers—the Buddha was one—prefer to avoid theistic terms in order to communicate better. Their intent is to bypass the deep cultural conditioning which occurs through such language and which blocks understanding.) We are manifestations of Being, but like the cosmos itself, we are also in the process of Becoming—always changing, developing, growing, evolving to higher and higher states which express ever more beautifully the perfection of the source of existence. Thus we are not only human beings, we are also human becomings. Enlightenment is understanding the perfect poise of being-amid-becoming.

The truth of all existence and all experience, then, is none other than the seamless here-and-now, the already present, the prior nature of that which seeks and strives and asks: Being. *The spiritual journey is the process of discovering and living that truth*. It amounts to the eye seeing itself—or, rather, the I seeing its Self. In philosophical terms, enlightenment is comprehending the unity of all dualities, the harmonious *composite* of all *op*posites, the oneness of endless multiplicity and diversity. In psychological terms, it is transcendence of all senses of limitation and otherness. In humanistic terms, it is understanding that the journey is the teaching, that the path and the destination are ultimately one. In theological terms, it is comprehending the union of God and humanity. In ontological terms, it is the State of all states, the Condition of all conditions which transcends the entire cosmos yet is also everyday reality, since nothing is apart from it or ever can be.

When we finally understand the Great Mystery, we discover our true nature, the Supreme Identity, the Self of all. That direct perception of our oneness with the infinite, that noetic realization of our identity with the divine is the source of all happiness, all goodness, all beauty, all truth. It is beyond time, space, and causality; it is beyond ego and all socially conditioned sense of "I." Knowing ourselves to be timeless, boundless, and therefore cosmically free ends the illusion of separateness and all the painful, destructive defenses we erect, individually and societally, to preserve the ego-illusion at the expense of others. The *Maitreyana Upanishad* puts it this way: "Having realized his own self as the Self, a person becomes selfless. . . . This is the highest mystery."

Involution, Evolution, and Return to Godhead

Although we are essentially Being, we are not simply static. We are also active, also Being-in-the-process-of-Self-induced-change, which is traditionally called Becoming or cosmic evolution. However, *evolution* is only one aspect of that mysterious process underlying creation. The other is *involution*—that "breathing out" by God, that "emptying" or *kenosis* which brings forth the cosmos and involves divinity in matter so that it may work itself through stages of growth in awareness, from nescience through simple consciousness, self-consciousness, and cosmic consciousness to that Great Remembrance-Resurrection of itself as none other than the One-in-all.

We are *in*volved in matter to become *e*volved as Spirit. We are developing, individually and as a race, through the levels of existence—physical, mental, and spiritual—that are in their ultimate nature simply gradations of God, the Great Chain of Being. Original creation of the cosmos was the materialization of Spirit; all which follows is the spiritualization of matter, in all words, high and low. Thus we are ultimately

God in a Self-imposed drama—a drama in which a part of God "forgets" itself, believes itself to be "lost" or separate and thereby is motivated to seek reunion with the Whole, the One-without-a-second. The act in which we become lost and forget our god-nature is involution, the fall from unity and bliss; the act in which we find ourselves and remember our true condition is evolution, the conscious return to godhead. When we understand that, we begin to live what Sri Aurobindo calls "the life divine."

Existence Is the Play of God

From the cosmic perspective, the situation we find ourselves in is a drama in which we are sleepwalking actors. We go through life unaware of the fact that everything is the play of God (pun intended). To awaken from that drama is enlightenment. You discover that God is the author, actor, and stage for an infinitely playful, and therefore delightful, drama. But what do you do after you wake up? Why, just the same as in daily life. You go about your business and get on with what must be done in the world—in all worlds. You become, in a sense, a co-creator with God in "saving" the universe by doing what you can to help others see the light and love of divinity shining in all things—indeed, *as* all things.

Enlightenment, then, is an endless process, not simply a one-time event. True, quantum leaps in awareness mark the spiritual path, as "maps of reality" developed by sacred traditions show, but one white-light experience does not a mystic make, nor a saint. Even the most spiritually elevated people have found there are states of being beyond their present level of development. This lifetime is sufficient to reach enlightenment but not to complete it. Self-realization is not the same as self-transformation. As Sri Aurobindo puts it, God-realization is a "middle term" in the process of higher human development. Thus self-realization, however radical, is not the end of the human journey. Higher states of development await, calling us to further transformation in our evolutionary destiny. Understand, however, that all such future stages of Becoming are nevertheless expressions of infinitely and eternally present Being and thus our ultimate identity is, in the words of Da Love-Ananda, "always already God." Always, that is, already enlightened.

Names and Symbols for Enlightenment

Enlightenment has been given many names. *Buddha* means "the enlightened one," as do *Christ* and *Messiah*. Saint Paul called it "the peace of God which passeth all understanding" and Richard Maurice Bucke named it "cosmic consciousness." In Zen it is *satori*, in yoga it is *samadhi* or *moksha,* in Sufism it is *fana* or *tawhid,* in Taoism it is *wu* or The Ultimate Tao. Gurdjieff labeled it "objective consciousness," Sri Aurobindo spoke of the Supermind, mystery schools and occult paths speak of "illumination," "liberation," and "self-realization." Likewise, enlightenment has been symbolized by many images: the thousand-petaled lotus of Hinduism, the Holy Grail of Christianity, the clear mirror of Buddhism, Judaism's Star of David, the *yin–yang* circle of Taoism, Freemasonry's royal arch, the mountaintop, the swan, the still lake, the mystic rose, the eternal flame.

And enlightenment has been described by saints, sages, and scholars in many ways. For example, Ken Wilber offers this summary in the final chapter of his *Eye to Eye:*

> The Ultimate State of Consciousness is universally described in mystical literature as union with the Absolute, where the Absolute is known not as one among many but one without a second. Further, it is specified that to know the Absolute is to be the Absolute. It follows that the Ultimate State of Consciousness is itself the Absolute, and thus the Ultimate State is not a state of consciousness set apart from other states, not one state among many, but rather one state without a second—that is to say, absolutely all-inclusive. Hence, the Ultimate State of Consciousness is not an altered state of consciousness, for there is no alternative to it.[1]

Likewise, Da Love-Ananda has commented at great length on the subject. His point of view, elaborated in his discourses and writing, is succinctly given in *The Bodily Sacrifice of Attention:*

> The usual man or woman thinks that Enlightenment is the having of a vision. Enlightenment is the most subtle, or tacit, unspeakable understanding. It is the Bodhicitta, the ultimate realization of Being, the ultimate Wisdom. On its basis, all kinds of radiant transformations may develop, but the Realization itself is so fundamental, so tacit, so simple, so direct, so obvious, so transcendental, that it is not identified with any phenomenon of experience or knowledge. The means of the transmission of this Realization is an awakened individual, the Spiritual Master, but the Realization is most tacit, perfect, simple, direct, and obvious. When you come to the point of acknowledging the Divine Identity and Condition of manifest existence, then you are Enlightened.[2]   *A m E N !*

Thaddeus Golas, author of the brief but wise *The Lazy Man's Guide to Enlightenment,* describes it like this: "Enlightenment is any experience of expanding our consciousness beyond its present limits. We could also say that perfect enlightenment is realization that we have no limits at all." And to paraphrase still another contemporary source, Maharaj-ji, the guru of ex-Harvard professor of psychology Ram Dass, enlightenment is never casting anyone out of your heart: that is, living as infinite and unconditional love, the way God loves.

Enlightenment Is Beyond Words and Symbols

Regardless of the name or symbol, however, and no matter how poetic and inspiring the verbal description, there is no substitute for direct experience. Enlightenment is ineffable—beyond words, images, and concepts. It cannot be grasped by intellect, logic, analysis, or any aspect of our egoic–rational–mental being, no matter how keen and penetrating the mind, no matter how cunning the intelligence. A symbol conceals as much as it reveals and words are only *about* truth; they are not truth itself. They are therefore only guides, not guarantees. Reading about enlightenment is not a substitute for practice of a spiritual discipline or a sacred way of life. There must be actual experience; pictures of pancakes do not satisfy hunger.

To experience enlightenment yourself, then, the only thing which absolutely *must* be "read" is the Great Mystery, and for that you read with the eye of contemplation, not the eye of reason, and certainly not with the various glittering goods of the enlightenment industry. Furthermore, no matter how hard you seek, no matter how great your effort, enlightenment can never be achieved—only discovered. And for that we are all dependent upon what spiritual traditions call grace.

But grace abounds—amazing grace. As Jesus said, if you ask for bread, you will not be given stones. Seek and you shall find. Knock and it shall be opened unto you. A universal intelligence provides everything you need every step of the way. Its entire purpose is simply to awaken you to your true nature. Enlightenment, or the kingdom of heaven, is your birthright.

Walking the Path to Enlightenment

Claiming our birthright, however, is no easy matter. As I noted in Chapter 2, grace falls like rain on everyone but, also like rain, it can only be received by a vessel properly prepared to catch it. The preparation involves a change of consciousness. Without that, we are mere stones from which the rain slides off; with it, we become worked stone hollowed into urns or chalices which can receive and retain what falls from heaven.

Nor is claiming our birthright a straightforward matter. On the spiritual path there are many side trails which are essentially dead ends, if not traps. (Psychic development, for example, is not the same thing as spiritual growth.) There are also periods of chaotic upheaval in the mind, moments of insight and partial breakthrough, intervals of exhaustion and utter apathy, and times of intense struggle and doubt when faith in the ultimate importance of the spiritual journey alone carries you stumblingly forward. What can we say about this process of what the mystic poet William Blake called "cleansing the doors of perception," of finding our true self?

Sacred traditions emphasize right living and awareness of the present moment, rather than offering minute descriptions of higher worlds intended for intellectual study. That is not to say they have no such descriptions—they do. However, their attitude is "Don't talk—experience! And make haste slowly. You will eventually learn all you need to know at a pace best for you. That makes the difference between knowledge and wisdom—between rote learning and real understanding."

If you were to ask a Zen master, for example, to explain satori, he might stoop down, pick up a rock, and hand it to you, or he might bark like a dog or do something else equally startling. Such behavior is intended to help you burst through your ordinary state of awareness, which is so object-oriented and language-bound, so conditioned by culture. Or he might puzzle you with a koan, an apparently insoluble riddle, like: "Before enlightenment, I chopped wood and carried water. After enlightenment, I chopped wood and carried water."

What is the spiritual seeker to understand by such "crazy wisdom"? The answer is this: Reality is reality—period. *It* is unchanging, but *your perception* of reality changes as you change consciouisness. As the rishis of ancient India said, knowledge is structured in consciousness. The difference before and after enlightenment, therefore, is in you—not in reality. To quote Meher Baba, the founder of Sufism Reoriented, "The infinite Truth which is at the heart of Reality . . . does not suffer any limitation even if the entire universe is dissolved." The limitation is in you—in your consciouisness—and when that limitation is transcended, you perceive existence differently and therefore relate to it in a new way. Your sense of identity changes. You experience the cosmos as unified and intimately one with your own essential being rather than experience yourself as a separate, isolated physical form apart from all the rest of existence. You recognize yourself as an individual who, although outwardly differentiated from all others in the boundless diversity of forms, is nevertheless one with them on the basis of prior inner unity.

Maps of Reality Which Guide You Along the Spiritual Path

But is it that simple? No. Although, as the *Brihadaranyaka Upanishad* declares, "By understanding the Self, all this universe is known," the discovery of Self-as-All is far from simple. What can be said about this process of coming to see things as they are, infinite?

Another Zen koan is appropriate here. "Before I came to Zen, mountains were only mountains, rivers only rivers, trees only trees. After I got into Zen, mountains were no longer mountains, rivers no longer rivers, trees no longer trees. But when enlightenment happened, mountains were again only mountains, rivers again only rivers, trees again only trees."

Here you can see the same perspective as in the other koan, but there is an additional element: the suggestion of an intermediate stage of growth in the process of enlightenment. If you follow this notion of states of growth, you find that sacred traditions have very soundly mapped the major landmarks on the spiritual journey. Their maps are called, in contemporary language, esoteric/transpersonal psychologies.

In traversing the planes of being, the higher worlds, as you ascend/ evolve in consciousness, it can be an enormous help to have a guidebook—something which offers sound advice and trustworthy directions. Of course, as Krishnamurti said, Truth is a pathless land. Or as Thaddeus Golas puts it, enlightenment doesn't care how you get there. All this is perfectly true, but why reinvent the wheel? There are already time-tested and world-honored maps of reality for bringing spiritual travelers through the mazes of mind and labyrinths of inner space with relative ease and safety. You wouldn't begin a long trip without some sense of where you're going and without asking questions about what is likely to be experienced along the way. Perhaps you'd go to a travel agency or automobile club for advice. Just so, the spiritual traveler should take advantage of the best guidance available when the self-realization journey is begun.

Humility, Selfless Service, and Unconditional Love

As I have said, from the cosmic perspective the human situation is a kind of sleepwalking from which we awaken by grace and no small effort of our own. But it is nothing to be proud of. Since you and all things are ultimately one, a genuine realization of God-as-yourself does not give you exclusive status, however intelligent, talented, charismatic, or otherwise distinguished you may be. You realize you are nobody special because, beneath outward form and name, everyone else is also you as expressions of the One Great Being. Thus, the true response to self-realization is humility.

The true response is also selfless service—the behavioral reflection of unconditional love. When you realize your true Self, you automatically respond to the call of humanity. That call, however unconsciously uttered, is: Show me the way to God. Thus, the enlightened are more involved in human society than any other group is, even though they may live retiringly or reclusively, because they alone see the truth, beauty, and love at the heart of existence. They alone live in accord with that perception to help others change consciousness and thereby discover the essential perfection of all things. Purpose, meaning, direction in life, understanding, happiness are what all people are searching for, however ignorantly. And that is what the enlightened seek to help others find, patiently, humbly, lovingly, without concern for reward or recognition, status or power (all of which imply an "other") because ultimately it is all being done for oneself. "By their fruits ye shall know them."

Saving the World

Planet Earth today is facing unprecedented threats. But those dangers looming over us—socioeconomic, environmental, nuclear/military—are, ironically, productions of our own minds, our ignorance and self-centeredness. Now, a problem can't be solved at the level which generated it. Therefore, resolution of the dangers facing humanity requires getting beyond the usual mind or self-sense. Political action, social programs, humanitarian work, and so forth are good but not enough. Only trans-formed consciousness can transform the world. The ultimate action, then, is no action at all except to change consciousness.

Enlightenment is liberation, freedom. But so long as one person is not free, no one is free. That is why, throughout history, the truly enlightened have always taken upon themselves a mission of devoted service to the world. Self-realization leads to a transformation of one's total being—both inner awareness and outer behavior. The illusion of separate self melts away. There is a marvelous release from all the corrosive scheming, manipulation, and defensiveness people "e-go" through to protect their illusory self from the truth of existence. Self-pity, self-righteousness, anger, lust, envy, sloth, and so forth evaporate—egoing, egoing, egone! What is left has a human form to ordinary perception. It eats, sleeps, walks, and functions like other human beings. As the koan says, it continues to chop wood and carry water. But the personal has changed into the universal by the recognition of one's total union with the infinite. Energy and intelligence are freed to make heavy work light and to be creative in tasks and relationships. Saintliness and sageliness emerge. Life becomes simple and unitive. The world becomes wonderful, the ordinary becomes extraordinary. Circumstances previously regarded as a problem become a challenge, even an exciting opportunity to learn and to grow and to relieve a bit of the world's burden.

The Key to Understanding and Happiness

Understanding is a function of your state of consciousness. So is happiness. As long as there is an "other" in your consciousness, there will be a limit to your understanding and happiness. Ignorance and suffering are directly proportional to the degree of ego or self-centeredness you bring to your circumstances. But when there is no one but the One, when you are the Self of all, you are infinitely assured, infinitely fulfilled, infinitely happy. In such a state, existence is seen to be inherently blissful. Then whatever occurs in your life and whatever you are required to do is perfectly acceptable. Your mere being contributes to the liberation of all and the salvation of the world.

There are many paths up the mountain to enlightenment. But when the paths get to the top, they all come together in the realization that truth is one. That is when the ego dies and you are reborn into life, into reality. In the enlightened condition, you discover that you are not just the traveler—you are also the path and the mountain. That is why Jesus died on the Cross with forgiveness in His heart. That is why *bodhisattvas,* Buddhist saints, vow not to accept final enlightenment until all sentient beigns are ready for it first. And it is possible for you to realize that right now because it is your very condition at every moment.

What is enlightenment? Look around you. Everything is yourself. That is it—just that. So open your "I" and see the wonder of chopping wood and carrying water. And then share it lovingly with others. That is enlightenment.

21

The Judeo-Christian Tradition and the New Age

In its best aspect, the New Age movement aims at manifesting a new mode of being, a radically transformed world inhabited by a new humanity. That new creation would involve a social order based on love and wisdom (as envisioned by many traditions, both sacred and secular) which resolves societal disharmonies and allows people to fulfill their deepest longings for peace, truth, self-expression, and freedom from the perennial problems of man's inhumanity to man. What precisely does this mean? How does it relate to Jesus and the Bible?

The emergence of a higher humanity is a perennial theme in world affairs. The images drawn from this theme vary in form and purity, ranging from the inspired visions of mystics such as Sri Aurobindo to the deranged fantasies of madmen such as Adolf Hitler. Nietzsche's *Das Übermensch* or Overman was distorted into the racial supremacy doctrines of the Third Reich, and Hitler sought through genocide to create a super-race. Übermensch also became, in a more benign form, the basis for a comic book hero, Superman. Pierre Teilhard de Chardin wrote of this emergence in quasi-scientific terms; Gopi Krishna addressed it more rigorously in his examination of the next evolutionary development in man via the kundalini experience; psychologist Kenneth Ring finds evidence for it in the widespread phenomenon of the near-death experience. Occult traditions such as Theosophy, Anthroposophy, Rosicru-

212

cianism, Freemasonry, alchemy, Cabbalah, and the genuine mystery schools also present the notion of the evolution of humanity to still-higher states. One of the most memorable statements is that of M. Bucke, on the last page of *Cosmic Consciousness.*

> . . .just as, long ago, self-consciousness appeared in the best specimens of our ancestral race in the prime of life, and gradually became more and more universal and appeared in the individual at an earlier and earlier age, until, as we see now, it has become almost universal and appears at the average of about three years—so will Cosmic Consciousness become more and more universal earlier in the individual life until the race at large will possess this faculty. The same race and not the same; for a Cosmic Conscious race will not be the race which exists today, any more than the present race of men is the same race which existed prior to the evolution of self-consciousness. The simple truth is, that there has lived on the earth, "appearing at intervals," for thousands of years among ordinary men, the first faint beginnings of another race; walking the earth, and breathing another air of which we know little or nothing, but which is, all the same, our spiritual life, as its absence would be our spiritual death. This new race is in the act of being born from us, and in the near future it will occupy and possess the earth.

For the majority of Westerners, however, the most familiar term for this experience—the emergence of a cosmically conscious race—was given two millennia ago by Jesus of Nazareth.

When Jesus spoke of himself, why did he principally use the term *Son of Man?* Others called him the Son of God, but Jesus most often referred to himself as the Son of Man, the offspring of humanity. Moreover, he told those around him that they would be higher than the angels and that those things which he did, they would be also, and greater (John 14:12), for that is the estate of Man.

The reason for this declaration by Jesus is that he was aware of himself as a finished specimen of the new humanity to come—the new humanity which is to inherit the Earth, establish the Kingdom, usher in the New Age. His mission and teaching have at their heart the development of a new and higher state of consciousness *on a specieswide basis* rather than the sporadic basis seen earlier in history when an occasional adept or avatar such as Krishna or the Buddha appeared. Jesus' unique place in history is based upon his unprecedented realization of the higher intelligence, the divinity, the Ground of Being incarnated in him—the ground which is the source of all becoming.

The Aramaic term for the Greek word for *Christ* is *M'shekha,* from which we get "messiah." It is a title, not a last name (as in Jesus Christ), and although it is conventionally translated "anointed," it really means "perfected" or "enlightened" or "the ideal form of humanity." Thus, Jesus was a historical person, a human being who lived two thousand years ago; but Christ, the Christos, the Messiah, is an eternal transpersonal condition of being to which *we must all someday come.* Jesus did not say that this higher state of consciousness realized in him was his alone for all time. Nor did he call us to worship him. Rather, he called us to *follow* him—to follow in his steps, to imitate him, emulate him, learn from him and his example, to live a God-centered life of selfless, compassionate service to the world *as if we were Jesus himself.* This is what is meant by the Latin phrase *imitatio Christi,* "the imitation of Christ." Jesus called us to share in the new condition, to enter a new world, to be one in the supramental consciousness which alone can dispel the darkness of our minds and renew our lives. He did not call us to be Christians; he called us to be Christed. In short, he aimed at fostering the development of *many* Jesuses. He aimed, as the New Testament declares, to make all one in Christ. And who is Christ? Paul tells us that Christ is the Second Adam, the founder of a new race.

The Kingdom is within us. Divinity is our birthright, our inheritance, nearer to us than hand and foot, but the eye will not see and the ear will not hear. Jesus called people to awaken, to change their ways, to repent. The very first words he spoke to humanity in his public ministry were "The time is fulfilled, and the kingdom of God is at hand; repent, and believe in the gospel" (Mark 1:14; Matthew 4:17). This is his central teaching and commandment, what is called the *kerygma.*

But notice the word *repent.* Over the centuries it has become misconstrued and mistranslated, so that today people think it merely means feeling sorry for their sins. This is an unfortunate debasement of Jesus' teaching. The Aramaic word Jesus used is *tob,* meaning "to return," "to flow back into God." The sense of this concept comes through best in the Greek word used to translate it. The word is *metanoia;* like *tob,* it means something far greater than merely feeling sorry for misbehavior. Metanoia has two etymological roots. *Meta* means "to go beyond" or "to go higher than." And *noia* comes from *nous,* meaning "mind." It is the same root from which Teilhard de Chardin developed his term *noosphere* and from which the word *noetic,* meaning "the study of consciousness," comes. It is also the term Plato used to designate the creative source of the universe prior to the Logos, the Word, which in the gospel of John refers to Jesus. So the original meaning of metanoia is literally "going beyond or higher than the ordinary mental state." In modern terms, it means transcending self-centered ego and becoming God-centered, God-realized.

This is the central experience Jesus sought for all people. This is the heart of Jesus' life and teaching, although it is now largely absent from the institutional Christian churches. Metanoia indicates a change of mind and behavior based on radical insight into the cause and effect of one's previous actions—insight arising from entry into a condition beyond the realm of time, space, and causality. Metanoia is that profound state of consciousness mystical experience aims at: the state in which we transcend or dissolve all the barriers of ego and selfishness which separate us from God. It is the summum bonum of human life. It is a state of *direct knowing unmediated perception* of our total unity with God, not through anything we have done or ever could do in a final sense (although we *must* seek to cleanse ourselves through spiritual discipline or there can be no transcendence), but simply through God's grace and unconditional love. Paul described it as "the renewing of your mind in Christ." Jesus said it even more simply: "I am the way" to metanoia.

In its best sense, then, metanoia means a radical conversion experience, a transformation of self based on a new state of awareness, a new state of higher consciousness. It means repentence in the most fundamental aspect of our existence—that of "a turning about in the deepest seat of consciousness," as Lama Govinda phrases it. That turning-about is for the purpose of rebinding or re-tieing ourselves to the divine source of our being, the source we have lost awareness of. That is what religion is all about. The word *religion* is etymologically derived from the Latin *re ligare,* "to tie back, to tie again." That is true repentence, when we "get religion" in the sense of becoming aware of our inescapable ties to God, the creator, preserver, and redeemer of the cosmos.

Failure to realize that is the source of all the world's troubles. But when we are rebound to God, the true meaning of sin becomes apparent. Sin means, literally, "missing the mark." Sin is not merely misbehavior; that is only the outer, behavioral aspect of it. The inner aspect, the deeper dimension of sin, is transgression of divine law or cosmic principle. It is failure to be centered in God—to be "off target." Religion, then, is in its most fundamental and truest sense *an instrument for awakening us to the evolutionary process of growth to godhood,* which is the aim of all evolution, all growth, all cosmic becoming. When we are guilty of sin, we are fundamentally missing the mark by failing to be God-conscious and all that this means for our behavior and thought.

Thus, the world is indeed in sin, but there is no remedy for it except to change consciousness. For in truth, God does not condemn us for our sins. Rather, we condemn ourselves *by* our sins. And thus forgiveness by God is not necessary; it is there always, as unconditional love, the instant we turn in our hearts and minds to God. As *A Course in Miracles* puts it, forgiveness must be offered *from ourselves to the world* for all the offenses, real or imaginary, we have stored in our hearts with rancor, bitterness, and longing for revenge. *That* is the turning point; that is when ego transcendence truly begins and the glory of God starts to be revealed to us. As Jesus said, the first and great commandment is to love God with all your heart and soul and mind.

To understand all is to forgive all. God understands all and forgives all and loves all. Thus, the essence of higher consciousness is never casting anyone out of your heart—to love as God loves. As Jesus said, the second great commandment is to love your neighbor as yourself. When we love as God loves, unconditionally, we are beyond the reach of the unloving. We may receive injury from them and we may feel pain, but we are incapable of being hurt or offended in spirit, and therefore are always happy under all circumstances, even in the face of monstrous ill will and injustice. For this reason, love is the greatest "revenge" we can seek against enemies and those who treat us spitefully and wrongly. Is that not precisely what Jesus taught? And is that not precisely how Jesus taught it—by preaching a sermon with his life as well as his lips?

There will never be a better world until there are better people in it, and the means for attaining that condition, for "building better people," are democratically available to everyone through the grace and unconditional love of God. If that grace and love were withdrawn for even the slightest instant, the entire cosmos would be annihilated. To become experientially aware of that fact is no easy task, but there is no substitute for growth to higher consciousness: the recognition that all is God and there is only God. The metanoia process, when completed, results in the state of awareness Jesus himself had when he said "I and the Father are one."

That is what Jesus taught and demonstrated: cosmic consciousness, the Christic state of mind, the peace which passeth understanding, the direct experience of divinity dwelling in us and all things, now and forever, creating us, living us, preserving us, urging us on to ever more inclusive states of being so that "he that believeth on me, the works that I do shall he do, and greater than these shall he do." That is the human potential, the potential for growth to godhood. That human *potential* is what can change the human *condition* and redeem the world from sinfulness—that alone. It is none other than recognition of the divine character of all existence in which, as Paul said, we live and move and have our very being.

The institutional Christian churches tell us that Jesus was the only Son of God, that he incarnated as a human in order to die on the Cross in a substitutionary act as a penalty for our sins, and thereby save the world. But that is a sad caricature, a pale reflection of the true story. It turns Jesus into a magical fairy-tale hero and Christianity into a cult of personality. As Ralph Waldo Emerson pointed out a century ago, Christendom has become a religion *about* Jesus rather than the religion *of* Jesus. The religion *about* Jesus puts him on a pedestal, regards him as Big Daddy in the Sky, and petitions him to be responsible for us. The religion *of* Jesus calls on every human being to take personal responsibility for growing to that same state of cosmic unity and wholeness which Jesus himself demonstrated. There is no substitute for personal responsibility.

Jesus did not "save" people; he *freed* them—from the bondage of ego. The significance of incarnation and resurrection is not that Jesus was a human like us but rather that *we are gods like him*—or at least have the potential to be. The Christian tradition, rightly understood, seeks to have us all become Jesuses, become one in Christ—beyond all the darkness of mind which results in the evil and suffering so widespread in the world. Jesus himself pointed out that this is what the Judaic tradition, which he fulfilled, is all about when he said "It is not written in your law, 'I said, you are gods'?" (John 10:34).

Jesus showed us the way. He demonstrated in his life and explained in his teaching that we all have the God-given right to enter the Kingdom, to be healed of our sense of separation and alienation, to overcome time and sin and fear of death (all of which are rooted in the egoic self-sense) and to enter into eternity-timelessness and become whole and holy. We all have this potential, given not by "my" Father but, as the Lord's Prayer says, by *our* Father. Jesus showed in his life, his death, and his resurrection that we are eternal celestial beings whose home is the universe. He showed that heaven is a present reality, not a future reward. He showed that the death of the body is not the destruction of our consciousness, that the Christ consciousness which embodied itself in the man Jesus transcends the facts of physics and biology and actually controls physics and biology as conventionally understood. He showed that the Christ consciousness was, is, and ever shall be present among us, faithfully calling us to reunion, world without end, because it is the source of all creation.

So rather than saying that Jesus was the Christ, it is more accurate to say: the Christ was Jesus. That allows for *other* Christs: you and me. As Vitvan says in his profound book, *The Christos*,[1] this capacity is a developmental process available to everyone. "If it is not operating in all universally, then it has no value to me."

Jesus, therefore, should not be seen as a vehicle of salvation but as a model of perfection. That is why the proper attitude toward him is one of reverence, not worship. Jesus showed us the way to a higher state of being and called upon us to realize it, to make it real, actual—individually and as the race. This is the true meaning of being born again: dying to the past and the old sense of self through a change of consciousness. To enter the Kingdom we must die and be born again, we must become as a little child. From the perspective of metanoia, the meaning of Jesus' injunction is clear. To re-enter the state of innocence infants exhibit, we do not merely regress to an infantile level, forsaking our mature faculties. Instead, we *progress* through transcendence of the illusion of ego and all its false values, attitudes, and habits. We attain a guileless state of mind without giving up the positive qualities of adulthood. We grow into what is called "the higher innocence." We optimize, rather than maximize, childhood, becoming childlike, not childish. Superficial values and capriciousness are simply outgrown, so that we function in the service of a transcendent purpose, offering our life's work to God moment-to-moment rather than seeking self-glorification and some consoling distant reward in this world or the next. We discover that heaven and hell are not remote places; they are states of consciousness. Heaven is union with God, hell is separation from God, and the difference is measured not in miles but in surrender of ego and self-centeredness.

Jesus showed us the way to the Kingdom, but he will not—indeed, cannot—magically take anyone there. That depends on our own effort and willingness to sacrifice our false self. And even then, the timing is unknown. God's grace is still the final factor in crossing the planes of consciousness. Nevertheless, the effort should be made, *must* be made. Like the climber who went up Mount Everest simply because it was there, sooner or later every human being will feel a call from the cosmos to ascend to godhood. That is our historical love affair with the divine. And as Jesus said, if you ask for bread, you will not be given stones. Seek and you shall find; knock and it shall be opened unto you.

There is no way to enter the Kingdom except to ascend in consciousness to the Father, to that unconditional love for all creation which Jesus demonstrated. That is what the Christian tradition (and, indeed, every true religion) is all about: a system of teachings, both theory and practice, about growth to higher consciousness. But each of us is required to take personal responsibility for following Jesus on that way. That is the key to the Kingdom. Self-transcendence requires honesty, commitment, and spiritual practice to cultivate awareness. The result of such discipline is a personal, validating experience of the fact that alteration of consciousness can lead to a radical transformation of consciousness, traditionally called enlightenment. But this, by and large, has been lost to the understanding of contemporary Christendom. Instead, Jesus and the Bible are idolized, and heaven is said to be located somewhere in outer space. Awareness of inner space—of consciousness and the need to cultivate it—is sadly lacking. *Exoteric* Judeo-Christianity must reawaken to the truth preserved in its *esoteric* tradition.

For example, the original form of baptism, whole-body immersion, was limited to adults. It apparently was an initiatory practice in which the person, a convert who would have been prepared through study of spiritual disciplines, was held under water to the point of nearly drowning. This near-death experience was likely to induce an out-of-body projection such as many near-death experiencers report today. The baptized person would thereby directly experience resurrection—the transcendence of death, the reality of metaphysical worlds, and the supremacy of Spirit. He would receive a dramatic and unmistakable demonstration of the reality of the spiritual body or celestial body of which Paul speaks in I Corinthians 15:40–44 (apparently referring to his own personal experience with out-of-body projection). The forms of baptism practiced today, even those involving bodily immersion, are from the esoteric perspective debasements of the original purpose and meaning of baptism in the Judeo-Christian tradition. (I am not implicitly advocating a return to that esoteric practice; much safer, less risky methods of inducing out-of-body projection are available today. The present symbolic use of baptism is justifiable *if* it is supplemented with the necessary understanding of its true but esoteric significance.)

Matthew 11:29–30 suggests other spiritual practices which Jesus taught to his disciples and an inner circle: "Take my yoke upon you . . . my yoke is easy." The word *yoke* is conventionally understood to mean "burden" or "work." However, it is better understood in the sense of the Sanskrit *yug,* meaning "to yoke or join." It is the root from which *yoga* comes, and yoga, as I pointed out earlier, is a system of spiritual practices designed to accelerate personal growth and development, physically, mentally, and spiritually, so that the yogi attains union with the Divine. That yoking with God was precisely the aim of Jesus' teaching. Thus, esoteric Christianity understands the verses to mean "the practices I prescribe for growth to Christ consciousness."

So long as people believe in an unbridgeable gulf between themselves and what Jesus demonstrated, Christianity will not have accomplished its mission. So long as the focus of attention remains on a naïve, romanticized image of the historical person Jesus as the King of Heaven rather than on his transpersonal Christic demonstration of how to bridge the gulf between God and humanity, Christianity will not have carried out its founder's intent. "Building bridges" should be the main thrust of Christianity. Interestingly, this is explicitly acknowledged in the Roman Catholic tradition—whose supreme authority, the Pope, is technically termed the *Pontifex Maximus,* Latin for "supreme bridgemaker."

At present, Christianity tends to demand blind faith, rote words, and mechanical behavior. This leaves people feeling empty and unfulfilled. But the cosmic calling we humans have will not be denied forever, despite the ignorance of religious institutions which, in effect, prohibits people from direct access to God. The Holy Spirit, the life force, will simply move on to create new forms of religious expression, leaving ruins called churches behind.

But it need not be that way. If the human potential which Jesus demonstrated is understood to be within us, if the capacity to grow to godlike stature is directly experienced by all Christendom as the key to the Kingdom, Christianity will fulfill its purpose by encouraging people to evolve, to transform themselves, to rise to a higher state. For we are not simply human beings. We are also human becomings, organisms in an evolutionary process, standing between two worlds, two ages: an old one and a new one. The marvelous thing about us as nature-becoming-aware-of-itself-as-God is that each of us has the latent ability to take conscious control of our own evolution, to build our own bridge, and thereby become a member of the new age, the new humanity. As John recorded the words of Jesus during his visionary experience on Patmos, "Behold, I make all things new." (Revelation 21:5)

There are stages of growth in the course of this transformation which can be presented in a simple formulation: *from orthonoia to metanoia through paranoia*. We grow from orthonoia—the common, everyday state of ego-centered mind—to metanoia only by going through paranoia, a state in which the mind is deranged ("taken apart") and rearranged through spiritual discipline so that a clear perception of reality might be experienced. Conventional Western psychologies regard paranoia as a pathological breakdown. It often is, of course; but, seen from this perspective, it is not necessarily always so. Rather, it can be breakthrough—not the final breakthrough, to be sure, but a necessary stage of development on the way to realizing the Kingdom.[2]

Paranoia is well understood by mystical and sacred traditions. The disciplines practiced under the guidance of a guru or master or spiritual director are designed to ease the passage through paranoia so that the practitioner doesn't get lost in the labyrinth of inner space and become a casualty. But because metanoia has, by and large, not been experienced by the founders of Western psychology and psychotherapy, paranoia has not been fully understood in our culture. It is seen as an aberrated dead end rather than a necessary precondition to higher consciousness. It is not understood that the confusion, discomfort, and suffering experienced in paranoia are due largely to the destruction of an illusion, ego. The less we cling to that illusion, the less we suffer.

The world's great spiritual systems, however, understand the psychology of this situation very well and have developed procedures for curing it by disburdening people of their false self-image, their false identity. It is no accident that society's models of the ideal human being include many saints and holy people. These self-transcendent, God-realized individuals have been revered for many reasons: their compassion, devotion, and serenity; their inspirational words of wisdom; their virtuous service to the world. What has been their motivation? Each of them, in his own way arising from his particular tradition or culture, has discovered the secret of the ages, the truth of the saying "Let go and let God." When the ego-sense is dissolved, when a sense of the infinite and eternal replaces our usual narrow self-centeredness with all its passing, unsatisfying fantasies, there is no longer a mental basis for fear, hatred, anxiety, anger, attachment, desire. Instead, the perfectly harmonious functioning of the cosmos operates through us—and the cosmos is always in balance, always at peace with itself.

The Christian message is essentially a call to be universal, a call to become cosmically conscious. It is not a fundamentalist warning to beware of false gods but a transcendental urging to *be aware* of True God. It is a call to place the Divine at the center of ourselves, not through blind faith but through insightful awareness, not through rigid adherence to ritual and dogma but through graceful expression of cosmic principles. It is a call to recognize God as the transcendent creator of all things, the immanent self of all things, and the omnipresent matrix from which all things arise. This is the true meaning of the Trinity—the three principal aspects of God and the three primary modes of God-realization: the transcendent Father, the immanent Son, and the omnipresent Holy Spirit. The Christian message is a call to live as that recognition, to "be as gods."

Thus Jesus could speak of what is called the Second Coming as the end of the age, the end of history, the end of the world. Waking up from the illusion of ego, from the dream of worldly life, into God-conscious reality does indeed end the world. However, it ends the world not as global destruction but as transcendence of space, time and causality, and all false sense of identity based on that. In reality there is no Second Coming at all (a point I elaborate in the next chapter).

Today the world stands close to global disaster. But remember, a problem cannot be solved at the level which generated it. The solution can only be found at a higher level, through transcendence. The answer to our global emergency is emergence. That is, the solution to the problem of history will not be found within history, within the state of consciousness which generates time, temptation, and trouble: ego. The only way out of history into the Kingdom of God, the only way out of our precarious world situation into a New Age is a change of consciousness, a transcendence of the false sense of self from which all destructive human behavior arises. Only metanoia, the emergence of Christ-in-us, can provide the means whereby reality is seen clearly and an enlightened global culture is possible. And that is precisely what the Son of Man showed us.

But if the Son of Man showed us the way to that higher state of being, so have other enlightened teachers of humanity shown us the same beckoning evolutionary advance. I do not mean to present Jesus as the sole path to cosmic consciousness. That would be further debasement of his teaching and therefore contrary to the spirit of the New Age. We have been taught by the Buddha and Krishna, Lao Tsu and Moses, Muhammad, Zoroaster, Mahavira, Quetzalcoatl, Guru Nanak. The human race has been guided by many other evolutionary forerunners of a new Earth and a new humanity—a new age—who have given us the world's religions, sacred traditions, spiritual paths, esoteric psychologies, metaphysical philosophies, hermetic disciplines, and genuine occult mystery schools. They have differed in emphasis and cultural orientation, but the core truth of them all is the same: *Thou shalt evolve to a higher state of being and ultimately return to the godhead which is your very self, your ever-present Divine Condition prior to all conditions, names, and forms.*

Salvation *as liberation or enlightenment* is possible for us at every moment. This is what our spiritual teachers and sages and saviors have told us throughout history, and the unanimity of their voices transcends the dogmatism of any sect or religion or organization. Buddhism, for example, has no concept of sin or God, so many Christians feel it is antagonistic to their beliefs. But from the point of view of metanoia—of theosis—Buddhism and Christianity are reconciled because Buddhism, which does recognize there is wrongdoing in the world, says that it arises in people because they have become separated from their True-self, their Buddha-mind: the higher mind which is known in enlightenment. The Buddha-mind and the Christic mind are one.

If Planet Earth should end up as just a nuclear flash in the sky or a polluted pile of rubble, from the cosmic point of view it will be the loss of just one lifebearing planet circling a minor star in a middle-sized galaxy among billions of galaxies—just an evolutionary experiment which failed. There are probably billions of other worlds, exobiologists tell us, where the evolution of intelligent life forms is going on, with many of them well beyond our own state of development. That terminal flash can happen, but it need not. The source of our being is calling to us through innumerable forms and channels—through nature and through enlightened teachers—calling us to awaken to our true identity and carry that knowledge forward in the emergence of a higher form of life, a new structure of human society, a new social and political order characterized by God-centered consciousness. That, as I have said earlier, is why bodhisattvas vow not to obtain final enlightenment until all sentient beings are first ready for it; that is why Jesus forgave his oppressors before he died.

That selfless, compassionate service, that behavioral expression of enlightenment is the key to avoiding global catastrophe and to transforming, rather than destroying, the Earth. Each of us must become our own messiah and thereby redeem the world from sinfulness.

The Kingdom is already among us as the source of our being. To the extent that it is realized in consciousness by people, is it being manifested. So if you want to see the present ruler of the world, Satan, who is the deceiver of the heart, the obstacle to establishing God's kingdom on Earth, the one who leads us astray from the paths of righteous—go look in a mirror. If the one who looks back is the ego, if the one who looks back does not have Christ in his or her heart, that one is the antichrist, the adversary, the blasphemer, the one who leads the world into hell. But even in the depths of sin, you are never apart from God. Even if you flee into hell, as the Psalmist says, there are Thou also, O Lord. We have only to realize it and surrender to Reality.

The way to God-realization or messiahship is through an ascent in consciousness to that unconditional love for all creation demonstrated by Jesus. In that regard, I'm sure Jesus the Christ would be in perfect agreement with Gautama the Buddha, who taught his followers to work out their own salvation by steadfastly seeking truth. For, as Jesus said, "the truth shall set you free."

Nothing less than this will bring the New Age, and everything else is superfluous—an unsatisfying distraction or a bogus consolation. Holistic haircuts and transpersonal teabags are silly but innocuous distortions of the New Age movement; Jonestowns and other mind-manipulations are tragic perversions of it. Neither is a true expression of self-transcendence and God-realization. The real meaning of the New Age is a renewing of our minds and hearts through awakening to the presence of God, not simply within us but among us (in other people) and around us (as nature), as well as above us and prior to us—as the All and Only Reality. Only that, only enlightenment or union with God, will transform the world and produce a new humanity. Thus Jesus is the prime exemplar of the New Age.

22

The New Age and the Second Coming of Christ

Advent is the time of year when Christendom celebrates the incarnation of Christ through the birth of Jesus. However, the term *Advent* also refers to a future event conventionally known as the Second Coming of Christ or, more technically, the Second Advent, the Parousia. At the Second Coming, it is widely believed, Jesus will return to Earth from his celestial dwelling place to judge humanity, accompanied by angels with mighty trumpets and by other heavenly signs. He will separate the saints from the sinners, establish the Kingdom of God, and raise the believers into heaven while the damned burn in hell for eternity.

Those who watch television have heard this message often; the electronic evangelists make it the subject of their preaching again and again: the Kingdom is coming; the end is near; these are the last days; Jesus is coming in glory to rule the world in peace as Lord of heaven and Earth.

And as the threat of nuclear annihilation looms, as famine stalks the planet, as environmental assaults upset the balance of nature, as earthquakes and volcanic activity increase, as crime and poverty seem to resist all effort to eradicate them, it is understandable that people should look for a savior, for someone who is wholly beyond the human order to impose a divine scheme of things on wayward humanity. They hope for the physical reappearance of a man crucified some two thousand years ago who, it is said, rose from the dead in a demonstration of his divinity and ascended into heaven, from whence he shall return.

The event awaited by some Christians is paralleled in other world religions, which also have their adherents who look for a savior or god-man. To Jews, he is the Messiah. To Muslims, he is the Imam Mahdi. To Buddhists, he is the Maitreya Buddha. To Hindus, he is the avatar of the age. To esotericists, he is the World Teacher. To practitioners of the ancient religion of Meso-America, he is Quetzalcoatl.

The search for the good life, utopia, the New Age has been a perennial theme around the globe for the last two millennia, not just in the religious sphere but also in the secular. For example, it was foremost in the thought of Karl Marx, Adolf Hitler, and Mao Zedong. Of course, their views of the ideal society were decidedly out of alignment with that of institutional Christianity, but in the broadest sense each of those men, in his own way, mobilized resources and took steps to establish what he thought of as a better world.

Who's right, Mikhail Gorbachev or Jerry Falwell? Or is it something else altogether? Is there some way to distinguish reality from illusion, truth from falsehood?

My answer is "Yes, there is a way," and in seeking to get at the truth of the matter, I've gone through a process which has three aspects: reason, research, and personal experience.

Let's begin with reason. It *is* logical and reasonable to consider a Second Coming on various grounds. First, the Old Testament has many prophecies and references to the First Coming, to the appearance of a messiah who will remove the wicked from among us and lead us in the path of righteousness into an age of peace. Second, if Jesus of Nazareth fulfilled those prophecies, his own words point us in the direction of what is called the Second Coming. Third, world affairs today certainly could benefit from the wisdom and guidance of a superhuman source of knowledge and power. Fourth, as noted above, many religious traditions project the appearance of a divine teacher who will bring the world to a new condition of harmony and love. So on both biblical and extrabiblical grounds, it is logical to consider the idea of the Second Coming. It is reasonable.

But is it plausible? After all, something can be logical and reasonable without necessarily being true. That is, if no data support the argument—no matter how reasonable or logical it may appear—the subject may be only an illusion or a delusion, a fanciful invention of unbridled imagination or wishful thinking and not worthy of a mature mind with clear vision. So, is there evidence to support the notion of a Second Coming? What does biblical research have to say about the scriptural passages people point to in support of the notion?

This question confronts us with the truth of the Bible. For Christendom, by and large, has departed from the Bible, and the Bible itself is by no means an impeccable document, as some fundamentalists claim when they say there is no error or contradiction in the Bible.

What do I mean when I say Christendom has departed from the Bible? I mean, as I remarked in the previous chapter, that it has become a religion *about* Jesus rather than the religion *of* Jesus. The original intent of Jesus, the true meaning of his words and his teachings have, for the most part, been lost by the institutional churches. And the concept of the Second Coming illustrates that vividly.

All kinds of things have been said and taught and fervently preached about Jesus which Jesus himself never said or meant and (I am sure) would thoroughly repudiate today if he were here to speak directly on the matter. If we are to understand the religion of Jesus, we must study his own discourses, not what others have said about him—and we must do so by drawing upon our understanding of the language and the culture of Jesus. Over the centuries, translations of translations have allowed all sorts of foreign concepts and dilutions of Jesus' teaching to creep into Christian doctrine, so that today we have such a splintering and fragmentation of Christianity that, I daresay, if Jesus were here he would be utterly appalled at what is being done in his name.

What did Jesus himself say about the Second Coming? Here I am drawing upon the scholarship of Dr. Rocco Errico, an Aramaic scholar and president of the Noohra Foundation in Irvine, California.[1] Errico studied with the late George M. Lamsa, a biblical scholar who translated the Bible from early Aramaic manuscripts. Lamsa's version is called *The Holy Bible from Ancient Eastern Manuscripts*. The work of Lamsa and Errico clarifies many dubious points and removes many questions about the meaning of the Bible. It goes directly to the language of Jesus to elucidate the idioms, colloquialisms, nuances, symbolism, and cultural meanings which have been lost over the years in the process of taking Jesus' teaching from the context of Palestine 2000 years ago and disseminating it through translation after translation in societies and cultures which lack many important points of reference for the words Jesus spoke to those around him.

In Matthew 24:3, a primary reference to what is popularly called the Second Coming, we see Jesus being questioned by his disciples. "Tell us," they ask, "when these things be, and what shall be the sign of thy coming, and of the end of the world?" (King James Version). Jesus then describes three great events: the fall and destruction of Jerusalem and the Temple; the success and triumph of his teaching; and the end of the age.

Now, in Aramaic, *coming* means "to come into your own." In other words, the disciples were wondering when Jesus would begin to rule triumphantly over the kingdoms of the world. They had not yet understand that Jesus was not a political or military figure. They had not yet understood the spiritual dimension of Jesus' mission. They understood his teachings primarily in literal and political terms—in a material rather than a metaphysical way. They saw themselves as reigning in his kingdom as typical Eastern potentates.

But Jesus' answer, using Aramaic metaphors, idioms, and a Near Eastern style of speech, meant something quite different than we understood from the King James translation. Jesus instructed his disciples, in verse 29 (King James Version): "Immediately after the tribulation of those days shall the sun be darkened, and the moon shall not give her light, and the stars shall fall from heaven, and the powers of the heavens shall be shaken: And then shall appear the sign of the Son of man in heaven: and then shall all the tribes of the earth mourn, and they shall see the Son of man coming in the clouds of heaven with power and great glory."

Lamsa and Errico tell us this means the universe is mourning over the tragic events and it also indicates there will be changes in the government. Stars are symbolic of political and religious leadership in ancient Aramaic thought. The apocalyptic nature of Jesus' words are meant metaphorically, not literally. "And then shall appear the sign of the Son of man in heaven" means the followers of Christ will know of his coming by means of a revelation because "heavens" or "sky" means "a high spiritual consciousness," a consciousness alert to the sudden change about to take place. "And then shall all the tribes of the earth mourn, and they shall see the Son of Man coming in the clouds of heaven with power and great glory" is an Aramaic idiom for "to succeed in a mission" or "to be highly acclaimed and successful." In Jesus' time, clouds were used as a figure of speech to suggest the greatest heights a person could reach; it was also believed that God rode the clouds as one would ride a chariot. As Errico put it in an article about the Second Coming, "Jesus, therefore, was assuring his disciples that his gospel, his teaching, would eventually triumph all over the world. His power and presence, which is the power and presence of God, would be realized and recognized among all nations."2

It is crucial to realize that the Bible does *not* speak of two comings. The proper biblical term is "the coming of Christ." As Jesus himself says at the end of the gospel of Matthew, "Lo, I am with you alway, even unto the end of the world." But, again, the sense of his words doesn't come through accurately in the King James Version because "end of the world" does not mean the destruction of the physical planet. It means the end of an age, the end of history. It means a radical discontinuity, with the termination of one mode of being and the emergence of another. What ends is the egocentric state of consciousness: the self-centered mind state which is the root of all evil, all fear, all suffering. What emerges is the paradisal condition which has been ours all along, even though we haven't realized it. That paradisal condition is the Christ consciousness Jesus demonstrated, the Christic state of mind, the peace which passeth understanding, the direct experience of divinity dwelling in us and all things, now and forever, creating us, living us, preserving us, urging us on to ever higher states of being through the process which is the central teaching of Jesus: metanoia.

Remember that the key to understanding the meaning of *Second Coming* is dependent on reason, research, and personal experience. That is, it depends on use of all our faculties and capacity for knowing, the rational and the spiritual, the intellectual and the intuitive. I've already said that the Second Coming is a reasonable concept to consider. I've also said that the research of some biblical scholars indicates it is a legitimate concept—but not as popularly understood and preached, where Jesus is Big Daddy in the Sky. To get at the final truth of the matter, we now must turn to the third aspect of our method for knowing reality, personal experience.

If you were to ask a six-month-old infant about the meaning of Christmas, what would his or her answer be? Not a word, not a response in any way connected with the question. An infant hasn't the capacity to understand the question, or to reply. It hasn't grown sufficiently in awareness to even learn language, let alone the deeper dimensions of experience to which language points. To an infant, the idea of Christmas is meaningless.

Now ask a four-year-old what Christmas means. Probably he will answer in terms of getting presents, or Santa Claus and his reindeer, or a Christmas tree with ornaments. In other words, the significance is grasped only in a superficial and personally centered way. Again, the consciousness of the individual hasn't matured sufficiently to talk about the spirit of Christmas or the symbolism of Christmas. Only the literal and material aspects are understood by the young child.

To an adolescent, whose experience and mentality is far beyond the infant and the child, Christmas can be understood in a deeper sense. Teenagers have the capacity to sense the meaning of Christmas as a religious event. They can tell you the Christmas story of the three Wise Men, the Babe in the manger, and can intellectually understand the celebration of a divine event in which a new way of living was patterned on Earth for humanity. They can understand intellectually that Christmas is a time for giving, and that the gifts given are tangible tokens of an inner attitude—of caring, of sharing, of reconciliation at year's end for whatever wrongs were done and of looking ahead to a new year and a new beginning.

They may not relate to all that emotionally, however. In fact, few adults do, let alone adolescents. How many people do you know who have so transcended their egotism, their self-centeredness that they actually live the spirit of Christmas all year long? How many do you know who are like the fourth-century bishop in Asia Minor named Nicolas, who acted with such loving-kindness, generosity, and apparently miraculous powers that he is revered centuries later as Saint Nicolas, the original Santa Claus?

My point, made millennia ago by the sages of India, is that knowledge is structured in consciousness. We can know only to the boundaries of our awareness. Or as Carl Jung put it, freedom extends as far as the limits of consciousness. Beyond that are ignorance, constraint, and bondage.

Furthermore, the expansion of consciousness is not something done merely by gathering more and more facts through scholarship. That's merely horizontal movement, not vertical ascent to the higher realms of spirit which all religions, including Christianity, tell us we must undertake if we are to know God or truth or ultimate reality. Jesus did not call us to worship him or even to be Christians. He called us to follow his example and become like him. He called us to a radically new experience: to be Christed. And that is not a matter of mere scholarly study of the Bible. It is a matter of removing from our heart all self-centeredness, all pride and anger and lust and jealousy and envy and hatred, so that only love of God resides in our being. It is a matter of seeing the light of God shining in all things and relating to everyone as if they are our very own being. As Jesus put it, "Thou shalt love the Lord thy God with all thy heart, and with all thy soul, and with all thy mind. This is the first and great commandment. And the second is like unto it, Thou shalt love thy neighbor as thyself. On these two commandments hang all the law and the prophets."

On those two commandments also hangs the judgment of whether you and I are worthy to enter the Kingdom, to do the things Jesus said we would do as He did, to become one in Christ. To repeat the point, the term *Christ* is a title, not a name. It is the Greek translation of the Aramaic *M'shekha*, "messiah." As noted, it is conventionally translated "anointed" or "consecrated," but the deeper meaning is borne in the phrase Jesus used to refer to himself: Son of Man. Messiah means "enlightened" or "perfected" or "the ideal form of humanity." That is what the Son of Man is—the offspring of humanity, the perfected or ideal form of the race presently inhabiting the Earth. Jesus understood that he was the Christ, the perfected form of humanity, but nowhere did he say that he alone was entitled to that condition. Nowhere did he say it was exclusively his for all time. Rather, he called humanity to rise to the condition he demonstrated. That is what the Christian tradition is all about. It is an experience of spiritual maturation beyond all childish dependence on a magical savior who will do it for us. It is transcendental knowledge, or *gnosis,* which confirms spiritual truth beyond mere belief while clarifying error and highlighting the important from the trivial.

So as we accept Christ in our hearts and minds and lives (not just the simple emotional conversion the electronic evangelists call for but a powerful, radical transformation of consciousness, called metanoia), as we become Christlike, we experience personally the coming of Christ, now, here, at this time, in this place, wherever that enlightening experience occurs for us. We realize the truth of his statement: "Lo, I am with you alway, even unto the end of the world." For when we truly awaken in Christ, the world ends. But it does not end in the sense the fundamentalist preachers mean, as global destruction. It ends the world for us in the transcendence of space and time into the divine domain which is always our true condition, our true self. It ends for us as the awakening from the illusion of ego, from the dream of worldly life, from the bondage of time and matter into the reality of God-conscious living.

As Jesus said, the Kingdom is *already* among us as the source of our being. To the extent it is realized in consciousness by people, is it being manifested. The separate-self-playing-God is the antichrist, the blasphemer, the one who leads you into hell. But even if you flee into hell, as the Psalmist says, there are thou also, O Lord. We are *never* apart from God, no matter how hardened in our hearts we become. The *illusion* of separateness is our own creation. It is called ego. When we drop that initial *e* and add a final *d,* we find ourselves released—into God, into Reality, into the peace, joy, and love which are hallmarks of citizenship in the Kingdom.

There is no Second Coming of Christ. As *Harper's Bible Dictionary* notes, "No [New Testament] passage refers to Jesus' *second* Parousia or coming as such. . . . Usually . . . reference is simply to the *coming* of the Son of man or Christ as Lord." The Second Coming is a false concept and an unwarranted doctrine. There is only, as the Bible puts it, the coming of Christ, through you and through me, as we ascend in consciousness to the truth of life and the source of being, as we awaken at the heart to God and realize ourselves—become—the sons and daughters of the Most High, reclaiming our estate. That is precisely what Jesus called us to do, and as that occurs on a global scale, the need for a world savior such as the electronic evangelists depict will be seen for what it is: a childish wish, a fantasy based on immature awareness and poor biblical scholarship. As that occurs on a global scale, there will be a collective salvation of a kind beyond the present understanding of TV preachers and their followers, who are still in spiritual infancy, still inexperienced in the ways of growth to higher consciousness and not yet capable of going beyond their childish, anthrophomorphic conception of the Christ to a more mature understanding of God as the immanent–transcendent–omnipresent divine dimension of all existence.

The final appearance of the Christ will not be a man in the sky before whom all must kneel. The final appearance of the Christ will be an evolutionary event marking the disappearance of egocentric Man (who might better be described as subhuman) and the ascension of God-centered Man. A new race, a new species will inhabit the Earth, people who collectively have the stature in consciousness which Jesus had. And in that process, the kingdom of God will truly be established on Earth through the governance of the Christ and in the hearts, minds, and souls of all people.

23

The Meaning of
the Christ

I have glorified thee on the earth: I have finished the work which thou gavest
me to do. And now, O Father, glorify thou me with thine own self with the glory
which I had with thee before the world was.

John 17:4–5

In these verses from the most mystic and metaphysical of the gospels,
Jesus says he is ready to return wholly to the Christic state—an
eternal state which transcends the entire cosmos, a state which is timeless, spaceless, and prior to the manifestation not simply of "the world"
(as John puts it) but of the entire universe. It is that aspect of God which
calls humans to ascend to godhood through the evolutionary drama
working itself out in time and space. It calls us to rise through all the
planes of nature and return to the source of being, the Supreme Identity,
the Self of all. Simply, the Christic state—the Christos or Christ—is the
archetype of the Self beyond all separate selves.

So, although Jesus of Nazareth is popularly called the Christ, it is
more accurate to say that *the Christ was Jesus,* just as the Christ was also
Gautama, Krishna, Lao Tzu, and other avatars, sages, and saviors of
humanity who realized their true Self. None of them, I daresay, would
claim to be the Christ exclusively, but all of them would claim to be
Christed: to have entered the state of unity-in-Only-God. So the historical
event upon which Christianity is founded, the incarnation of the Christ as
Jesus of Nazareth, is one of the points of insertion of Eternal Spirit into

time and human flesh. Its origin is totally transcendental: the Precosmic Void, the Source of creation, that realm wholly beyond all the planes of creation, no matter how sublime or celestial the plane may be.

But is that event unique, as Christian tradition claims it to be?

Yes and no. No, because others have been Christed. Yes, because when Spirit descended into Earth to take on human flesh and form as Jesus of Nazareth, it was then subject, as the person Jesus, to the scheme of biological development governing human growth through all the stages of self-unfoldment until at last it, as Jesus, transcended the laws of physics, biology, and the physical planes. And that act of transcendence—that return to the Father—fundamentally and forever altered human evolution and human destiny. In that act salvation was assured. (But that salvation, while fundamental, must not be understood in any fundamentalist sense, as explained below.)

At birth Jesus was probably as helpless and ignorant as any other babe in swaddling clothes. Undoubtedly he was a precocious child, though, and developed through the stages of ego-formation very, very quickly, passing soon into the transegoic realm. By the age of twelve, when most humans have barely grown into the mental-egoic stage, Jesus was well into the transpersonal, as shown by his speech in the temple and afterward to his mother.

During the "lost years" (from ages twelve to thirty) Jesus probably was trained in at least one mystery school of higher human development. There is a rich extrabiblical tradition of legends which claim this, although hard evidence is lacking. During this training, it is said, he mastered physics, physiology, and biology, so that he could refine his innate ability to heal, perform psychic phenomena, and so forth (although those abilities are not necessarily marks of Christhood). Toward the end of that period he fully realized his godhood. And at his baptism in the River Jordan, he demonstrated his authority to begin his ministry: God-realization. However, he had not yet fully transformed himself upon the basis of that realization. That would come only after the crucifixion.

Upon his full God-realization, Jesus took upon himself a mission to show forth the Gospel. To show forth means to teach, preach, and demonstrate in one's total being. Of teachers and preachers there have been many, but Jesus alone demonstrated the Gospel—and the world has never been the same. At the end of his life Jesus became the first human to fully demonstrate complete transformation of the psychophysical complex—the body-mind—in which we live as apparently separate individuals. There are hints and slight indications, in the yogic tradition of India, the hermetic mystery tradition of Egypt, and in the Hebrew tradition that others (such as Melchizedek and Enoch) achieved this transformation previous to Jesus, but I am unaware of any historical documents or other records which offer unquestionable evidence of this.

Thus, if Jesus was the first to fully show the Way to godhead, his effect upon the world is metaphysical in the most profound sense. He fundamentally altered the etheric blueprint or morphogenetic field upon which Man's destiny is unfolded. He actually injected into the total scheme of ontogenetic (individual) and phylogenetic (racial) human development, through all the planes of nature, the necessary and sufficient means for Man to complete evolution and return to God, transformed and resurrected as the Son of Man.

In the tomb, Jesus demonstrated conquest of death—the total transcendence of biology and physics—by creating a body of light (what esotericism calls a solar body) and functioning through it with complete control of matter and energy. The Shroud of Turin offers its enigmatic image as silent witness to the event.[1] Apparently, a self-induced nuclear "explosion" was the means by which Jesus "translated" or passed wholly from the physical to the metaphysical realm. (As Frank Tribbe tells in his *Portrait of Jesus?*, the closest science can come to explaining how the image of the Man in the Shroud got there is by comparing the situation to a controlled burst of high-intensity radiation similar to the Hiroshima bomb explosion, which "printed" images of disintegrated people on building walls.)[2] For the next forty days Jesus revealed to humanity what had never before been shown (except possibly in the mystery schools). In a body of light—a resurrection body—Jesus appeared and disappeared at will. "O death, where is thy sting?"

At the end of the forty days, Jesus "went before to prepare a place" by ascending to the Father. As this is popularly interpreted, he floated upward through the air and now waits somewhere among the clouds in a form and substance similar to what he had on Earth. From my point of view, that interpretation of scripture is naïve. What actually happened, I think, was that Jesus of Nazareth dissolved utterly out of time and space, leaving not the slightest trace—physical or psychic—behind. He left behind even his body of light and returned to "the glory which I had with God before the world was." He vanished entirely out of space-time, ceasing to exist in any form whatsoever. He returned wholly to the Formless state of being. His return was to the Preluminous Void, that condition which preceded creation of the universe and is the ever-present Ground of Being sustaining all the universe. It is the precosmic condition before God said "Let there be light." It is the timeless, spaceless (and therefore formless) Unmanifest from which all creation, all existence, all manifestation flows. It is the Original Face which Buddhism says is ours before we were born.

If that is so, you may ask, what do people experience when they see Jesus in visions, meditation, or dreams? My answer: an image from their own minds. But I am not denigrating that image because the image is not based on fantasy or imagination in the ordinary sense of those words. It *is* from a higher level of reality, but it is not ultimate.

Consider this. Science is now showing there is an energy associated with thought, and that the energy can be externalized by the person directing it, as in telepathy and spiritual healing. If energy, including the energy of mind, is neither created nor destroyed, then all the thoughts ever thought are, theoretically speaking, still accessible in some form. (The energy-substance of thought has been called a hundred or more names by various prescientific and scientific traditions, as noted earlier.)

Consider further how much thought and thought-energy has been directed by people around the world to the life of Jesus, especially to the idea of Jesus as the Perfect Human. It is *that* image which people perceive in visions, meditation, and dreams—not Jesus as an infant, not Jesus as a boy, but Jesus as a model of perfection.

What is the nature of the image? It is a psychologically created thoughtform of the romanticized, glamorized Jesus. It is a composite picture built up over the centuries from the mental impressions of millions and millions of people who—through prayer, study, and heartfelt yearning for self-transcendence via the Christian path—have unknowingly added their psychic energy to a worldwide field of thought energy and thereby built up a "charged" repository of "mindstuff" which stores the image holographically in a planetary thoughtfield. That repository is accessible to people in altered states of consciousness.

To put it another way, what people see during their visionary experience is the psychic equivalent of a 3-D picture. Undoubtedly their perceptions are colored to some degree by personal experience and unconscious factors in their own minds. But just as a hologram or animated film of someone is not the living individual, the apparitional image of Jesus seen during visions is not in any way whatsoever the personal presence of the man who walked in Palestine two millennia ago. It is the embellishment of an archaic image from the past—a stereotyped picture from history. It is visionary but not veridical.

One strong indication of this is the phenomenon of stigmata. Since the thirteenth century, when Francis of Assisi became the first stigmatic, several hundred cases have been recorded of people with flows of blood supposed to be in imitation of Jesus' crucifixion wounds. The wounds are always in the palms of the hands, and sometimes in the feet and the side of the body. But modern biblical research, anatomical studies, and evidence from the scientific study of the Shroud of Turin all indicate that crucifixion involved nails through the *wrists,* not the hands. (Nails through the hands wouldn't be able to hold the weight of a human body against the pull of gravity. The nails would be pulled right through the hands because soft flesh couldn't hold on to them. Only the wrist-juncture, where the radius and ulna bones of the arm come together, offers sufficient strength to support a body nailed to a cross.)

As Tribbe points out, the Greek *cheir* can mean hand, wrist, or forearm. The King James and other versions of the Bible mistranslated the language describing the crucifixion.

All that has been learned only in this century, in recent decades, in fact. And until very recently all the stigmatics have had their "wounds" in the hands! Why? They were simply externalizing their mental image of Jesus as popularly pictured. The image was projected through the ages via stories, paintings, carvings, and statuary until this century, when forensic medical investigation showed the error of popular thought. If Jesus of Nazareth were really existent in space-time after the ascension, if he were accessible through visions, dreams, and meditation, those claiming to have seen him would have seen *realistically* where the nail wounds actually were. Yet no one, including the hundreds of stigmatics, has ever done so. This strongly indicates that their guiding, albeit unconscious, image of Jesus was not veridical. They identified psychologically with a wrong idea about Jesus and then manifested it physically.[3]

The same can even be said about visionary experiences in which people "see" Jesus in their waking state. It is all hallucinatory—perception of an eternal event which has no physical reference—or is based on a false impression. It is simply the externalization of their own subconscious but mistaken mind-image. As such, it is not "wrong"—it is simply nonultimate. It is spiritually valid, but only as a phenomenon characteristic of an intermediate stage of self-unfoldment. It is a form of experience to be understood and transcended, what Zen calls *makyo.* The true significance of Jesus is not as a vision or apparition.

If I am correct about this, channeled writings and spoken discourses alleged to be from Jesus are actually not so because Jesus is not accessible that way, or at all. For example, consider *A Course in Miracles,* which I regard as a truly profound, inspired document. It is probably the most important channeled writing of the century and possibly of all time because it is the most practical, as well as the most coherent, eloquent, and enlightened set of instructions for God-realization. It is extraordinarily insightful, and certainly worthy of attribution to Jesus. But from my point of view, its source cannot be Jesus of Nazareth, no matter what proponents of the *Course* may say, including the channel herself, Helen Schucman, who claimed to have questioned the source and said that it identified itself as Jesus.

Now, I can't state absolutely that Schucman was wrong. After all, various spiritual traditions describe ascended masters and avatars who, although masters of all the planes of existence, nevertheless choose because of compassion to return to the lower planes from time to time, even taking on a flesh body for certain missions, or at least remaining near the Earth in such a way as to be accessible by people. My friend Swami Radha of Kootenay Bay, Canada, has three times experienced the visible presence of Babaji, one of the kriya masters in Paramhansa Yogananda's lineage; Babaji is said to be at least several hundred years old, and probably more like a thousand or two. He is described as an ascended master, the same as Madame Blavatsky's and Alice Bailey's mentors are. And Radha has interacted with Babaji in such a way as to convince me of Babaji's reality as a spiritual entity.

So it is theoretically possible that Jesus, who certainly attained the same degree of development as Babaji and the others, has chosen to remain on Earth in such a form. The historical Jesus, I must acknowledge, might be the author of *A Course in Miracles* (although I believe its author is simply an unnamed spiritual entity of great age and wisdom who can claim, with legitimacy, to speak in the name of the Christ), and visions of Jesus may indeed be true perceptions of the historical Jesus in spiritual form. Even the gospels tell us he said, "Lo, I am with you always, even unto the end of the age." In some sense, Jesus has never left us.

But is that sense the popularly held one: the man Jesus of Nazareth residing among the clouds in a body of light-energy? I don't think so. Here's why.

Some people today claim to have met Jesus as a being of light face to face during a near-death experience. But their accounts don't convince me that the being was Jesus because many others who have had the same experience say (more accurately, I think) that the being of light they met did not identify itself. In fact, NDE researcher Dr. Kenneth Ring told me in personal correspondence that he doesn't know of a single instance when the light-being identifies itself as Jesus, Krishna, the Buddha, or any other known figure. The identification, he said, is provided by the percipient, not the perceived.

Thus, the NDErs' identification of Jesus as that light-being is probably an interpretation based on their cultural and religious traditions and their personal beliefs. This conclusion is further supported by the fact that other NDEers have variously identified the being they met as an angel, a prophet or a mythological figure. And, of course, beings of light have been noted in other contexts. In the Hindu tradition, for example, beings of light are known as devas—the equivalent of angels, conceptually speaking.

My opinion is that the beings of light whom NDErs meet are ontologically real entities native to higher planes of Nature. Normally, such beings are invisible to us. But when a person is in an out-of-body condition, unfettered by the perceptual filters of the nervous system, such beings may be perceived. Some of them—angels, for example—are indigenous to those planes. Others, however, are our "elder brothers." They are emissaries from a far-distant stage of evolution which preceded humanity by many eons—a stage Jesus was (probably) the first human to attain. (Of course, others have claimed that he was such before he was born, so his "return" was only to that prior light-bodied condition and, as such, it was not attainment at all.)

In my opinion, however, that is not what is truly unique about Jesus. His awesome gift to humanity is this: he was the first to transcend even that phase of evolution and totally, utterly "return to the Father," who is the prior and primal condition of all the universe. No matter how that return is viewed, Jesus "saved" the world by showing the Way and making it possible for the entire human race to be Christed. His "return to glory" paradoxically places him here in the world more truly, more fully than if he were still residing in a body of light-energy and located somewhere in space. Jesus' departure from space-time as a separate and distinct entity paradoxically returned him to the universe at each and every point—not as a personality but as its very Ground of Being, as the formless and omnipresent source of life, as that truth and consciousness and bliss which "lighteth the world." As Jesus of Nazareth, he is to be found nowhere. As a manifestation of the Christic state, he is to be found everywhere and has been from the beginning of time. As Paul said in his epistle to the Ephesians (4:10ff), "He who descended is he who also ascended far above all the heavens, that he might fill all things."

Thus, the historical Jesus does not exist as a spirit entity. Jesus will not return to Earth on a cloud with angels playing trumpets because he is truly here already—in the very center of you and me as our deepest nature, our very essence. Instead of being *somewhere,* he is *everywhere.* He, as the Christ, is that in which we live and move and have our very being. He pervades every level of creation. He is in our mind and hearts, our blood and DNA and nervous system, our relationships and aspirations and ideals, beckoning at the doorway of higher consciousness for us to open it and enter, that we might realize our true self, ascend through evolution to godhood and become "one in Christ."

24

What Is Spirituality?

The New Age is characterized by spirituality. In essence, spirituality is simply living with intention to realize God in every circumstance of your being—thoughts, emotions, words, deeds, relations, aspirations—in short, the totality of your life, right through its very end (as saints and sages do by "dying the good death"). As I have said before: That attitude, that stance in life is the only thing which can truly create a better world. There will never be a better world until there are better people in it. The way to build better people is to begin with yourself by realizing God. To realize God means to know God on every level of reality and in every mode or aspect of God's being. Thus, spirituality can be defined, level by level of reality, this way:

In *physical* terms, spirituality is recognizing the miraculous nature of matter and the creative source behind the mystery of matter.

In *biological* terms, spirituality is realizing that a divine intelligence underlies all life-change and that such change is evolving all creation to ever greater degrees of wholeness in order to perfectly express itself.

In *psychological* terms, spirituality is discovering within yourself the ultimate source of meaning and happiness, which is love.

In *sociological* terms, spirituality is giving selfless service to others, regardless of race, creed, color, gender, caste, or nationality.

In *ecological* terms, spirituality is showing respect for all the kingdoms in the community of life—mineral, vegetable, animal, human, spirit, and angelic.

In *cosmological* terms, spirituality is being at one with the universe, in tune with the infinite, flowing with the Tao.

In *theological* terms, spirituality is seeing God in all things, all events, and all circumstances, indwelling as infinite light and unconditional love, and seeing all things, events, and circumstances in God as the matrix or infinite ocean in which the universe occurs.

Enlightenment or God-realization is the object of spiritual life. There are three modes of God-realization, corresponding to the three primary modes of God: immanent, omnipresent, and transcendent. Saints and sages have realized God in one or another of these modes; thus, to a degree, they are enlightened. But *all* aspects of God must be personally realized in the process of higher human development and consciousness expansion.

To realize God as immanent is to discover God in the center of your own being—the subject of yourself. To realize God as omnipresent is to discover God as the center of all other beings and all which has being— the subject of all objects. To realize God as transcendent is to realize God as the source of all subjects and objects—all being itself—and to realize God as the source which will abide when the entire cosmos in all its levels of creation and all its life forms has passed away and utterly vanished into the Void, annihilated.

All this is summarized in the Christian tradition by the concept of the Trinity. The triune nature of God has commonly been conceived as having three personalities or even three personages: the Father (who looks very much like the gray-bearded man in Michaelangelo's Sistine Chapel painting of "Creation"); the Son named Jesus; and the Holy Ghost, who looks like a dove.

But that personification of God is a naïve misunderstanding. The Trinity is really a means of articulating the insight, apprehended by sages and mystics in exalted states, that God has three principal *modes* or *aspects,* which in their totality describe the Great mystery.

God-as-immanent is God the Son, the Christ consciousness dwelling within us. This aspect can be regarded as masculine. Traditionally, it is also regarded as the Redeemer—that which brings salvation, that which brings us back from the hell of egoic existence and opens for us the gates of heaven as conscious union with God.

God-as-omnipresent is God the Holy Spirit, the means by which miracles are performed. This aspect can be regarded as feminine. Why feminine? The Holy Spirit is the creative force which miraculously and mysteriously gives rise to the entire cosmos and thus is the matrix of all Nature. The Latin *matrix,* "womb," is derived from *mater,* "mother." *Mater* is also the etymological source of the word *matter,* meaning "physical substance" or that from which the universe is composed. Thus, the Holy Spirit is that aspect of God which brings forth, nurtures, and supports the creation. Traditionally, it is also regarded as the Preserver, that which keeps creation going. The feminine nature of the Holy Spirit—the Cosmic Creatrix—should thus be apparent. It was apparent to artisans who first depicted the Holy Spirit as a dove, which is also a symbol of the feminine.

God-as-transcendent is God the Father, the ultimate source from which the cosmos arises. This aspect, though denominated "Father," is actually genderless—even more so than angels are. Duality, or the division into the sexes, does not exist in the transcendent Void which is prior to all creation. God in the transcendent aspect therefore cannot be assigned gender.

Enlightenment is an endless process in which we grow more and more godlike, evolving to ever greater orders of complexity and ever higher planes of being until the self reaches universal proportions—a universe supremely conscious of itself as a unified living entity. Beyond that? The Hindu myth of cosmogeny perhaps expresses it best through the notion that Spirit is the breath of God: Brahman exhales and the outgoing breath manifests a universe, Brahamn inhales and the inflow of breath annihilates the creation. In between, during the billions and billions of years of cosmic drama, the New Age is a relatively local event. Not unimportant, of course. But the New Age movement needs to keep itself in perspective—keep its Self in perspective. The efforts of New Age-oriented people are necessary and admirable, but the full advent of a New Age of humanity is not the end of the human adventure in consciousness. As T. S. Eliot expressed it at the conclusion of his magnificent "Four Quartets":

> We shall not cease from exploration
> And the end of all our exploring
> Will be to arrive where we started
> And know the place for the first time.

In Reality, there is only God!

Afterword: Toward
Homo Noeticus

"When we are in tune with a consciousness of the cosmos, we become members of a new species."

R. M. Bucke

In 1973 I created the term *Homo noeticus* to denote a higher form of humanity which I saw emerging among us. Since then, the term has been adopted approvingly by some. It has also been criticized as imprecise and unscientific by others. This afterword will describe more clearly what I mean by the concept.

As I pointed out earlier, *noetics* means the study of consciousness. The primary method for studying consciousness is going within oneself to discover Ultimate Reality. The "experts" in that, the ones who have done it, the models I had in mind when describing the features of the coming race were men and women recognized throughout history as enlightened sages and adepts, such as Jesus, Lao Tzu, Guatama, and others mentioned throughout this book. They are the awakened ones—awakened to Ultimate Reality.

I see *Homo noeticus* as the next stage of human evolution precisely as Cro-Magnon superseded Neanderthal. That evolutionary advance didn't happen overnight. It took many generations. It was an event which anthropologists demark rather than date precisely because the end of one race and the beginning of the other overlapped, sharing common ground. Apparently a few mutant Neanderthals recognized themselves as "different" and sought out like-minded individuals with whom they shared their lives. From an anthropological perspective, we can say they speciated. They thrived and grew in numbers, crowding out, through various means, the Neanderthals from whom they sprang. That is also the situation today, as I see it, although the evolutionary process is accelerat-

243

ing rapidly. *Homo noeticus* may speciate far more quickly than Cro-Magnon because science, technology, and communications are now affecting human evolution, allowing greater control and range of choice, greater freedom from random forces directing the process.

Paleontologists tell us that during the Age of Dinosaurs there were little tarsierlike creatures. They apparently remained small and stayed under cover because the great lumbering dinosaurs would crush or otherwise easily exterminate them. In order to survive, they lived "on the fringe," so to speak. But when the dinosaurs died, these tiny creatures emerged from cover and began to grow. It was a very slow process, but eventually they evolved into primates, then hominids, and beyond—into the first protohumans.

Evolution didn't end there, however. Especially in Africa, Nature experimented with various ancient forerunners of humanity, most of whom died out. But some survived and became our progenitors.

When life reached the human level, the drama of speciation continued. First, the Neanderthal people appeared about 300,000 years ago. Then, about 50,000 years ago, they were superseded by the Cro-Magnon people. That spelled doom for the Neanderthal. The Cro-Magnon were a qualitative advance, a higher form of life yet genetic change was not a significant factor. Physically speaking, there wasn't much difference between the two. Both had the same biological functions; both needed food and shelter. The primary change seems to have been mental capacity—a change in consciousness. The Cro-Magnon had superior tool-making ability. They were the world's first artists, as their cave paintings demonstrate. Altogether, they showed a superior degree of consciousness. Evolution had clearly moved into a mental realm.

And now, here *we* are: masters of Earth, more powerful and knowledgeable than anything else on the planet has ever been (so far as the historical record shows, at least). Powerful and knowledgeable—but, sadly, unwise. Perhaps we've become too narrow and specialized; perhaps we are incapable of going along with the process of change. Homo sapiens may be a dying species near the end of its life cycle. As we flex our technological muscles, raping and plundering the planet, we stupidly promote ecocide. As we shake a nuclear fist at our brothers and sisters, spending for weapons instead of food and homes and education, we irrationally flirt with genocide.

The new species can see this happening and, like those little creatures in the Age of Dinosaurs, has until lately remained under cover and on the fringes of a society which may be entering its death throes from its own nuclear, chemical, and environmental insanity. But now the new breed is emerging from cover. As an historical epoch draws to a close, it is asserting its right to live.

An evolutionary advance is taking place in the world today as a higher form of humanity takes control of the planet. By "control," I mean living in respectful recognition of intimate interdependence. Control means living in harmony with the entire community of life—and therefore positioning itself to survive whatever global crises occur while the older species dies out from a massive overdose of irrationalism. Quite simply, the new breed is psychologically adapted to the altered conditions nature is imposing as it restores the balance Homo sapiens has ignored nearly to the point of no return. The larger dimensions of this process are not recognized at present by most evolutionary forerunners or are only dimly intuited by them. The process is still fragmented and leaderless—an Aquarian conspiracy. And the number of conspirators is still quite small in proportion to world population. Nevertheless, higher intelligence is working through them, calling them to self-recognition of their role in preserving and enriching the fabric of life.

Because of their deepened awareness and self-understanding, the traditionally imposed forms, controls, and institutions of society are barriers to their full development. Their changed psychology expresses rather than suppresses feeling. Their motivation is cooperative and loving, not competitive and agressive. Their logic is multilevel/integrated/simultaneous, not linear/sequential/either-or. Their sense of identity is embracing and collective, not isolated-individual—but transpersonally so, not prepersonally. Their psychic abilities are used for benevolent and ethical purposes, not harmful and immoral ones. The conventional ways of society don't satisfy them. The search for new ways of living and new institutions concerns them. They seek a culture founded in higher consciousness, a culture whose insititutions are based on love and wisdom, a culture which fulfills the perennial philosophy of self-transcendence and God-realization. (I indicated in the introduction some of the major themes and movements at work today to achieve that sacred culture.)

Such an achievement is not inevitable, but the evolutionary thrust of life is clearly distinguishable and by no means a vain hope for humanity's future. Physicist Ilya Prigogine, whose work in physical chemistry won a Nobel prize in 1977, demonstrated an evolving life force in a thermodynamically dissipating universe. His work can be summarized thus: If an entity—which could be anything from a chemical reaction to a society—is both unstable (i.e., changeable) and self-organizing (i.e., capable of structuring and maintaining itself), and the entity is "perturbed" (i.e., challenged, stressed, damaged) by some force, then the entity will reorganize itself taking the perturbing force into account. It will tend to maintain its previous talents, while adding to them something which contends with the offending perturbation. It will become "more clever" in existing.

In other words, Prigogine said, evolution is a natural response to crisis. He declared the reality of a "deep cultural vision" which poets and philosophers have articulated over the ages as they perceived perturbations taking society to a new, higher order.

So I wasn't the first to declare that evolution is still occuring. Throughout this book I've mentioned Nietzsche, H. P. Blavatsky, R. M. Bucke, Sri Aurobindo, Teilhard de Chardin, Gopi Krishna, Oliver Reiser, Kenneth Ring, Ken Wilber, Jean Gebser, Georg Feuerstein, and various occult/esoteric traditions such as Theosophy, Anthroposophy, Rosicrucianism, Freemasonry, cabbalah and alchemy. To this list I would add Henri Bergson, Walt Whitman, L. L. Whyte, Erich Newman, Jean Houston, Dane Rudhyar and Haridas Chaudhuri. All these people and traditions have given some insight to the nature of the higher humanity, the qualities and characteristics of the new race. But while they have had a shaping influence on my perspective, the idea itself came from a higher source prior to meeting them through books and conversation.

In 1963, I discovered the human potential for growth to godhood through a spontaneous mystical experience. In a moment of grace, nirvikalpa samadhi happened to me. Time stopped. "I" ceased to exist. Limitation and boundary dissolved into infinite consciousness of unity. All was light, unending light, and love the foundation of the cosmos. I saw that divinity is our very essence *sub specie aeternitatis,* that our evolutionary journey is purposeful, and that purpose is the return to godhead. So the basic notion of *Homo noeticus* was derived from personal experience. In my past I saw the human past; in my future I saw the human future.

Although I had a legitimate insight gained through an experience of higher consciousness, when I dropped back into the world of time and matter and the stubborn resistance of egoic people—including myself—I naïvely thought that god-knowledge would be more easily transmissible than it is. I knew our noetic potential; I'd seen the arc of it amid the transpersonal splendor of Being. But to translate that transcendental knowledge into the realm of time and matter required greater wisdom and experience than I had then. In other words, simply saying that humanity can accelerate its own evolution is not the same thing as convincing humanity it can, let alone, should. I had some wishful thinking to jettison.

Through my life's wanderings, it eventually became obvious that my timing isn't always God's timing. Prior to that, like some biblical prophets who'd likewise seen the Messiah during visionary experience, I fell victim to what biblical scholars call "prophetic foreshortening." I thought it all would happen in a generation. It was the tenor of the times—the psychedelic hope of the 1960s for "paradise now." As a wise man once said about himself, "Like every young fool, I thought utopia was just 'round the corner."

But as I cleared away the illusory time scale, I saw that the vision itself remained valid. There *is* acceleration in the evolutionary process—and it is *both* globalization *and* spiritualization. In a meeting of science and spirit, I saw what some others have seen: an exponential shortening of the timespan from one dominant lifeform to the next.

Here is what science has said about that. The prebiotic planet may have existed in an inchoate-to-semiformed state for several billion years or longer. (As I will point out in Appendix 4, since geological dating depends on solid material, it is theoretically possible that our planet existed as a protoplanet with unsolidified matter for much longer than the four billion years measurable by radioactive dating of rocks.) Then life appeared. In the Archeozoic Era, simple organisms held sway for perhaps one and a half billion years—a period markedly shorter than the preceding one. Next, the fish family dominated the planet for half a billion years. Again, there was a notable abbreviation of the time scale until the succeeding period emerged. The Age of Reptiles lasted only 150 million years or so, the Age of Mammals about 75 million years. Primates emerged some 20 million years ago. By then the timescale for the lifespan of the dominant species was measurable in tens of millions rather than hundreds of millions of years. With the appearance of hominids some four million years ago, the timescale had compressed to mere millions of years. Homo sapiens' life cycle was a few hundred thousand years. And Homo sapiens sapiens—us—emerged only 50,000 years ago, within a time frame measurable by comparatively brief ten-thousand-year units.

The image suggested by this is what becomes visible when a chambered nautilus shell is cut in half: a spiral of ever-larger segments. Each segment is a chamber in which the nautilus lived until it outgrew the space. Then it moved forward and replaced the previous segment with another, larger one. By following the chambers backward from last to first, the inward spiral symbolizes what I've described here: a quickening pace, a rush toward the metaphysical center of our being in which each succceeding chamber-stage of our own growth occurs more intensively and in a briefer period.

The logic of it all says to me: If we don't blast ourselves off the planet or commit ecocide, there will most likely be a proportionally shorter time before the next major form of life gains ascendence and is clearly recognizable as such. If the present dominant life form emerged in a timespan measured in tens of thousands of years, the timespan for *Homo noeticus* would be measured in mere thousands of years.

The full emergence of *Homo noeticus* thus is probably several thousand years away. It will be at least that long before a majority of the world-community's population (including that in many far-flung space colonies) is stabilized and fully functional in the mystical stage of human evolution characterized by nirvikalpa samadhi—ego transcendence and formless perception of God as the ground of all being, the One behind the many. But the forerunners of *Homo noeticus* are here *now,* in increasing numbers, making their presence felt, crowding Homo sapiens, creating their own niche in the eco-psychosystem and pointing out to him his own potential to change consciousness and thereby evolve, directing his own evolution and accelerating the process. I am one of them. So are you—or you can be. A change of consciousness leading to a change of species is your human potential.

If evolution is essentially the unfolding of consciousness, *Homo noeticus* will be characterized by the mystical state of consciousness. It will not be a momentary experience but rather the basic and constant mode of awareness through which all experience is registered. As Bucke stated, it will enter the human species more and more fully, manifesting at a younger and younger age in individuals until, just as ego-consciousness now begins to emerge in people after infancy, the transpersonal identity discovered in mystical experience becomes grounded in the life of people during childhood. Jesus in the temple at age twelve, stating "I must be about my Father's business" illustrates this condition. As it was for Jesus, so it will be for all the children of *Homo noeticus:* "And the child grew, and waxed strong in spirit, filled with wisdom: and the grace of God was upon him."

There are stages of human development beyond *Homo noeticus,* so I do not mean to present the new breed as the ultimate form of humanity. Even a world in which the majority of people are Christs and Buddhas will not be the end of the evolutionary drama. We—they—will eventually be succeeded by—what?: *Homo illuminatus, Homo magnus.* That form of humanity, as I dimly perceive it, will largely have left behind its physical structure and will function in solar bodies or resurrection bodies, as do the "beings of light" whom people meet now in meditation and in near-death experience. Those "elder brothers" are representatives of a still more distant state of humanity.

But one step at a time. For now it is enough to understand that we are unfinished and that the conclusion of the human journey depends to some extent on you. To hear the cosmos calling is profoundly empowering. It also carries a profound responsibility. The kingdom of heaven is yours if you dare to seek it within yourself. But it is not yours exclusively. Only in community—indeed, only in communion—can we safely and sanely grow godward.

Sleeper, awaken!

Liberation Literature: A New Age Approach to Literary Studies

As a youngster in the 1950s, I thrived on literature of all kinds, from comics to classics—Sherlock Holmes, Tarzan, the Oz stories, Penrod and, especially, science fiction and fantasy. It did more than merely entertain me; it also caught me at the aesthetic level, sensitizing me to the uses of language to thrill the inner senses and capture the imagination. The best of it made me *think* and *feel* and *wonder* about the nature of reality and my place in the universe. What an adventure to wander with Ray Bradbury through *The October Country* and to ride with E. M. Forster on "The Celestial Omnibus"! Once, during a two-week stay in bed for pneumonia, I gloriously roamed the heavens and Earth through such stories in *Collier's, True, Argosy,* and *Saturday Evening Post*—and always wanted more.

That yearning for fulfillment through literature led me to become an English major at Dartmouth. I thought I would later be a poet or a novelist dispensing wisdom through my books, speaking reassurance to the confused and hopeless, leading readers to sing in their hearts, weep for joy, feel sadness, terror, pity, and all the tender emotions springing forth from my adolescent dreams of heroism and glory. A highlight of my freshman year was the moment in a first-semester English class when the professor chose my essay about childhood to read aloud in class, sharing with everyone my "immortal" and long-since forgotten lines about running through a field until I was breathless and then flinging myself upon a patch of long, cool grass as ecstasy overtook me and I was lost in bright images of the future. Heavy stuff, you know?

But it wasn't to happen quite that way. "The world" crept in bit by bit and I soon found myself grinding out papers and hour exams and making forced marches through Milton, Henry James, the Romantic poets, Pepys' diary, the variorium Shakespeare, and other apparatus of academia which accumulated heavily in my head and seemed to squeeze the vitality out of me. The endless study became grubbing for grades just to stay on scholarship. No time for fun, no time for dates, no time for athletics. As Wordsworth asked in his ode on immortality: Where was it now, the glory and the dream?

I remember a period in my senior year when I felt so desperate to escape from what seemed the irrelevance of being an English major—because Life was calling me—that I barely cracked the textbook for a Victorian literature course. Not that I was goofing off. I got an A on both papers for the course because the assignments interested me and I was busily reading in my other courses and, on my own, in psychology, philosophy, and religion as well. I was searching for myself, trying to make sense out of the perplexities of head versus heart, individuality versus social membership, body versus spirit, mortality versus eternity, and all the rest of my unavoidable but unfathomable circumstances. With a shock of recognition I read Young Yeats' statement. "The antinomies cannot be resolved" and felt an invisible blow to my solar plexus. Existence had come to seem almost totally absurd to me. It was a classic case of identity crisis at twenty-one.

Today, the antinomies have indeed been resolved and I've returned to my love of literature with a perspective formed by having taken the long way home. As an adult who has spent more than three decades in consciousness research and the exploration of higher human development, I know now what I was seeking through those longing moments of absorbtion in adventure stories about awe and manliness and Earth's salvation and new worlds discovered. I was seeking enlightenment—ultimate certitude, the Answer to the Cosmic Mystery, understanding of the Truly Big Questions: Who am I? Why am I here? Where am I going? What is life all about?

In an earlier era such knowledge was readily available through literature because literature was sacred, not secular. It was centered in a world view that bespoke absolutes to audiences and left no room for doubt or deviation. Nor was there much capacity in people for that, anyway.

But the emergence of ego in the human species brought Man from the bliss of personal ignorance to the agony of personal identity and the suffering of separate selfhood. That was my dilemma at twenty-one as ontogeny recapitulated phylogeny. Intuitively, groping I sought help through bibliotherapy. If I could understand the urge of Ahab, if I could penetrate the significance of Oedipus, if I could grasp the meaning of

Molly Bloom, if I could make "Fern Hill" and Alfred Prufrock and "In Memoriam" yield their secrets, I might emerge from the labyrinthine hell of confused individuality which became my condition as I was relentlessly urged into the world by duty and demand.

By the amazing grace of God, I did. From literature I gravitated to psychology, then levitated to parapsychology and kept going, upward and onward, exploring the limits of mind, past the first star on the right and into the realm of noetics and mysticism where science and spirituality merge in the experience of self-transcendence, the illusion of egoic life is seen for what it is, the arc of human evolution melts into godhood, and the extraordinary splendor of transpersonal being at the core of the cosmos illuminates even the most perfectly ordinary experience of moment-to-moment existence.

The outward aspect of that journey followed a variety of conventional and unconventional forms. But through it all I've arrived at the place of universal peace. My yearning is fulfilled; my destiny is clear; my life is content. I am constantly blessed.

This leads me to propose, as a way of sharing that blessing, that a new concept in literary criticism be recognized: liberation literature.

Liberation is one of the traditional names for God-realization or enlightenment: the discovery of your ultimate identity, resolution of all dualities into cosmic unity, blissful recognition of divinity at the center of yourself, the peace which passeth understanding. Literature has been one of the best means throughout history for conveying to people that sense of wisdom and peace with the universe. When a work of literature touches us deeply, when it moves us out of our usual narrow self-concerns and into a larger, more sympathetic relation with existence, we naturally accord the work and the author high regard.

The degree to which people experience self-transcendence through a novel, short story, poem, play, or film is regarded as a primary criterion in assessing literary greatness. Although this is generally recognized, so far as I know this characteristic has not been considered by literary critics the basis for a genre in its own right, let alone been examined in a significant way. I can think of only a handful of critical texts which touch on the subject.

In an article "Liberation and the Unity of Opposites in *Romeo and Juliet*" (*ReVision,* Spring 1983), I coined the phrase *liberation literature,* "works of fiction whose primary concern is fostering self-transcendence and higher human development by expanding the audience's consciousness beyond the egoic-mental realm into the transpersonal, thereby accelerating human evolution." The concept is grand; the definition, I trust, is not grandiose.

Some may object to the term *liberation* because in recent years it has been widely and vocally associated with political ideologies and the literature supporting various programs for radical socioeconomic reform. I recognize the validity of such writings and the possible confusion my designation may create. I nevertheless choose to describe the concept as liberation literature because the term *liberation* is far older than the contemporary body of writings against oppressive economic systems and political regimes. It goes back millennia and is a synonymn for enlightenment, which is the core truth of all the world's sacred traditions and the aim of all human development.

The foremost function of liberation literature is self-discovery beyond ego. Liberation literature is rooted in a vision of human evolution and the human potential for growth to higher states of being which ever more beautifully express the Ground of Being, which is the source of all becoming. Liberation literature embodies, to varying degrees, an enlightened understanding of the nature of God and the human condition—a condition which is an expression of godhead working through the vast processes of time and space to bring Man from humanity to divinity, from the Fall to the Resurrection.

Strictly speaking, therefore, the genre I designate is ancient—at least as old as Vedic times, when the rishis of India created short tales as teaching devices for spiritual aspirants. What is new is its recognition as an artform whose principal aim is not plot, character, delineation, style, aesthetics, or any of the usual literary considerations. Though these are nevertheless important, the aim of liberation literature is transformation of the world through inducing the reader into altered *states* of consciousness which can lead to altered *traits* of consciousness. That change of consciousness takes the reader or viewer in the direction of the transpersonal and, ultimately, the liberating realization of his or her true identity as the Self of all. It cannot lead to ultimate discovery of the Supreme Identity (that is impossible through words alone) but at least the reader or viewer may gain a new freedom through awareness of self beyond individualism and therefore beyond ego.

There is a Tibetan Buddhist saying: Insightful wisdom requires skillful means to produce effective action. With regard to liberation literature, effective action means that which can lead to self-transcendence. Since ego is itself the ultimate fiction, liberation literature uses fiction as skillful means to expose the illusion by transcending it. Through reverse psychology, so to speak, the reader is drawn *into* the work and *out of* the egoic shell which armors him against the world and cuts him off from the saving grace of human community and divine love. By coaxing him to go beyond his ordinary bounds of awareness and conventional sense of reality, the author gently expands and deepens the reader's or viewer's consciousness, leading him into higher realms of existence—those realms which first present themselves to us in childhood as appealing stories of fantasy and imagination and later in adulthood as noble ideals, inspired visions, quiet service, heroic acts, and selfless sacrifice.

The best liberation literature exhibits mastery of the traditionally recognized aspects of great literature. The plots are believable, the characters are well drawn, the dialogue realistic, the settings plausible, the style fresh and engaging. Thus, the authors of liberation literature display thorough knowledge of the conventions and traditions of their craft but are not bound by them. They simply use them for a purpose beyond both entertainment and information alike: liberation. Insofar as "lib lit" works are entertaining, the entertainment is inspirational; insofar as they are informative, the information urges transformation.

What are some examples? Liberation literature is found in all categories of British and American fiction. In drama, there are many striking works, such as Shakespeare's *King Lear* and *Romeo and Juliet* and Thornton Wilder's *Our Town*. As for novels, Melville's classic *Moby Dick* comes to mind, along with all of Joyce's work, Michael Murphy's *Jacob Atabet* and its sequel, *An End to Ordinary History*, J. R. Salamanca's exquisite *Lilith,* Aldous Huxley's *Island,* and Adrian Malone's recent *The Secret.* Certain short stories by classic and contemporary writers also fall (or should I say ascend?) into this genre. Consider Nathaniel Hawthorne's "Young Goodman Brown," "Roger Malvin's Burial," and "The Minister's Black Veil" or J. D. Salinger's "Teddy." They are marvelous studies of ego seen from a transegoic perspective. Likewise, Salinger's *Franny and Zooey* lead to deeper self-knowledge, as does Joseph Conrad's *Heart of Darkness.* Poetry is perhaps the major literary form in which examples of liberation literature can be found; think of Blake, Wordsworth's "Ode: Intimations of Immortality," Whitman's *Leaves of Grass,* Emerson's "Brahman," T. S. Eliot's *Four Quartets,* and Allen Ginzberg's "Howl."

Beyond British and American literature there are other notable examples: Dante's *The Divine Comedy;* Hermann Hesse's *Steppenwolf* and *Siddhartha;* some of the works of Tolstoy and Balzac; Sri Aurobindo's epic poem *Savitri,* Goethe's *Faust.* Other titles may come to mind; I would welcome hearing about them.

Likewise, the cinema is rich with liberation literature: *Citizen Kane, High Noon, 2001: A Space Odyssey, Zardoz,* and, yes, even *An Officer and a Gentleman, Saturday Night Fever,* and *Yentl.* Why the latter three? Zack and Tony grow from self-immersed users of women into open, honest, caring people; Yentl's passionate commitment to learning, despite a multitude of cultural obstacles, and her selfless love for Avigdor provide an inspiring image of human development. None of these three characters are themselves enlightened, of course, but for an audience whose narcissistic defenses are every bit as hardened as a Zack or a Tony, they are to some degree enlightening. They've just begun to enter the transpersonal realm; they have much to learn about higher planes of being and about living in community. Nevertheless, they call us out of the illusion of separate selfhood with all its suffering—call us to liberation, to fulfillment of our humanity.

How might the subject be approached most effectively? I've found that theme-oriented courses can be created to answer the deeply felt needs of students. Here are four examples.

1. "The Evolution of Consciousness and Humanity's Future as Seen in Science Fiction." The books I'd include are Arthur Clarke's *Childhood's End,* Dane Rudhyar's *Return from No Return,* John Boorman's *Zardoz,* Roger Zelazny's *Lord of Light,* Piers Anthony's *Macroscope,* Olaf Stapledon's *Star Maker,* Adrian Malone's *The Secret,* and the first (and possibly the second and third) volume in Frank Herbert's *Dune* series. I'd also work in films: *2001: A Space Odyssey* and, again, *Zardoz.* All of these make very powerful statements about transpersonal and transhuman development and are commanding studies in the possible future of our race and our planet.

2. "The Nature of Madness." Questing individuals can find a mirror for their inner situation—and a revelation—in works such as *King Lear,* Ken Kesey's *One Flew Over the Cuckoo's Nest,* J. R. Salamanca's *Lilith,* Hannah Green's *I Never Promised You a Rose Garden, Moby Dick,* and J. D. Salinger's *Fanny and Zooey,* and, of course, the film versions of *Lilith, Cuckoo's Nest, Rose Garden,* and *The Snake Pit.*

3. "The Hero and Heroine in Film." Among the titles appropriate for this theme are *High Noon, Shane, On the Waterfront, An Officer and a Gentleman, Norma Rae, Citizen Kane, Siddhartha,* and *Yentl.*

4. "The Agony and the Ecstasy of Youth." I'd include literature such as *Romeo and Juliet* (both the text and Franco Zefferelli film), *A Portrait of the Artist as a Young Man, Our Town, The Yearling, The Catcher in the Rye, Huckleberry Finn,* John Knowles' *A Separate Peace,* and, on film, *The Graduate, Dead Poets Society,* and, again, *The Yearling.*

The germ of my thoughts about the liberating function of literature began, as I said, in my struggle for self-understanding during my high school and college years. About 1975 my now-deceased friend and colleague, Jerome Ellison, professor of English and Humanities at the University of New Haven, gave me a copy of his 1966 article "Criticism for a New Age." It was the first time I'd seen formal expression of my idea in print. Writing in the *Southwest Review* more than twenty years ago, he stated his literary manifesto:

Evolution of consciousness has greatly increased its tempo in the twentieth century, and with cause. Humanity may not survive a third such destructive outbreak of the archaic mind as occurred in 1914 and again in 1939. Literary criticism stands in imperative obligation to hasten psychic evolution by discriminating between the more and the less evolved. By taking its place among the other great progressing inquiries into the meaning of man in the universe, literature and its criticism can regain their lost significance. Criticism might even become what in its highest function it always was supposed to be: the unifying agent, the catalyst that makes of man's multifarious inquiries something essentially and significantly one.

That is a profoundly important statement, deeply aligned with the idea of a New Age, but at the time of its publication it wasn't recognized as such by scholars and literary critics. Nor, so far as I can see, has it been since. But its time has nevertheless come. The now-global search for self-transcendence and higher human development is Nature's way of dealing with the egoic-based nuclear/ecological threat to human existence—and, indeed, the entire community of life—which hangs over our planet. Awareness of that must surely touch the educational establishment sooner or later—not just in political demonstrations outside the classroom but in its core curriculum. It can no longer stand aloof, irrelevant and powerless, or evolution will pass it by. I therefore point to Ellison's statement in hope that the spirit of his transpersonal approach to literary criticism will settle upon academia, so that the too-often-sterile scholasticism and just-plain-dull teaching which deadens students' appreciation for literature as a source of perennial wisdom and self-transcendence becomes (my apologies, dear Joyce) instead of a wake, awake.

Children, Computers, and Consciousness

As many as 30 million Americans are functionally illiterate. Why? Educators and noneducators alike have lamented the effect of television on younger people, and research has shown that the many hours of tube-watching children do can reduce literacy and word skills for nearly all except slow learners. The ridiculously unintelligent programming which fills the airwaves is apparently producing a semiliterate generation. Not only can't Johnny read, he doesn't want to. Further, he can't write or spell well.

It's sad that this situation should exist in the country which pioneered free public schools. I see reason for hope, however, in the form of computers and computer software which will make their way into the classroom and home. Little more than a decade has passed since Steven Jobs and Steve Wozniak, co-founders of Apple Computer, Inc., built what was to be the first commercial personal computer, yet look at what has occurred with PCs since then. There are millions in homes and schools across the nation, and children love to play with them.

The PC revolution is still in its early development, but in the future students will interact with computers from their earliest school years, and even earlier at home. Computers will have software to check spelling, punctuation, capitalization, grammar, syntax, and other mechanics (such as incomplete sentences and ambiguous references) as children compose at their keyboards; style-evaluating software will add a higher dimension to the process.

Moreover, the process will be highly interactive. Information will be presented with graphics and sound which rival Saturday-morning cartoons or music videos. The programs will be loaded with goodies such as artificial intelligence, high-resolution full-motion animation, and 3-D image processing which yields better image quality than current TV sets.

In other words, from the very beginning it will be *fun* for kids to learn the formal aspects of written language, just as they easily and naturally learn how to speak. This benign interaction, with instant feedback from the computer, will gently and enjoyably condition kids to spell perfectly, to think in well-formed sentences, and to experiment with language and composition. It will relieve teachers, parents, and students alike of the burdensome aspects of learning English or any other language.

This process will be accelerated by "talkwriters," which have just come on the market. They are still expensive and quite limited in their capacity to understand spoken language. However, judging by the speed of change in the computer industry, it's likely that talkwriters will be available for home use at moderate prices within a decade at most. Then, users will simply speak to a computer (shades of HAL in *2001!*, which will instantly display the utterance in written form, with spelling and other mechanics executed perfectly. Unclear or incorrect material will be flagged for clarification or correction by the user. Talkwriters will even be able to speak back to the user with synthesized speech.

Thus, standardized pronunciation of "broadcast" English (or any other language) will be encouraged. The ability to be articulate, even eloquent, will naturally follow as young people grow up with a computer-based teacher of language, rhetoric, composition, grammar, spelling, and so forth.

The breathtaking result: linguistic competence in children which will be the envy of the world and will facilitate their development of still-higher faculties at increasingly younger ages without damaging or arresting their growth as whole human beings. And who knows—some of it may rub off on parents (and even teachers!) who presently aren't so competent themselves.

What about learning foreign languages? Here, too, computers will function as teachers of infants. The children will grow up with multi-lingual abilities made possible by translation machines. Research and development is proceeding strongly in this field; translation machines with vocabularies of several thousand words are already available for a number of foreign languages, although the user must input words through a keyboard.

Beyond that, there is the possibility of an automatic-translation telephone system which can be used in international communication. Users will be able to speak to someone in another country—say, Spain or Japan—and will hear the reply in their native language via voice-generation equipment and translation software, with the reverse process operating similarly for the person being called.

Transpose such technology into the home environment and parents will have the capability to speak to their children in languages they've never learned. Children will be able to learn the languages at a young age, as easily as they learn their native tongue. And ¿*quien sabe?*, parents might also pick up some knowledge of other languages, *nei?*

Technology is here to stay; the question is how to apply it wisely, benevolently. If events unfold as I've projected here, I foresee a very positive effect upon human consciousness—and a major contribution to a New Age.

Justice, Compassion, and the New Age

s a person responsible for his behavior if insane or brainwashed? In the past, legislative and judicial proceedings in American have answered no, allowing for what is called the insanity plea. The U.S. Supreme Court's recent decision to exclude insane murderers from the death penalty finalizes the position for America. To that action I say: the decision is itself crazy. The Constitutional grounds used in supporting it are dubious at best—witness the close 5–4 vote by the justices. In addition, it makes a mockery of logic and justice. It is incompatible with enlightened living in a New Age.

I am not discussing the death penalty here. Rather, my concern is personal accountability for crimes and enlightened treatment of criminals. Even in the New Age, there will be some crime and cruelty from evolutionary holdovers—those Shaolin bandits I mentioned in "Empty Self, No Sword." Citizens of the New Age should be clear about the basis for punishment and incarceration. My position begins with this principle: *There is no substitute for personal accountability and nothing more dangerous for society than to allow a person, regardless of his state of mind, to escape the consequences of his actions.*

Because of murder trials in which the accused have pleaded not guilty by reason of insanity, admitted killers have literally gotten away with murder—legally. The insanity plea allowed judges to sentence them to mental hospitals for observation and treatment. There they were found sane and then released because they cannot be tried twice for the same crime. That acquittal is nothing less than a psychiatric atrocity.

It is *legislative* and *judicial* insanity that this should be allowed to

259

happen. Ensuring citizens safety from violence ought to be a prime objective of legislation in any enlightened society. Yet many lawabiding Americans live in fear of crime in the streets and in their homes because "law and order" isn't working effectively. When things get to the point of absolving confessed killers, that's just plain disorder and benightedness.

Some people feel the legal system should be compassionate with criminals. Others feel it should be tougher. Can compassion and judicial sternness work together? I say they can, but only if each is properly understood.

In a free society such as America, laws are made to control behavior, not states of mind. So the second principle in my position is this: *A defendant's mental state should have no bearing whatsoever on whether he is found guilty of commiting a crime.* He may be insane, brainwashed, drug-crazed, hypnotically programmed, "possessed" by an evil spirit, have multiple personality disorder or be otherwise *non compos mentos* and incapable of telling right from wrong (e.g., retardation or mere adolescence with it incomplete moral development), but that should only be taken into account *after* the finding. If a person is genuinely unbalanced, he can be given a sentence which includes appropriate treatment to restore mental health, whether the treatment be psychiatry, deprogramming, detoxification or even exorcism. Then, if treatment is successful, the case should be reviewed. The person should serve the rest of his sentence unless the preponderance of expert opinion feels that pardon or commutation is in order. At that point compassion becomes proper—but not before.

This position applies across the entire spectrum of mind states and motives leading to criminal behavior. I include in that even mercy killings where a spouse or family member terminates the life of a hopelessly incurable invalid. Although the murderer's motivation may be love and tender concern rather than hatred, greed or some other negative emotion, that is no excuse. It is only an explanation to be considered in sentencing.

Our judicial system is intended to deliver justice, not compassion. Ignoring this crucial distinction had led to the shameful and dangerous situation in which admitted murderers are declared innocent and released into society without punishment and without even simple restitution for the victim's survivors.

We can agree that Jim Jones of Guyana was insane, but does that mean that if he had survived the Jonestown massacre he should have been found not guilty by reason of insanity? Or Adolf Eichmann?

Unconditional love tells us to hate the sin, not the sinner. But loving someone unconditionally does not mean condoning misbehavior and unethical conduct. Wrongdoing may be forgiven—that's compassionate—but it should never be overlooked or ignored—that's foolish. Doing that for children leads to spoiled brats. Doing that for adults leads to anarchy and rampant violence. When lawbreaking occurs, it should be recognized and dealt with according to law. That is what justice is all about. Only when guilt or innocence has been determined does compassion become proper. If a finding of guilt has been made, there may be reason for a lighter sentence or even a pardon. On the other hand, there may be reason to "throw the book" at the convicted person. But letting someone "get away with it" is misplaced compassion, inappropriate Christian charity, "sloppy agape."

"Tough love" is the contemporary term for what Buddhists have traditionally called "ruthless compassion." Tough love does not mean casting someone out of your heart; compassion or unconditional love never does that. Tough love means allowing a person to experience the consequences of his wrongful or foolish behavior. Only that way will the antisocial or dangerous person learn to be responsible for his behavior and learn to respect the rights of others. Tough love is love, but first of all it is tough.

The Nuremberg trials declared loud and clear that people must be responsible for their acts, even in time of war. Trials in America today, however, declare that people are *not* responsible for their acts because their state of mind excluded reason. Consequently, criminals have been handed the legal means to get away with murder, and they, aware that their lives are at stake, quite reasonably use it. As the saying goes, they may be crazy but they're not stupid!

Legislators should correct this most gross miscarriage of justice—a miscarriage based on the foolish idea that a person's state of mind has a bearing on his innocence or guilt in criminal proceedings. If the person committed the act, he's guilty—period. Whether he remembers doing it or whether he could make a rational decision at the time doesn't matter at that point in the judicial proceedings. His state of mind and other possible mitigating or extenuating circumstances should be taken into account only in passing sentence. Irresponsible behavior should never be condoned to the point of murder. The failure of legislators to recognize and correct this outrageous situation only contributes to the general deterioration of respect for law and social order. And it certainly is a major roadblock on the way to the New Age.

At the Borderland of Matter: The Case for Biological UFOs

P art of the difficulty in understanding the UFO experience is the term itself. It lumps together a wide variety of dissimilar phenomena, leading the public and even many ufologists to think there is a single solution to the problem. Most theories attempt to reduce the entire body of ufological data to a unified explanation. Yet the data, in my judgment, show that qualitatively different phenomena are occurring. To speak of *the* UFO experience is to confuse rather than clarify the situation.

There seem to be at least three categories of phenomena comprising the UFO experience: terrestrial, extraterrestrial, and metaterrestrial. Extraterrestrial and metaterrestrial UFO cases are well reported (if not well explained) in the literature, but except for the conventional notions of hoax, hallucination, and craft secretly built by some human agency, the first category has hardly been considered. Yet there is one little-known contribution to ufology within this category which could be a breakthrough and which deserves the most thorough consideration: biological UFOs.

The data on this phenomenon have been gathered principally by Trevor James Constable of Hawaii. A merchant marine radioelectronics officer and an internationally known aviation historian, Constable is a longtime researcher in borderland science. Basing his work on the etherian physics of Rudolf Steiner and the orgone energy discoveries of Wilhem Reich, Constable claims to have discovered and photographed a form of life heretofore unknown to official science, although, he says, long known to occult science. The strange creatures shown in Constable's still photographs and movie films can explain an enormous number of UFO sightings which were thought at the first to be craft.

"Not all UFOs are sapcecraft from another world," Constable says. "Quite simply, many UFOs are living organisms. They are invisible biological aeroforms living in the sky unknown to official science. I know. I have developed simple methods for attracting them and photographing them directly from the invisible state. Others have since done likewise."

Thus Constable claims to have done what thousands of astronomers, biologists, and exobiologists should be most interested to hear: captured on film a form of life which offers startling new data and insights for all these fields and many others.

Astronomer-planetologist and UFO skeptic Dr. Carl Sagan, testifying before the U.S. Congress during the 1968 Symposium on Unidentified Flying Objects, said: "A bona fide example of extraterrestrial life, even in a very simple form, would revolutionize biology. . . . It would be truly immense." Constable feels he has begun the revolution.

The full story of this potentially momentous discovery is told in Constable's 1976 book *The Cosmic Pulse of Life,*[1] in which he demonstrates, through text and photographs, that animals live invisibly in the sky. Pictures taken on infrared film show organisms which look like gigantic amoebas. Constable believes they are life forms in the plasma state. That is, the creatures are not solid, liquid or gas, but exist in the fourth state of matter—plasma—as living heat-substance at the upper border of physical nature.

Fire is the most common example of plasma. Constable's pictures appear to show unicellular aerial fauna whose substance might be called "living fire." Yet if they are fire, they are cold fire—or at least they have a capacity to change temperature radically. Constable refers to these creatures simply as critters, on the grounds that classification of such bioforms is premature. Others have coined names for them: plasmoids, aeroforms, ideoplasms. But whatever the term, he says, the important point is to recognize that this class of UFO exhibits animal-like behavior for a simple reason: They are, in fact, animals. (An illustration of animal-like UFO behavior can be found in a 1979 report from Brisbane, Australia, where a glowing aerial object had been seen for a decade, showing up and chasing people almost as regularly as if it were a habit, like coming to a watering hole in the evening.)

Characteristics of Critters

Critters are normally hidden from human gaze for three reasons, Constable says. First, in their natural condition they are invisible because they exist mainly in the infrared range of the electromagnetic spectrum. Second, their native habitat is the stratosphere and beyond at distances greater than unaided sight can penetrate. (Constable claims to have seen them in the background during television coverage of the lunar landings and pointed them out to friends.) And they propel themselves bio-energetically at extremely fast speeds, often appearing like meteors before vanishing from view.

According to Constable, critters occasionally emerge into the visible portion of the electromagnetic spectrum, however, through their ability to change their density. Consisting of matter in its most tenuous form, they can become more dense and thereby pass from one level of tangibility and visibility to another. How they do this is unknown to Constable, but he says some of these variable-density creatures in discoidal form have been seen close up on the ground in full physical density. If seen by humans in such a condition, they are quickly labeled UFOs (which they are, of course). But they are not mechanical spacecraft; they are living creatures. When the late Ivan Sanderson, well-known naturalist and investigator of the unknown, saw some of Constable's photos, he wrote in this book *Uninvited Visitors,* "They don't look like machines at all. They look to a biologist horribly like unicellular life-forms, complete in some cases with nuclei, nucleoli, vacuoles and all the rest."[2]

Critters, Constable says, pulsate with "the cosmic pulse of life." When visible, they usually emit a characteristic red-to-orange glow, sometimes with blinding intensity. They travel in pulsatory fashion, swelling and shrinking cyclically as they move through the air, much as we humans pulsate with our heartbeat and swell and shrink with our lung movements.

Although critters can change their form like amoebas, they generally are discerned as discs or spheroids. They have a diaphanous structure, transparent like mica or the sheerest cloth, which allows a limited view of the interior. British author Harold T. Wilkins remarked that Constable's photos reminded him of "looking through the side of an aquarium tank."

As living organisms, Constable says, critters appear to be an elemental branch of evolution probably older than most life on Earth, dating from the time when our planet was more gaseous and plasmatic than solid—hence before the geological record began. He states that they are an upper-border counterpart to the microbic world, and like the microbic world, require a removal of human optical limitations in order to become visible to us. Critters are part of what occultists term "elementals," he says, and they live invisibly like fish in the ocean of atmosphere. Like fish, he judges them to be of low intelligence. They will probably one day be better classified as macrobacteria inhabiting the aerial ocean we call the sky, he predicts.

Furthermore, he notes, these plasmatic aerial creatures are not the only organisms in the upper atmosphere. It supports a veritable aerial jungle, an idea suggested by Arthur Conan Doyle in his story "The Horror of the Heights" and by pioneer investigator of the paranormal Charles Fort. Some of these critters are serpentine, virtually as described by Conan Doyle seventy years ago.

Critters range in size from that of a coin to 100 feet or more in diameter, Constable says. As do most plasmas, they give a solid radar return, even when unseen by the naked eye. This characteristic explains those many UFO reports where fighter pilots, scrambled aloft to intercept unidentified incoming "bogeys," have found nothing when vectored to the location by ground-control radar operators, even though the radars have continued to track the objects on their scopes. The mysterious "foo fighters" which World War II and Korean War pilots reported as miniature UFOs can be explained as critters in the visible, luminous state.

So, perhaps, can some reports attributed to the phenomenon of ball lightning. Recent experiments in plasma physics, according to Dr. Stephen Bardwell, have shown with "astounding regularity the occurrence of spontaneously ordered structures in plasmas."[3] There is, he says, an "inherent nonlinear quality" in them which gives rise to "large-scale coherent motion that is self-concentrating." Bardwell discusses these "self-ordered phenomena" and calls for a research program to develop "a zoology of these global, structured phenomena." Although Bardwell does not discuss the possibility that such plasma phenomena may cross the threshold from physics to biology and may actually be living creatures (albeit of a very low order of intelligence), his use of the term *zoology* is curious. It brings us to the field of exobiology, the scientific search for life beyond Earth.

The Search for Extraterrestrial Life

What does exobiology say about the possibility of life originating in space? First, consider how varied the conditions are under which life on Earth can arise, and how varied the lifeforms. Organisms have adapted to hot acidic springs where the water temperature approaches boiling; to the heat of deserts and the cold of the Arctic and Antarctic; to the nocturnal world; to the darkness and pressure of undersea deeps; and even (in the case of anaerobic bacteria) to the absence of air. What might go beyond even that?

Michael Grant, writing about "A New Energy of Life?" in *Science*

Digest, points out that our notions of biology are founded in the idea that all life is photochemically based—fundamentally solar-powered. But, he notes, there are other forms of energy which vibrate *outside* the wavelength range used in photosynthesis. Magnetism is an example. "We may . . . discover someday organisms that use portions of the electromagnetic spectrum other than that used in photosynthesis. All such an organism would need is a molecule that could, for example, take in high-energy ultraviolet light and bleed off excess energy in the form of electricity."[4]

Exobiology has found that organic compounds—the basic building blocks of life—are present in deep space itself; this supports the possibility that other forms of life could exist in the universe. Scientists participating in the search for extraterrestrial intelligence (SETI) gathered at the International Astronomical Union Colloquium on Bioastronomy at Balatonfured, Hungary, in June 1987. They heard Otto Schidlowski of the Otto Hahn Institute in Mainz, West Germany, present the case that the emergence of life on Earth some four billion years ago, scarcely 500,000 years after the solar system formed, can best be explained "if the ancient Earth had been inoculated by extraterrestrial protobionts." The conference was reported by astronomer-author John Gribben, who commented: "This does not require the guiding hand of intelligence, but suggests that prebiotic molecules arise naturally in space and infect *all* suitable planets with life."[5]

A recent *New York Times* article discussed the possibility advanced by Dr. Frank Drake of Cornell, an eminent astronomer involved in SETI work, that a sort of life could evolve on the surface of a neutron star, where the temperature hovers around 14,000°F and the pull of gravity is enough to squash atoms. Conventional chemical processes would therefore be impossible on a neutron star, but perhaps nuclear fragments might survive and combine with neutrons to "create forms of matter inconceivable in a terrestrial environment." Drake suggested in the 1970s that the bare nuclei of atoms in direct contact with each other might interact, giving rise to a kind of nuclear chemistry analogous to the electronic chemistry which governs our own world.[6]

Another possibility for exobiological life in free space is denoted by the term *zeroidal.* Dr. Franklin Ruehl, a nuclear physicist and former professor of physics at UCLA, described the body of scientific evidence suggesting zeroids in a 1979 *Canadian UFO Report* article.[7] He concluded that "abundant opportunity exists for entities of limitless diversity to develop throughout the universal expanse, and exist with high probability!" In a thought-provoking summary, he said: ". . . zeroids could easily have trod many different evolutionary paths, so that they may now range in dimensionality from the microscopic to the macroscopic, with morphologies varying from the utterly simple to the extraordinarily complex."

Critter Research

Beginning in 1957, Constable and his colleagues, James O. Woods and Robert A. McCullough, over twenty years took hundreds of still and motion pictures of critters with the aid of an infrared film and filters, standard 35mm cameras, and a Rolex 16mm and Minolta XL400 Super 8mm camera in the case of the motion pictures. In this way they appear to have opened a vast new field of life which had been veiled from normal human visual ability. The same methods have also produced a substantial number of photos of construct-type UFOs—objects propelled by fields of force which can be seen in the photographs. Constable emphasizes that the constructs and the critters have been mutually confused since 1947, the year of Kenneth Arnold's epochal "flying saucer" sighting.[8] "I have given proof of a basic qualitative element in UFOs," says Constable, "and provided irrefutable evidence of the biological and bioenergetic base upon which the whole subject rests technically."

Constable has been accused of both ignorance and fraud because of his photos. What appears, his critics say, is due either to defects or errors in film handling and developing by Constable, or else he has deliberately tampered with the film to produce images he then claims are genuine UFO phenomena. He denies these charges categorically, stating that for several years he was the largest consumer of Kodak high-speed infrared film west of Chicago and learned processing from professionals. Major laboratories have handled all his film for many years. As far as deliberate tampering is concerned, he says, this would be strange conduct indeed for a man internationally respected by the aviation community for the integrity of his histories or for a man entrusted with the responsibility for communications of a multimillion-dollar vessel of the U.S. merchant fleet.

Nevertheless, I put Constable's photographs to the best test so far devised by science: computerized electronic analysis and evaluation. In 1975, through the director of Ground Saucer Watch, William H. Spaulding, I had the negatives of photos "Alpha 1" through "Alpha 4" (as Constable numbered them in *Cosmic Pulse*) examined. On the basis of computer analysis, Spaulding concluded that Constable's photos could be duplicated with what could be called "a little darkroom magic," but that this alone did not prove they were faked. Rather, he told me, he felt the photographs showed something genuinely paranormal and outside the range of the computer's program, which is based on all known phenomena, natural and human, which have been shown to account for UFO sightings.

Constable welcomes interested parties to try his methods of photography. "If they carry out the experiments they will get results," he says, "but it will not be much." He gives full instructions for taking infrared photos in *The Cosmic Pulse of Life*. He includes specifics of the means by which critters may be attracted. In 1975 he developed a different technique but did not publish details of it until after *Cosmic Pulse* was in print. The new method is called the "reverse spectrum" technique, and it simply uses Ektachrome Super-8mm movie film and an 18A (ultraviolet) filter to objectify the portion of the spectrum in which critters live invisibly. With this method UFOs appear in color out of a black background in full daylight. Instructions for taking photographs this way can be found in the abridged paperback edition of Constable's book, retitled *Sky Creatures: Living UFOs*.[9]

Constable supports his photographic work with scholarly research showing there were many cases of critter sightings by others both in the U.S. and elsewhere long before he began photographing them. Some cases occurred prior to his birth. The most startling and comprehensive record is the ancient cave paintings at Lascaux, France, dating from 30,000 to 10,000 B.C. These, Constable declares, show "discs, doughnuts, large fusiform shapes accompanied by lines of small discs . . . collections of shapes indstinguishable from many UFOs reported and photographed in the twentieth century."

Is Constable the only person who has captured critters on film? No. According to Vincent H. Gaddis, in his *Mysterious Fires and Lights,* as long ago as the early 1960s Constable's photographic success "was duplicated by others who have not sought recognition for their work, particularly Miss Doris LeVesque, of Joshua Tree, California, whose film and prints have been processed and developed by H. D. Clark, a retired professional photographer, and formerly a photo instructor with the Chicago Board of Education."[10]

Since the publication of *Cosmic Pulse,* half a dozen readers have reported to Constable the success of his infrared method. One such photo appears in *Sky Creatures*. It and several others were taken in 1977 by Richard Toronto, a Californian, at two locations in that state. Toronto reported his experiences in a 1980 *Fate* magazine article entitled "Living UFOs." Like Constable, he got results on infrared film when he could not see anything in the viewfinder. Like Constable, he has had his films expertly examined. And, like Constable, he has had his results explained as errors. Toronto wrote:

"I sent Kodak three strips of film but made no claims about their origins. I simply asked if something was wrong with the film. Over a month later I got an official answer: no. The film was in good condition at the time it was shot, Kodak said. The effects were caused, the company suggested, by nothing more than drying spots and finger marks on the film—or maybe I had hastily unloaded the film canister.

"This was a bit hard for me to swallow, since by that time I had been poring over these things for months and was well aware of what drying spots and finger marks look like. As one who had been handling film for over nine years, I considered the Kodak suggestions a blow to my photographer's ego. So I snapped another roll and sent it to a laboratory without opening it. More critters. Either everyone out there smudges his fingers all over the film or someone at Kodak didn't interrupt his coffee break long enough to check these things out thoroughly."[11]

Toronto tried Constable's reverse spectrum technique and again got results. "I have on file," he said, a "panchromatic shot of a small critter, taken unknowingly in Orlando, Florida. . . . And I have seen ideoplasm photographs, which others have taken purely by chance, on black-and-white panchromatic film. Obviously, this phenomenon, while far from cooperative, is definitely there."

Although he has done more than anyone to establish the case for the critters, Constable wrote in *Cosmic Pulse* that "I was not the originator of the theory that some UFOs could be living organisms." Credit for that, he says, goes to author-ufologist Meade Layne, who preceded him by about ten years, and also to veteran UFO researcher John Philip Bessor.

It was Bessor who coined the term *ideoplasm,* designating a type of primitive ectoplasmic creature "originating in the stratosphere, capable of materialization and dematerialization." He has also described them as "gelatinous meteors," and his research has turned up a number of instances (the earliest dating to 1650) in which such objects have troubled scientists. In 1819, for example, a Dartmouth College lecturer in chemistry found an odd material after a meteor shower. It was a "buff-colored, pulpy substance of the consistence of good, soft soap, of an offensive suffocating smell. A few minutes' exposure to the atmosphere changed the buff into a livid color resembling venous blood. It was observed to attract moisture readily from the air." Readers will probably recognize the similarity between this 1819 report and some modern reports of "angel hair" from UFOs. Might this also explain some of the "falls of blood" recorded by pioneer investigator of the paranormal, Charles Fort?

Work supporting Constable also came from the GRCU UFO research group in Genoa, Italy. Luciano Boccone, spokesman for the engineers and technicians comprising the group, sent Constable a letter in 1979 which corroborates his work entirely and independently.

Boccone, who died several years ago, wrote: ". . . we have got irrefutable documentary evidence of the presence of such 'plasmoids' at low altitude over our mountain and marine research areas, close to us on the ground, and inside our houses, too. I repeat, we have objectified them many times directly from the invisible state on infrared, panchromatic, and color still pictures, most of which have been taken on instrumental detection only. . . .

"This is the reason why, sticking to the facts and failing for the time being any exhaustive, satisfactory explanation other than their 'biological nature,' we agree to your interpretation, according to which most of the UFOs that have mystified men for generations are not extraterrestrial spaceships at all, but are generally invisible, ultradimensional, ultraterrestrial, biological, etheric organisms that are of our planet, that have been living with us, side by side, unnoticed, since the beginning of time."

The most significant aspect of the Italian work is that it was undertaken in the 1976–1979 period, without any prior knowledge on the part of the Italians that Constable even existed. Only when their work was complete did they learn of Constable's pioneering efforts twenty years previously, through author Brad Steiger.

A comprehensive, mutually corroborative 144-page presentation of the Italian photos and those of Constable was published in 1979 in Italy, entitled *UFO—La Realtà Nascosta.*[12] Boccone shows dozens of stills and movie film frames of critters. The color and black-and-white photos are often quite dramatic.

Virtually identical photographs have been made behind the Iron Curtain, Constable reported in 1981. A group of Romanian engineers directed by Florin Gheorghita of Cluj-Nopoca used an instrumental approach to certain objective evidence of critters. The Romanian group was in touch with Boccone, who reported their work to Constable. But, Constable told the *Journal of Borderland Research,* their efforts "have been rewarded with police surveillance and a severance of [Gheorghita's] contacts with his Italian friends."[13]

The most dramatic critter pictures, however, were made by people who apparently did not recognize the true nature of their photographic subjects. I am speaking of the NASA space programs, which through its astronauts and remote-control spacecraft has brought back to Earth dozens of UFO photos. NASA's official explanation for these strange objects floating in space is either "space junk" or "light reflections on the camera or spacecraft window."

Such explanations are unsatisfactory, and exactly that has been publicly stated by at least one astronaut, Gordon Cooper. But even the astronauts who took pictures of UFOs in space failed to recognize the living creatures they apparently photographed. Nevertheless, some of the photographs have been released, and when compared with Constable's, the identity of "lens flares" and "space junk" seems to become immediately obvious: critters.

For example, astronaut Edwin E. Aldrin, Jr., during the Gemini 12 mission in November 1966, observed a UFO hovering in space with a second one nearby. He photographed them, just as astronauts Charles Conrad and Richard F. Gordon, Jr. had on their Gemini 11 flight two months earlier. Visual inspection of their photographs, performed by someone who is aware of the critters hypothesis, shows that plasmatic aeroforms seemed to be present in both cases.

Equally dramatic photographs of something in space which could not be identified were again taken by Aldrin when he was a crew member of the historic Apollo 11 lunar landing mission in 1969.[14]

And even more recently, Soviet cosmonauts in Salyut 7 sighted what was described "a band of angels," "celestrial apparitions," and "fields of pure energy and alien intellect," but what may actually be simply another instance of critters in the visible state. According to *Weekly World News*, Dr. Yury Manakov, a Soviet astrophysicist, said that in July 1985 the Salyut craft was engulfed in a brilliant orange glow caused by "seven giant figures in the form of humans, but with wings and mist-like halos. They appeared to be hundreds of feet tall with a wingspan as great as any jetliner. . . . The forms seem to change continually. The beings appear solid, then misty. They are nothing like the classic descriptions of angels, which are corporeal, like humans," Manankov told French journalist André Demazure. Manakov studied the ten-minute film shot by the cosmonauts and concluded that the entities "descended from a race of humanoids who shed their bodies after reaching the top of the evolutionary ladder." A strange and unlikely tale, indeed, considering the source. But if there is anything to it, critters—not angels or evolved humanoids—seem the more probable explanation.[15]

Even the NASA photos do not satisfy skeptics, however, and NASA has steadfastly stuck to its "explanation" of having no explanation. Not until December 31, 1978, when an Australian television crew flying over New Zealand filmed a UFO for twenty minutes, was what is probably the best proof of critters obtained. Dr. J. Allen Hynek pronounced the films genuine after exhaustive tests. So did Jack Acuff, president of National Investigations Committee on Aerial Phenomena (NICAP).

The film was shown on TV around the world. What appeared was a brightly lit object which at various times seemed to be round, triangular, and even bell-shaped. Its color changed from white to white-yellow to red and orange. Its size was estimated to be about 100 feet wide.

While it is possible to imagine a craft changing its shape (for example, folding its wings, as some do), it surpasses the limit of technology to say that a man-made craft changed its color as well in the manner observed. An objective consideration of the evidence, when viewed in light of the data on biological UFOs amassed by Constable and others, points most strongly to this conclusion: The object filmed over New Zealand on December 31, 1978, was a critter.

Thus, evidence not only shows that UFOs are real but also suggests a wholly biological dimension to the UFO experience.

When I first became aware of Constable's work in the early 1972, I took an active interest in it because I felt he presented a plausible case for the critters. Several years later, I showed Constable's photos and then-unpublished manuscript of *Cosmic Pulse* to Carl Sagan. He skeptically dismissed the entire project, saying that until there were 3-D photos (which involve simultaneous exposure of two negatives focused on the same object) he wouldn't want to waste his time because the photos looked too much like they were caused by improper development of the film. J. Allen Hynek, however, in a more open-minded fashion, showed great interest in Constable's work. He thought the photos and manuscript very intriguing and followed my suggestion to meet Constable. They got together briefly in Los Angeles International Airport, while Hynek expressed interest in going on a "critter hunt" with Constable. The expedition never happened, however, because of Hynek's busy schedule. Instead, he asked Constable to send him some rolls of exposed but undeveloped film taken of critters. This Constable did, but when an assistant of Hynek's developed the film, he reported it was completely exposed; only totally black negatives appeared. Constable, suspecting sabotage of his work and infiltration by a government agent, ceased contact with Hynek. He has now turned his research entirely to weather engineering and is no longer involved in the UFO question—critters or otherwise.

At this point the ball is in the court of ufologists. One data source for further study would be satellite photographs. Many infrared photos have been taken by scientists and the military, who are mapping planetary resources and features as well as observing military activities around the globe. Possibly some photographs evidence seemingly inexplicable heat sources in the atmosphere which have been interpreted as atmospheric thermal anomalies and then disregarded, since the purpose of the photo work is the surface of the Earth. If such is the case, it may well be there are many pictures of critters, but the scientific establishment is simply unaware of their significance.

Living heat-substance, life forms which predate the geological history of Earth, invisible animals existing in the sky: is it unreasonable to ask the scientific community to examine Constable's claim? If one aspect of the New Age is recovery of lost ancestral knowledge and a wider view of the nature of reality, the case for the critters seems to promise another point for the meeting of science and spirit.

If This Is the New Age, I'll Take Budweiser!

Recent articles in newspapers and magazines indicate an appalling lack of discrimination and integrity in some nominal New Agers, and an even more appalling lack of ethics, compassion, and just plain common sense among those who are supposed to be at the forefront of spiritual growth and the demonstration of higher consciousness. Sometimes I just want to throw up my hands in exasperation. If *this* is the New Age, I'll take Budweiser!

The sensationalism, ripoff, and outright danger has reached such horrible proportions that I've decided to take a drastic step. I'm going public with a unique spiritual instrument I obtained from a lama high in the Himalayas. He was my teacher in a previous life and taught me a secret mantra for novice New Agers: O-wa ta-na sigh-om. (To understand this mystical, enlightening statement, say it aloud five times quickly without pausing.) His temple kept the holy device for many centuries and then was instructed by an emissary from another galaxy to pass it on to me. Its origin is lost in the mists of time, but legend has it that it was removed from the Great Pyramid by a mystery-school adept and later brought to India via UFO by a "thirteenth disciple" secretly appointed by Jesus to develop an elite corps to guard the Gates of Heaven.

This most important piece of technology is called a spiritual crap detector (SCD). Based on an ancient Atlantean prototype, the SCD is designed to measure the spiritual development level of anyone you meet. As you operate this matchbox-sized unit discreetly from your pocket or purse, its crystal light probe will examine a person's bioenergetic field and its readout window will then tell you the highest chakra open in the person's aura. Now, for the first time anywhere, you can own one of these amazing devices for the incredible price of just $139.95. Send your check or money order to me c/o P.O. Box ∞, Nirvana, CA 66666. I'll send a unit to you astrally for quickest delivery. So order yours today and get in on the SCD action. Also ask about bulk sales discount prices and the multilevel marketing plan. As a way of saying thanks, I'll include a free gift—a miniature vial of antikarma lotion. Its new and improved formula is guaranteed to reduce your future incarnations by at least ten lives! (Batteries for SCD not included. Offer void where prohibited.)

Notes

INTRODUCTION

1 Robert Basil (ed.), *Not Necessarily the New Age: Critical Essays* (Buffalo, N.Y.: Prometheus Books, 1988), p. 351.

2 William I. Thompson, *Imaginary Landscape: Making Worlds of Myth and Science* (New York: St. Martin's Press, 1989).

3 George Feuerstein, *Jean Gebser: What Color Is Your Consciousness?* (Mill Valley, Calif.: Robert Briggs Associates, 1989).

CHAPTER 1

1 (England: University Press).

2 *International Herald Tribune,* March 31, 1981.

3 John Gliedman, "Scientists in Search of the Soul," *Science Digest,* July 1982, p. 77.

4 (Boston: Shambhala Publications, 1985), p. 176.

5 John Eccles, *The Understanding of the Brain* (New York: McGraw-Hill, 1976).

6 Wilder Penfield, *The Mystery of the Mind* (Princeton, N.J.: Princeton University Press, 1975), p. 48.

7 *MacLean's Magazine,* April 17, 1976.

8 Roger W. Sperry, *Science and Moral Priority* (New York: Columbia University Press, 1982).

CHAPTER 2

1 My reference to God as male/Father should not be construed as sexist. Whenever possible, I use gender-neutral terms, but sometimes I use the traditional forms simply to avoid awkward phraseology. Likewise, my references to collective humanity may sometimes be expressed as Man for aesthetic reasons. See Chapter 24 for my views on the nature of God with regard to gender.

CHAPTER 3

1 Michael Murphy and Steven Donovan, *The Physical and Psychological Effects of Meditation* (San Rafael, Calif.: Esalen Institute, 1988). Available from The Esalen Study of Exceptional Functioning, 230 Forbes Avenue, San Rafael, CA 94901.

CHAPTER 4

[1] Peter Warlow, *The Reversing Earth* (London: J. L. Dent & Sons, 1982), p. 195.
[2] Charles Hapgood, *Maps of the Ancient Sea Kings* (New York: E. P. Dutton, 1979), p. 239.
[3] Jeffrey Goodman, *We Are the Earthquake Generation* (New York: Berkley Books, 1979), p. 188.

CHAPTER 6

[1] Lawrence Fawcett and Barry Greenwood, *Clear Intent* (Englewood Cliffs, N.J.: Prentice-Hall, 1984). Reissued in 1990 as *The UFO Cover-Up*.
[2] Robert K. Temple, *The Sirius Mystery* (Rochester, Vt.: Inner Traditions International, 1987).
[3] Charles Berlitz and William L. Moore, *The Roswell Incident* (New York: Berkley, 1980).
[4] Trevor J. Constable, *The Cosmic Pulse of Life: The Revolutionary Biological Power Behind UFOs* (San Jose, Calif.: Merlin Press, 1976).
[5] Paul Devereux, *Earth Lights Revelation* (London: Blandford Press, 1989).
[6] C. G. Jung, *Flying Saucers: A Modern Myth of Things Seen in the Sky* (New York: Harcourt, Brace & World, 1959).

CHAPTER 7

[1] Ivan Sanderson, "Editorial: A Fifth Porce," *Pursuit* 5 (4), October 1972.
[2] Carl Jung, "The Archetypes and the Collective Unconscious," *The Collected Works of C. G. Jung* (Princeton, N.J.: Princeton University Press, 1959), p. 3.
[3] Ira Progoff, *Jung, Synchronicity, and Human Destiny* (New York: Julian Press, 1973), p. 91–92.
[4] Dilip Kumar Roy and Indira Devi, *Pilgrims of the Stars* (New York, Delta, 1974), p. 252.

CHAPTER 8

[1] Joseph S. Benner, *The Impersonal Life,* 43rd ed. (Marina del Rey, Calif.: DeVorss, 1983), p 171.
[2] Robert McDermott (ed.), *The Essential Aurobindo* (New York: Schocken, 1973), p. 38.
[3] *The Essential Aurobindo*, p. 83.
[4] Satprem, *Sri Aurobindo or The Adventure of Consciousness* (Pondicherry, India: Sri Aurobindo Ashram Trust, 1968), pp. 97–98.
[5] *The Essential Aurobindo*, pp. 100–101.
[6] *The Essential Aurobindo*, pp. 101–102.
[7] Jesse Roarke, *Sri Aurobindo* (Pondicherry, India: Sri Aurobindo Ashram Trust, 1973), pp. 42–43.
[8] Sri Aurobindo, *The Problem of Rebirth* (Pondicherry,: India Sri Aurobindo Ashram Trust, 1952), pp. 135–137.
[9] Roarke, *Sri Aurobindo*, p. 41.
[10] Satprem, *Sri Aurobindo*, p. 101.
[11] Satprem, *Sri Aurobindo*, p. 101
[12] *The Essential Aurobindo*, p. 105.
[13] Roarke, *Sri Aurobindo*, p. 44

14 The works of Sri Aurobindo and those books about him are not widely available in bookstores but can be obtained from the Matagiri Sri Aurobindo Center, Mt. Tremper, N.Y. 12457, and from the Sri Aurobindo Association, P.O. Box 372, High Falls, N.Y. 12440.

15 Sri Aurobindo, *The Problem of Rebirth*, p. 83.

16 M.C. (Mabel Collins), *Light on the Path* (Des Plaines, Ill.: Yogi Publication Society, n.d.), p. 92.

CHAPTER 9

1 Lobsang P. Lhalungpa, *The Life of Milarepa* (New York: Dutton, 1977), p. 124.

CHAPTER 10

1 Rammurit S. Mishra, *Fundamentals of Yoga: A Handbook of Theories, Practice, and Application* (New York: Crown, 1987), p. 2.

2 *Be Here Now,* (New York: Crown, 1971), p. 18.

3 Glenn H. Mullin, *Death and Dying: The Tibetan Tradition* (New York: Penguin, 1988), p. 241.

4 Swami Ajaya (ed.), *Living with the Himalayan Masters* (Honesdale, Pa.: Himalayan Publishers, 1980), p. 440.

5 Noted in *The New York Times,* January 19, 1988, p. C3.

6 See C. Louis Kervan, *Proof in Biology of Weak Energy Transmutations* (Paris: Maloine Publishers, 1975).

CHAPTER 11

1 Kundalini Research Foundation, P.O. Box 2248, Noroton Heights, CT 06280.

2 Gopi Krishna, *Kundalini, The Evolutionary Energy in Man* (Berkeley: Shambhala, 1970).

3 Gopi Krishna, "The True Aim of Yoga," *The Awakening of Kundalini* (New York: E. P. Dutton, 1975) pp. 92-95.

CHAPTER 12

1 The philosopher-yogi Dr. Haridas Chaudhuri said to me in a 1975 letter, "Strictly speaking, the basic *fact* of being aware is essentially and hierarchically different from the pure *act* of awareness which is the essence of pure consciousness. The *fact* of being aware is no less an object of consciousness than thoughts, ideas, feelings, and other psychic processes. Consciousness may mean *consciousness as experienced*—as an object or fact of awareness, as a phenomenon of knowledge. It may also mean the pure act of consciousness, the unobjectifiable element of transcendence in the human mind."

2 Watts adds, "Zen points out that our precious 'self' is just an idea, useful and legitimate enough if seen for what it is, but disastrous if identified with our real nature."

3 Quoted by Arthur Koestler in *The Ghost in the Machine*, p. 219, from J. C. Eccles' *Brain and the Unity of Conscious Experience*, Cambridge University Press, 1966.

4 Ken Wilber, "The Spectrum of Consciousness," *Main Currents in Modern Thought*, Vol. 31, No. 2, Nov.–Dec. 1974, p. 55.

5 The Institute of Noetic Sciences is located at 475 Gate Five Road, Suite 300, P. O. Box 909, Sausalito, California 94966-0909. It is open to public membership.

6 Theodore Roszach, "Letters," *Science,* Vol. 187, p. 792.

CHAPTER 13

[1] In the electrogravitic research of nuclear physicist Thomas E. Bearden, who has developed a theory of psychotronics which demonstrates how electromagnetism and gravity are unified, both negative energy and negative time are primary aspects. However, this does not lend credence to the popular misconception of "negative energy." Bearden's use of "negative" is specific and quantifiable, and he acknowledges that both positive and negative space-time are subordinate to consciousness.

CHAPTER 14

[1] Richard M. Bucke, *Cosmic Consciousness* (New York: E. P. Dutton, 1969), pp. 9–10.

[2] Pierre Teilhard de Chardin, *The Phenomenon of Man* (New York: Harper & Row, 1961).

CHAPTER 16

[1] J. Donald Walters, *How to Be a Channel* (Nevada City, Calif.: Crystal Clarity, 1987), p. 14.

[2] Actually, you're *gaining* your sanity by losing your everyday view of reality (which, insofar as it has excluded spirit realms, is itself insane in the sense that anything less than a clear view of ultimate reality is to some degree crazy). Ideal mental health is the condition known as enlightenment. Short of that, we're all insane to one degree or another.

[3] Jon Klimo, *Channeling: Investigations on Receiving Information from Paranormal Sources* (Los Angeles: Jeremy P. Tarcher, 1987), p. 320ff.

CHAPTER 19

[1] Miyamoto Musashi, *A Book of Five Rings* (Woodstock, N.Y.: Overlook Press, 1974), p. 86–87.

[2] Gichin Funakoshi, *Karate-do: My Way of Life* (Tokyo: Kodansha Interational, 1975).

[3] Joe Hyams, *Zen and the Martial Arts* (Los Angeles: J. P. Tarcher, 1979). (An inexpensive edition is available from Bantam Books.)

[4] John White (ed.), *The Highest State of Consciousness* (New York: Doubleday-Anchor, 1972), p. ix.

[5] Jay Gluck, *Zen Combat* (New York: Ballantine, 1962), p. 72–73.

[6] Randy F. Nelson (ed.), "From *Zen in the Art of Archery*," in *The Overlook Martial Arts Reader* (Woodstock, N.Y.: Overlook, 1989), p. 141.

[7] Richard Kim, *The Weaponless Warriors* (Burbank, Calif.: Ohara Publications, 1974), p. 109.

[8] *The Weaponless Warriors*, p. 105.

[9] Terrence Webster-Doyle, *Karate: The Art of Empty Self* (Ojai, Calif.: Atrium Publications, 1989).

[10] *Karate*, first page of main text.

[11] John Stevens, *The Sword of No-Sword: Life of the Master Warrior Tesshu* (Boston: Shambhala, 1989), p. ix.

[12] *Sword of No-Sword*, p. 39.

[13] Taisen Deshimaru, *The Zen Way to the Martial Arts* (New York: Dutton, 1982), p. 2.

[14] *The Zen Way*, pp. 1–2.

[15] *The Zen Way*, p. 5.

16 *The Zen Way,* p. 5.

17 John Stevens, *Abundant Peace: The Biography of Morihei Ueshiba* (Boston: Shambhala, 1987), p. 67 and back cover.

18 C. W. Nicol, *Moving Zen: Karate as a Way to Gentleness* (New York: Morrow, 1975), p. 45.

19 Paul Brunton, *Essays on the Quest* (York Beach, Me.: Samuel Weiser, 1985), p. 72.

20 Howard Reid and Michael Croucher, *The Way of the Warrior* (New York: Simon & Schuster, 1987), p. 172.

21 Personal correspondence, July 19, 1989.

22 *The Overlook Martial Arts Reader,* p. 100. The Rothpearl reference is to Allen Rothpearl, "Personality Traits in Martial Artists," *Perceptual and Motor Skills,* L (1980): 395–401.

23 *Essays on the Quest,* p. 72.

24 Gluck, *Zen Combat,* p. 183.

25 Don Ethan Miller, "A State of Grace" in *The Overlook Martial Arts Reader,* p. 153.

CHAPTER 20

1 Ken Wilber, *Eye to Eye* (New York: Doubleday/Anchor, 1983. The summary appeared in an early draft of the chapter but was deleted in publication.).

2 Da Love-Ananda, *The Bodily Sacrifice of Attention* (Clearlake, Calif.: Dawn Horse Press, 1981). pp. 127–128.

CHAPTER 21

1 Available from The School of the Natural Order, P.O. Box 578, Baker, NV 89311.

2 The stages of spiritual unfoldment have been described well in an excellent article by John T. Chirban, "Developmental Stages in Eastern Orthodox Christianity," in *Transformations of Consciousness,* edited by Ken Wilber et al. Chirban delineates the stages as: (1) Image, (2) Metanoia (conversion), (3) Apatheia (purification or transformation), (4) Light (illumination), and (5) Theosis (God-union). This more precise use of the term *metanoia* is a valuable clarification.

CHAPTER 22

1 Noohra Foundation, Suite 100B, 18022 Cowan Street, Irvine, CA 92714.

2 Rocco Errico, "Light from the Language of Jesus," *Science of Mind,* June 1981, p. 39.

CHAPTER 23

1 The recent scientific study of the Shroud, which dates it as a fourteenth-century artifact, is so flawed and open to question that many sindologists have publicly denounced the report and rejected the conclusions as unsupportable. The media have not given much attention to this, focusing instead on the alleged "disproof" of the Shroud's authenticity.

2 Frank C. Tribbe, *Portrait of Jesus?: The Illustrated Story of The Shroud of Turin* (Briarcliff Manor, N.Y.: Scarborough House, 1983).

3 However, according to Tribbe, Teresa Neumann, a twentieth-century mystic-stigmatic, and some other others acknowledged that their wounds were symbolic and that the flesh of the palm would not have supported Jesus' body.

APPENDIX 4

[1] Published privately by Constable under the imprint of Merlin Press, Tustin, California, and distributed by Borderland Science Research Foundation, P.O. Box 429, Garberville, California. Also available in a British edition from Neville Spearman, London.

[2] Ivan Sanderson, *Uninvited Visitors: A Biologist Looks at UFOs* (New York: Cowles, 1967), p. 75.

[3] Stephen Bardwell, "The Implications of Nonlinearity," *FEF Newsletter*, 1977.

[4] Michael Grant, "A New Energy of Life?," *Science Digest*, November 1983, pp. 22.

[5] John Gribben, "The Search for ET Goes On," *New Scientist*, July 23, 1987, p. 28.

[6] *The New York Times*, February 8, 1988, p. C4.

[7] Franklin Ruehl, *Canadian UFO Report* (Summer 1979): 18.

[8] Interestingly, Arnold himself came to believe that UFOs are biological, not mechanical. In the November 1962 edition of *Flying Saucers* magazine he wrote: "After some 14 years of extensive research, it is my conclusion that the so-called unidentified flying objects that have been seen in our atmosphere are not space ships from another planet at all, but are groups and masses of living organisms that are as much a part of our atmosphere and space as the life we find in the oceans. The only major difference in the space and atmospheric organisms is that they have the natural ability to change their densities at will."

[9] (New York: Pocket Books, 1978).

[10] Vincent H. Gaddis, *Mysterious Fires and Lights* (New York: Dell, 1967), p. 38.

[11] *Fate 33* (August 1980): 50.

[12] Edizioni Invaldi Editore, Via Fieschi 3/10, Genoa, Italy, 1979.

[13] *Journal of Borderland Research 37* (March–April 1981): 19.

[14] An Alternative explanation is offered for these photos by James Oberg in *Fate*, September 1980. They are "doctored" stills from a test sequence shot by Aldrin, Oberg says. The sequence, he claims, actually shows light refelctions of the lunar module's ceiling lights. I have reviewed the film footage, entitled *Photo Aberrations, Debris & UFO's* (Production #CL 79862, available without charge from NASA through AV Corp. in Houston, tel. 713-333-4980). Although I disagree with Oberg, I am not yet in a position to disprove his contention. I am awaiting photoanalysis of the footage. I would also like a statement from Aldrin, to whom I wrote some years ago, asking whether he saw and/or photographed UFOs or something in space which he felt was not a man-made artifact. I got no reply.

[15] *Weekly World News*, April 8, 1986, p. 24.

Index

The Meeting of Science and Spirit by John White

ABOUT THE AUTHOR

JOHN WHITE, M.A.T., is an internationally known author, editor, and educator in the fields of parascience, consciousness research, and higher human development. He has held positions as Director of Education for the Institute of Noetic Sciences, a California-based research organization founded by Apollo 14 astronaut Edgar Mitchell to study human potential for personal and planetary transformation, and as president of Alpha Logics, a Connecticut school for self-directed growth in body, mind, and spirit.

He is author of *Pole Shift, A Practical Guide to Death and Dying, Everything You Want to Know about TM*, and a children's book, *The Christmas Mice*. He has also edited a number of anthologies, including *The Highest State of Consciousness, What Is Meditation?, Frontiers of Consciousness, Psychic Exploration, Other Worlds/Other Universes, Future Science, Relax, Kundalini, Evolution and Enlightenment, Psychic Warfare—Fact or Fiction*, and *What Is Enlightenment?*.

His writing has appeared in popular magazines such as *Reader's Digest, Omni, Esquire, Science Digest, Woman's Day, New Age, Saturday Review, East-West Journal*, and *Body, Mind & Spirit*, in professional journals and in major newspapers such a *The New York Times, Chicago Sun-Times, San Francisco Chronicle, Philadelphia Inquirer*, and *Hartford Courant*. His books have been translated into seven languages and his articles have been reprinted in textbooks on linguistics, education, biology, psychology, yoga, and holistic health. He is general editor of the Omega Books series published by Paragon House.

He was born in New York City on August 16, 1939. He holds degrees from Dartmouth College and Yale University. He has taught on the secondary and college levels and has been on the governing and advisory boards of various academic and research organizations. He is also on the editorial and advisory boards of scholarly journals and popular magazines, including *New Realities, Science of Mind, ReVision, Yoga Journal, Venture Inward, Journal of Near-Death Studies, Balance, Mind-Expander, Journal of UFO Research* (published in Beijing), and *Body, Mind & Spirit*. He writes a monthly column for *Science of Mind* and edits *Mind-Expander* newsletter for The Phenix Society. He has lectured at various colleges and universities throughout the United States and Canada and has made numerous radio and television appearances.

He and his wife Barbara have four children and live at 60 Pound Ridge Road, Cheshire, Connecticut 06410, USA.